SPIDER FROM MARS

MY LIFE WITH BOWIE

SPIDER FROM MARS

WOODY WOODMANSEY

with Joel McIver

SIDGWICK & JACKSON

First published 2016 by Sidgwick & Jackson
an imprint of Pan Macmillan
20 New Wharf Road, London N1 9RR
Associated companies throughout the world
www.panmacmillan.com

ISBN 978-0-2830-7272-7 HB
ISBN 978-0-2830-7273-4 TPB

1 3 5 7 9 8 6 4 2

A CIP catalogue record for this book is available from the British Library.

Typeset by by Ellipsis Digital Limited, Glasgow
Printed and bound by CPI Group (UK) Ltd, Croydon, CR0 4YY

Visit www.panmacmillan.com to read more about all our books
and to buy them. You will also find features, author interviews and
news of any author events, and you can sign up for e-newsletters
so that you're always first to hear about our new releases.

This book is dedicated to my wife, June;

to my sons, Nick, Joe and Dan;

to my sister, Pamela;

to my brothers in the Spiders From Mars,
Mick Ronson and Trevor Bolder;

and to my friend David Bowie,
who changed my life.

Contents

Foreword
by Tony Visconti

As an American new to England I thought the name Woody Woodmansey might have been a Tolkien invention, like Tom Bombadil. I had never heard of such a name. Mick Ronson was singing his praises, though: Woody was Mick's favourite drummer and we had to import him from Hull immediately.

The 'we' was David Bowie and me. Months earlier David and I had been completely taken with Ronson's guitar playing and formed a backing group called the Hype with drummer John Cambridge, who'd suggested Ronson to us in the first place. Ironically, back in Hull, Woody replaced Cambridge in the Rats, Ronson's earlier group, and now at Ronson's behest he was replacing Cambridge yet again, this time in the Hype. Rock is a cruel mistress.

David and I occupied a huge Victorian flat in Beckenham, Kent, and Woody and Ronson moved in, sleeping on mattresses on the floor. Sometimes their girlfriends from Hull came down for a visit, and that would make nine of us all together, including our girlfriends and Roger the roadie. But most of the time we were downstairs in a disused wine cellar, banging out arrangements for the first songs of the new David Bowie album, later to be called *The Man Who Sold the World*.

Mick Ronson was right about Woody – he was an amazing drummer. His speedy hands were a blur, adapting quickly to the strange juxtaposition between sophisticated chord changes, sudden time signature changes and songs structured like operettas. From the USA I brought in concepts like the jazz bolero – the instrumental section of 'All the Madmen' – that Woody learned in five minutes. I got him to play instruments he hadn't heard of, such as the guiro and timpani. He mastered everything thrown at him. He had my respect, and I know as a bass player and producer that I certainly had to earn his.

We were a happy bunch of musicians when we entered Trident and Advision Studios in 1970. We blew their roofs off and we completed the album feeling triumphant. What happened afterwards will be told later . . . but in 2014 I received an email from Woody asking me if I would like to play *The Man Who Sold the World* live in concert, as we had never actually done that back in the day. I was iffy about it, because I was uncertain whether I still had it in me to play the Herculean bass parts which I'd busked so many decades before.

I didn't fully commit until I got this email from Woody:

> Hi Tony,
> Was It something I said? Mac stuck on SLEEP?
> Hiatus?
> Woody

That was the slap in the face I needed. I accepted the challenge.

At the time of writing this we have performed *The Man Who Sold the World* at least forty times to wildly enthusiastic audiences in the UK, Japan, Canada and the USA. We are still on tour with our core group of Glenn Gregory, James Stevenson and Paul Cuddeford and will play it at least twenty times more.

This is my story with Woody Woodmansey. Now let Woody tell his, how a young man from a blues band in the north of England ended up as the drummer in the Spiders From Mars.

Tony Visconti, 2016

PROLOGUE

'A rediscovered TV performance by David Bowie singing his classic song "The Jean Genie" live on *Top of the Pops* is being shown tonight for the first time in almost forty years,' newsreader Fiona Bruce announced. 'It was thought the performance had been lost for good . . .'

It's a funny thing to see a video of yourself from forty years ago pop up on the BBC's six o'clock news.

It was a few days before Christmas in 2011, and in amongst all the stories of scandal and conflict, there it was – a recording of Bowie and the Spiders, which had been broadcast on 4 January 1973 and not seen by anyone since. Although the BBC's tape had been lost or recorded over, one of the cameramen from the day, John Henshall, had made a copy for himself that had been kept in a drawer somewhere – until now.

Later that evening, they played the full video on the *Top of the Pops*' Christmas special and I sat down with my family and watched. Although I was sixty-one years old, as I watched my twenty-two-year-old self I was caught up in the excitement all over again.

At that moment in time, we'd had a hit single in the UK and US with 'Starman', and the album *The Rise and Fall of Ziggy Stardust and the Spiders From Mars* had been released in June 1972, so far having spent twenty-five weeks in the charts. 'The Jean Genie' had been released the previous November and was number sixteen in the charts (and about to climb a lot higher). We'd just come back from our first US tour and were in the middle of a small English one before heading back to the US again. It felt like things were really beginning to happen.

As I listened to Mick Ronson play that familiar guitar line harder and more aggressively than the recorded version, I remembered that when the BBC asked us to do *Top of the Pops* Bowie had been absolutely adamant we'd only appear if we could play live. Over the course of the tour the live version of the song had become more energetic and raw, and we all felt strongly that it would have more impact on the show than simply miming to a pre-recorded backing track, which was normal at the time. Luckily the BBC agreed, and we had time to fit in our appearance between our gigs in Manchester on 29 December and Glasgow on 5 January. Although we'd only had about three days off over Christmas, which hadn't really been enough time to unwind, none of us felt tired as we arrived at Studio 8 for the recording.

Our stage look was always evolving and our designer, Freddie Burretti, who was on a roll now, had made us new clothes for the show. Bowie was bare-chested, wearing a turquoise patterned jacket with blue trousers. He'd added a necklace and one single pendant earing. Mick wore his new black and gold suit, Trevor his black and silver suit.

It made me smile to see my get-up – a white- and black-striped jacket, with padded shoulders and very wide lapels, red Oxford-bags-style trousers, a black shirt and metallic-silver tie. It looked brilliant but Freddie tended to forget that I needed to be able to move my arms. The sleeves of the jacket were so tight that I wasn't looking forward to playing in it.

I was positioned at the front of the stage, which was not my usual spot for live performances but the producers had used the same set-up when we'd done 'Starman' the year before and that had obviously been successful. What was different this time was that we were playing a live version of the song with an extended guitar solo, which would last as long as Mick felt it should last, so eye contact was important – I knew Mick would give me a nod as he finished his solo. In the recording you can see me turning my head around to be able to see his cue.

By the time the show was broadcast we had been on our way to the Glasgow gig and never actually saw it. None of us probably thought about it much again.

Watching it now, though, it felt odd that this moment had been sitting in a drawer somewhere, one song from so many that we played together over those years. We didn't know then what those songs would come to mean to people all over the world. I had no idea that more than four decades later, people would still come up to me and tell me that watching us changed their life, made them think differently. We were just up there, playing the best we could.

If you'd have told me when I was starting out that all those years later a video of me playing the drums would be on the news, I'd have laughed in your face and told you not to be daft.

But that's the story I want to tell you now; how a boy from a small town in East Yorkshire became a Spider from Mars.

Woody Woodmansey, 2016

1

ROCKER IN WAITING

I remember, with absolute clarity, the moment when I knew I was going to be a rock musician.

It was a warm summer day in 1964 and I was fourteen years old. The Beatles' 'A Hard Day's Night' and the Rolling Stones' 'It's All Over Now' were riding high at the top of the charts. I was more of a Stones fan – the Beatles were a bit too smooth for me. Everybody liked them, including my parents, which was a real turn-off. I also liked the Animals, the Kinks and Johnny Kidd and the Pirates. *Top of the Pops* had started airing in January that year and like millions of teenagers I sat glued to the TV on a Thursday evening. But my epiphany didn't come as a result of hearing any of my favourite bands. I was standing on the edge of a farm machinery repair depot in the Yorkshire town of Driffield when everything changed.

My friend Frank's dad owned the place, and we'd often go down there to mess about on the machines and play football. That afternoon four of us were kicking a ball around in an open area of concrete between the huge combine harvesters and tractors. It was basically a bit of wasteland surrounded by tall banks of nettles. I kicked the ball at one of the other kids, but it shot over the nettles and vanished.

I went in search of it, finding it lying next to the door of a brick building that looked a bit like an air-raid shelter, maybe twenty foot long, with no windows. I'd never noticed it before. The ball had rolled up to a silver-painted door; the words 'The Cave' were painted on it, graffiti-style.

As I bent down to pick up the ball I heard music coming out of this building. At first I thought someone had a transistor radio in there, and then I realized that it was more dynamic than that. I could feel the vibration in my body, even standing outside the door. I shouted to Frank, 'What's that music?'

'It's my brother,' he replied. 'He's playing in there with his band.'

'What kind of band?'

'Rhythm and blues, or pop, or something,' Frank shrugged.

'Can we go in and listen?' I asked.

'No, you only get in there if you're wearing a dress,' he told me.

The music had really grabbed my attention, though, and I pestered Frank to ask his brother if I could go in and watch, even just for one song. A few days later Frank said, 'They're practising tonight, come down. My brother says you can go in and watch if you want.'

The first thing I noticed as I went inside the Cave was that it smelled strongly of damp. The second was how dark it was, lit only by a single red lightbulb. The band, who were called the Roadrunners, had hung what looked like fishing nets from the ceiling in an attempt at cool decor, which added to the atmosphere – to my eyes it looked very rock 'n' roll.

At the far end of the main room was a stage, about a foot high, that was carpeted. There were five musicians on it, so it looked pretty cramped. In the middle was a drummer sitting at his kit, on the left stood a guitarist and a bass player, on the right another guitarist, and the singer was out front. They were already playing when I arrived, a Bo Diddley song I recognized. I'd never seen a band play live before and, only 10 feet away from them, every sense I had was being assaulted. I was mesmerized. It was the most exciting thing I'd ever experienced. They all had long hair, but the singer stood out as his hair was ginger. He was wearing bell-bottom jeans and shaking a pair of maracas in time to the drummer's Bo Diddley beat. They all looked so cool and confident.

I was a shy kid, so even going in and watching the Road-runners was pretty nerve-wracking for me. But I had to do it: something was compelling me. I even tapped my feet and nodded my head to the music, by my standards a major display of exhibitionism. Watching the Roadrunners, I was so happy; the impact of the music hit me so hard. I thought, 'This is it. This is what I'm going to do, I'm going to be in a band like this and play music.'

Up to that point, if I'd thought about it at all, I'd have assumed my life would be spent in Driffield. It was a busy little town in a picturesque part of Yorkshire, surrounded by farmland, with turkeys, sheep and cows in every direction, as well as cornfields. There was a little bit of industry, but not too much: we had Bradshaw's flour mill on the outskirts of the town. There were a couple of factories, including Dewhirst, which made shirts for Marks & Spencer, and Vertex, a spectacles company.

That description makes the town sound pretty boring, I'm sure, but it could be exciting at times: there were a few local rock bands, and occasionally a big London band would come up and play. We had a couple of good coffee bars with juke-boxes, where we hung out.

Driffield was only twelve miles from the coast, where there were resorts like Bridlington and Scarborough, and then Hull was the nearest big city, about thirty miles away. Perhaps that's not such a long way to travel if you're driving or taking a train, but, believe me, the cultural distance between Driffield and Hull was huge in lots of ways. Driffield had one main street of shops and one main venue, the Town Hall, whereas Hull was a bustling city which at that time had the third busi-est port in the country, although this would change drastically in the seventies after the Cod Wars with Iceland saw the local fishing industry decline. It had a university and an art college as well as clubs and theatres. In Hull all the big names of the time – the Beatles, the Stones, Roy Orbison and Jimi Hendrix to name a few – would come play at the ABC Theatre.

My father, Douglas Woodmansey, was originally from the village of Langtoft, which is about six miles north of Driffield. He joined the army with a friend of his when he was in his teens, because they wanted to see the world. I don't recall which regiment he was in, but I know he served in the Far East, including a spell in Hong Kong.

My mother, Annie, was born in Driffield, and was part of a large family. She became a nurse at East Riding General Hospital in the town, and met my father when he was home on leave. They never really talked much about that time, perhaps because they weren't keen to admit that she got pregnant. Mum and Dad didn't get married at that point because they weren't sure if they would be together in the long term. He wanted her to be an army wife following him around the country, but she loved nursing and wanted to continue in the profession. They were both on their own career paths and hadn't got around to making big decisions yet. It took a bit of thinking through, especially with the stigma of having a baby out of wedlock. It was a hell of a big deal in a small, very traditional community like Driffield at that time.

Mum kept working right up until I was born, hiding her pregnancy with a sort of corset worn around her abdomen. It was so tight that she passed out on the ward one day, and I appeared shortly afterwards, on 4 February 1950.

My mother's father wanted to kick her out of the house, I later found out, because she'd got pregnant. He'd been in the army himself, and was a real disciplinarian. But her mother – who was a very no-nonsense woman – stepped in and said, 'Annie's staying in this house, and she's having her child here.' My grandfather was tough, but she was tougher.

So I spent my early years living in my grandparents' house at 18 Eastfield Road, which was also home to my mother, her uncle Edward, her sister Deanie and their two brothers, Harold and Ernest. It was on a new council estate, and I'd cycle around on my little three-wheel bike and chase fire engines, and go so far from home that my long-suffering relatives would be scouring the streets trying to find me and bring me back. My mother worked nights a lot and my dad was away most of the time, so essentially my grandmother raised me until I was five, when my dad left the army. Although I was christened Michael Woodmansey, I went by the name Mick Bradley then, using my mother's surname.

My grandfather was an engineer at the local gasworks in the centre of the town. I went to the works with him a couple of times when I was little; I remember burning my hand on a pipe. My grandmother was a housewife, looking after their four children and me. It was a really good period of my childhood. I was a happy kid.

The old cliché of neighbours being in and out of each other's houses was completely true for the families where we lived. People would leave their front doors open and you'd go round and have tea. The whole street was like that, except for one particular set of neighbours whose house you'd never go to. I remember very clearly that there was some animosity between our family and theirs. One day in 1954 those annoying neighbours complained to my family that I was keeping them awake with my drum kit – even though I didn't have one. I don't know what they'd actually heard, if anything, but this gave my uncles an idea . . . so they went out and bought a snare drum, sticks and a stand and took me upstairs to the bedroom next to the neighbours' bedroom.

'We're going to shut the door,' they told me cheerfully. 'Make as much noise as you can!'

Apparently I really went for it and beat the hell out of those drums – and that, looking back, was the very start of my career as a drummer. I like to think I've developed a bit of subtlety in my technique since then, but you never know.

When I was five years old my parents got married. I guess they must have slipped away and done it as they never mentioned it. They had finally come to the decision that my dad, rather than my mother, would give up his career so we could live as a family in Driffield. The outcome was that he left the army and the three of us settled down together at 49 Westgate, a terraced house divided into two flats: we had the ground floor and the garden, plus an outside toilet which was about thirty yards away from the house, and an outside bathroom which was about twenty yards away. This was an outhouse with a concrete floor and three tin baths of different sizes hanging on the wall. There was a boiler in there so you could heat water up for the baths, and it got very steamy: you couldn't even see your feet to wash them.

After you'd had a bath, it was too wet in there for you to put your clothes on, so you had to wrap a towel round you and sprint to the house through the wind, rain and snow, thinking, 'Fuck!' Being clean took courage! This was normal back then, by the way; we weren't a poor family, although there wasn't a lot of spare money. (After a couple of years we moved into the upstairs flat, a considerably nicer place with an inside toilet!)

It was quite a shock for me to leave the Bradleys, where I was part of a large, warm family who gave me a lot of attention. About a year after my parents married, my sister Pamela was born, which was something else to adjust to. But the most difficult thing was living with a dad I hardly knew, having only seen him when he was home on leave. He was very strict: I wasn't allowed to jump on furniture or walk on walls like you do as a kid. I guess I'd got used to the more relaxed atmosphere at my gran's when I had been the only child in the family. His viewpoint was that I was spoilt. To me he looked a bit like John Wayne, a bit of a hard man. I began to have a troubled relationship with my dad at this point. He carried a chip on his shoulder for quite a while, as I'd effectively come along and interrupted his army life. He had a lot of mates in the army, and none at home, so he didn't have much of a social life because he was a young dad. I was the object of his frustration, basically, and that took a lot of getting used to. It's tough for a kid to feel that his father resents him, although I realize that there were extenuating circumstances.

Sometimes my dad's annoyance would be frightening: my mum would set the table for Sunday lunch and if he was in a bad mood he'd grab a corner of the tablecloth and rip the whole thing off. My dinner would be in front of me, and then all of a sudden it was dripping off the wall. This was scary behaviour.

I can understand it to an extent, because I have three sons myself; although I love them and I'm close to them, being a parent can be hard work, and I think it was especially hard for my dad because he was so young and his life had been overturned when I arrived. My relationship with him wasn't all bad, fortunately: he had a great sense of humour, which I shared. We both loved listening to *The Goon Show* and watching *Hancock's Half Hour* on TV and he took me to see the comedian Jimmy Clitheroe in Bridlington. I remember Jimmy came and sat next to me during the show, and it freaked me out because he was an adult but barely four feet tall. Dad and I would have play fights, and he took me fishing, too, and did a lot of dad stuff like that. There were good times as well as less good times.

My dad had one record, a collection of blues songs by

Muddy Waters and others, although he must have played it at my grandmother's house because we didn't have a record player at home until much later. I must have wanted to play music rather than just listen to it, because I remember at the age of eight I had a tantrum in Woolworth's. Apparently I wanted a trumpet, of all things, although I have no idea why because I've never wanted to play a brass instrument since then. I kicked up merry hell, lying on the floor and shouting, and they had to carry me out. I didn't get the trumpet either. That was the end of my performing aspirations until I was fourteen, by which time I'd started to get into music properly, mainly through listening to Radio Luxembourg, which was the best source of contemporary music, although the BBC Light Programme had shows like *Pick of the Pops* where you could hear what was in the charts.

Even though I lived in a very small place, I was always interested in the outside world. There were American air force personnel based at RAF Driffield in the late 1950s and I had a couple of American friends; it felt very alien to have them in our schools, because they were so different from us. I remember playing baseball on the school field with George Smith, who had a typical American crew-cut and who wore sneakers and jeans which seemed a lot cooler than the ones we wore, better fitting and more stylish.

George was a nice guy, but quite a few kids at school didn't mix with him because he was different, and people didn't like things being different back then. But there was something about America that fascinated me from an early age: I used to wonder what it would be like to go into a diner in Texas and order dinner. When you were in a farming town in Yorkshire, the idea of ever doing that was almost unimaginable.

What I didn't know at the time was that Americans like George's dad were in Driffield because the US wanted to deploy their Thor ballistic missiles in Britain. RAF Driffield was home to three of these nuclear warheads, which were capable of reaching Moscow. Considering that made us a target should the Soviet Union ever launch a nuclear strike, I'm glad I was oblivious to this. But I do remember the Cuban Missile Crisis in 1962, when it seemed America and Russia were on the brink of nuclear war. It was made very real for us because our American schoolmates were so fearful.

My curiosity was also fuelled by reading science fiction comics. I bought every comic I could lay my hands on and so did two of my school friends, Johnny Butler and Graham Cardwell. Johnny's father was in the navy and he'd bring back American science fiction comics like *Amazing Stories* and *Weird Tales*. I was hooked on them; some of the stories really opened your mind up to different possibilities.

There was often a moral in these stories, which taught me right from wrong much more effectively than anything I ever read at school. There was one story about an astronaut who crashed on a planet, searching for an earlier astronaut who had been lost. It was raining heavily on this planet and there was mud everywhere. He saw what he thought was a monster, covered in lumps and hunched over, and assumed it was an enemy – he spent most of the story trying to kill this 'monster' but actually it was the lost astronaut. Then the rain started burning his own skin and raising lumps, and he began to turn into a monster himself – and that was the end. I thought, 'Whoa! So the moral of this story is that appearances are deceiving, and you can't judge things by how they look.' This was an interesting way for a kid to learn about life.

I liked thinking and talking about the meaning of life, although I do remember very clearly that my mother had no interest in these subjects whatsoever. I once asked her, 'Don't you ever wonder what life is all about, Mum?' and she sighed and said, 'Oh no – what do I want to think about things like that for?' That was always her attitude but I didn't hold it against her. She had a lot on her plate trying to run a household, with money and time in short supply.

Still, I was different from my parents in that respect, and from my sister Pamela too, who was going the same way as my mother in that she wanted to be a nurse when she grew up. Pamela and I were close, though; we had good times growing up together.

I was raised as a Methodist, and I got really into it and did all the scripture examinations. I was even thinking about becoming a minister at one point, which seems pretty amusing to me now. In church we'd discuss the nature of God, and where religion fits into life, but by the age of ten I found myself asking things like, 'Does God have a mother, if we're created in his image?' and was told not to come to any more discussions because I was disrupting them with my silly questions. I also noticed one of the members of the congregation taking money out of the collection box at a point when we were all supposed to have our eyes closed – which clinched it for me. So I grew out of Christianity pretty quickly.

My parents both worked, although making enough money

was sometimes a struggle for them. After my dad left the army he held down two jobs, one at the East Yorkshire Electricity Board and the other – more excitingly – as a fireman. Occasionally when I was at school I'd see him running across the field to the nearby fire station. In those moments he looked like a hero to me.

At the age of ten you don't really ask yourself why your father's got two jobs. I found out later that it was because my parents were saving up to buy a house, which they eventually did, at 30 Victoria Road in Driffield in 1961. That was a big place: a Victorian terrace with a bow window and three bedrooms, and the all-important inside toilet as well as one outside. The house was definitely a huge step up for us, socially and in terms of simple comforts.

My parents were ambitious for themselves and for their kids. My mother always insisted that I needed to do well academically. All through school I endured her saying things like, 'Mick, your cousin's working in the bank now, and you're brighter than he is. I hope you're going to work hard at school' and 'So-and-so in the family's done well: he's a lawyer. You could be a lawyer too, as long as you work hard', and so on and so on.

I passed my eleven-plus exam in 1961, and it was a real learning experience for me: it made me realize that the grammar school system wasn't remotely fair. When they were allocating places for the grammar and secondary modern schools, the teacher called me out and asked, 'What does your father do, Woodmansey?'

When I told him my dad worked for the East Yorkshire Electricity Board, as well as being a fireman, he said, 'We think you'd be better off going to a secondary modern school, young man.' That was the first time the class system really hit me: they were literally telling me that I couldn't go to a grammar school because of who my parents were, and what their jobs were – even though I was top of the class in most subjects.

The whole process was ridiculously unfair but it didn't really bother me, partly because even at that early age I wasn't planning to have a long-term education. School just didn't mean a lot to me, although I genuinely enjoyed some of the lessons. Perhaps most importantly from an eleven-year-old's point of view, all of my close friends were going to the local secondary school, so I didn't mind not going to the grammar school anyway. My parents didn't kick up a fuss because in those days you didn't argue with an authority figure like a teacher.

In September 1961 I started at Driffield County Secondary Boys' School; there was an equivalent girls' school 200 yards away. I was a good student at Driffield County, just as I'd been at my primary school. I really liked English and maths, and I was particularly good at art and football. I also did athletics; my father had been a sprinter in the army and it turned out I'd inherited his speed. I could do the 100 yards in 12.2 seconds, even at the age of eleven, and also raced in the 200 yards and the last leg of the 440-yard relay. Our gym teacher, Mr Wilson, asked me if I'd considered running as a professional, and entered me in a competition between the schools in the area – they wanted us to try out for selection to the English national team. I came second – pipped at the post.

I could have taken athletics further, but rock 'n' roll got in

the way in 1964, when I discovered the Roadrunners rehearsing at the Cave. Once I'd seen them play I knew I had to put
together a band of my own, so I suggested it to some mates
from school; they were Frank Theakston, whose dad owned
the farm machinery depot where I'd discovered the Cave,
Paul Richardson, John Flintoff and Michael Grice.

None of us had any musical experience, but that didn't
stop us: rock music was cool, and all around us, and we knew
that we had to be a part of it. We went down to the Salvation
Army shop and bought two acoustic guitars and a bass. I
didn't have a clue what I was doing, though. I didn't know
how to tune the guitar, let alone play it. You probably won't
believe this, but I simply sat at home with it on my knee,
thinking to myself, 'Something's bound to happen.' Strangely
enough, it didn't! I don't know why I never thought of getting
a book to teach myself how to play, because such books were
around. I had absolutely no idea how to get started. You can't
imagine today's kids being that clueless. All I can say in my
defence is that it was a different world back then. We had no
information.

So the band got together for a rehearsal the following
week in a shed which was in the same yard owned by Frank's
dad. The others all said to me, 'Go on, play your guitar.'
I couldn't play a note, of course, but Frank knew how to
play chords and he quickly showed me some. Obviously I still
couldn't play the guitar, even after he'd done that, so they said,
'You're rubbish', took it off me and gave it to Paul, who could
play it as he'd been practising it at home.

Now I looked like a complete loser. But then Frank pulled
a pair of drum sticks out of his back pocket and said, 'You're

the drummer.' I liked that idea a lot, so I took them and said, 'Cool!'

I went and got myself a drum kit for the equivalent of 50p in today's money from the Salvation Army shop. God, that kit was terrible. It was really old for starters: one of the cymbals was bent and sounded terrible when you hit it, and the skins were real animal skins, with old tears stitched up. Nowadays skins are synthetic and easily replaced. But it was a functioning drum kit, and I spent a lot of time tinkering with it. After a while I started experimenting with it, and, as time passed, I gradually learned how to play it.

We called our band the Mutations, which was the strangest name we could think of. And once we'd realized how badly the shed leaked in the rain, we got permission from the Roadrunners to move to the Cave for rehearsals. We used a little room next to theirs which had been blocked off from the rest of the Cave and had no door. It did have a large window – although there was no window frame or glass, just a rectangular hole in the wall. I had to put the drums through the window to set them up. I kept my kit at the Cave – my dad would never have let me play the drums at home – and I'd practise in there, on my own, at weekends.

The other guys in the band thought this was hilarious, and they used to throw sticks and stones through the window at me, just to piss me off. A stone would come sailing through and hit the cymbal, or a branch would come in and land on the drums. I'd shout abuse at them. I guess I took the band more seriously than they did.

I must have had a bit of native talent for the drums, because it only took me a week to master the all-important trick of playing different things with each hand. Once I felt a bit confident about that, I brought the bass drum in. I was dead set on getting a beat right; I was really motivated, actually. I remember finally getting it right one day, but I didn't dare stop playing in case I lost it. I kept going with a single drum beat for about an hour. That was the moment when I first thought, 'I can do this.'

Music began to mean everything to me from that point on, and I started listening to as much of it as I could. As I've said, my favourite band was the Rolling Stones, who made a huge impact on me because they were rebellious. I was starting to feel that way myself: pissed off with school, and having to study subjects that I thought were far less interesting than music and the drums. I got into earlier music too, thanks to the Stones who were influenced by the blues. American singers like Howlin' Wolf and Muddy Waters were my idols; I'd make a real effort to find old blues records and learn the drum parts from the songs.

The first style of drums I played was rhythm and blues; if you couldn't play that kind of music you weren't accepted in the circle of musicians that I was starting to move in. After that I moved towards soul and Tamla Motown, and then I got into more musical blues-rock. A friend called Dave Simpson, who later became a roadie for the Roadrunners, had a lot of albums. He lent me the first Stones records and *Five Live Yardbirds,* the first Yardbirds album which featured Eric Clapton. He introduced me to John Mayall too and over the next few years I'd borrow the Bluesbreakers albums from him. I had a record player of my own now, so I'd play them incessantly.

These guys were so advanced musically; that was why I was attracted to their music and the way they played it, although I certainly wasn't any kind of advanced musician myself at that point.

Around that time I had to make a decision between music and sport, because if I was going to take my running any further I would have to devote a lot of time to it, and the Mutations would have to go. So I asked myself if there was a career ahead of me in athletics, and I suppose there might have been to an extent, but it wasn't a passion of mine so I had to let it go. I didn't mind, though: I was too busy with the drums to go out and run every day.

Now I was in a band I needed to look the part, so I decided to grow my hair long, which was the start of the downward slope, academically speaking. There were only four of us at Driffield County Secondary who had the courage to sport long hair: Johnny Flintoff from the Mutations was one of them.

The teachers hated it and wouldn't let us eat our lunch with everyone else; they actually had a special table in the canteen for the long-haired boys. I guess it's hard to imagine this nowadays, but back then the whole school would walk past you, chanting 'Unclean! Unclean!' and pretending to ring lepers' bells.

I suppose that was moderately funny, but it didn't feel like that to us so we told them to fuck off.

You have to understand that 'long hair' back then just meant that you hadn't got a short back and sides; there was a little bit of hair over your ears. Look at any photo of a band from that era and you'll see what I mean. Nowadays a kid would just laugh if he had hair like that and the teachers got angry about it.

When those morons shouted 'Unclean!' I felt conflicted, because of course it was a major put-down, and it made you feel like an outcast – but at the same time it felt great, because it was rebellion: a real fuck-you to them.

My grades began to go down after that, simply because I was losing what interest I'd had in my studies. I just wasn't bothered any more because the drums were taking up so much of my attention. Worse, I also started to annoy the teachers, but not deliberately, and not just because of my long hair either. It was because I was trying to be funny. At the time I thought I wanted to be a comedian when I left school. I'd watch comedy shows on the TV trying to understand how humour worked. A lot of it was down to timing, which tied in with playing the drums, of course.

Perhaps unwisely I began to practise my comedy routines at school, repeating sketches I'd seen, because I was more interested in having a laugh than working. I was also fond of making what I thought were amusing comments in class. For example, one of the teachers had a mahogany stick, about an inch and a half square, and he would belt kids with it. He'd get it out and as a joke I'd say, 'Me next, sir!' That sometimes backfired and I'd get the 'mahogany' treatment myself. The idea was to lighten the atmosphere while some kid was getting beaten up. After a while the only reason for me to go to school was to get laughs.

When I wasn't performing, if I was ever in a small group

of three or four people, I would spend most of my time wondering what to say. I really was shy at heart, and it was painful.

While the teachers were gritting their teeth over my sarcastic remarks at school, I was also getting into trouble at home. The length of my hair had now become a serious problem for my dad. He used to say, 'I'll make a man of you if it kills me!'

I woke up one night to find that he was actually trying to cut my fringe while I was sleeping. The scissors were dangerously close to my eyes. I pushed him away, but I can understand what he was thinking, because all this was happening at a time when a boy with long hair was regarded as a sissy, less than a man, especially in a northern town. People would shout, 'All right, Mary, how are you doing?' in the street. It was more than annoying.

My mum was caught in the middle of all this. She understood my dad's point of view, because she wanted me to do well at school, but as my mother she also wanted to protect me. My grandparents were on my side to an extent, because of the fact that they'd raised me.

I get it, of course. My father didn't want any son of his to go down the route that I was obviously taking. Before I started rebelling against everything I'd been a genuinely good student and my school reports had always confirmed that I was bright. My parents seemed to regard me as some kind of kid genius who was going to go places, although to them that meant being a bank manager, or having my own firm of accountants, or some other respectable middle-class profession. In their minds I was definitely going to do something along those lines, anyway, although I myself had no idea what I was going to do. What teenager does? None of the possible jobs the career officer gave me held any appeal and when I tried to come up with my own list – anything from detective to train driver – I didn't want to do them either.

I have to give my parents points for perseverance: they really kept the pressure on me in the face of massive indifference from yours truly. I remember once I came home from school, delighted with a test result I'd got, and expecting them to be really pleased.

'I came second in English!' I said, bursting into the kitchen.

My dad looked up from his tea and replied, 'Why weren't you first?'

I was speechless, but he just looked at me.

Summoning up some words, I managed to say, 'Well, some other kid did better than me, but second is pretty good, I reckon.'

He just ignored me, and I began to feel a bit annoyed. This wasn't fair.

'Oh, piss off then!' I snarled, and turned to walk away.

That was the first and only time I ever swore at my dad. As I left the room, I heard him stand up and come after me. He grabbed my shoulders, spun me round and lifted me up by the lapels of my jacket so my feet were off the ground. There was nothing I could do except struggle: he was much stronger than me.

He carried me over to the coat pegs on the wall, hung me up by the back of my jacket and started thumping me. He completely lost it. Honestly, I'm not making this stuff up. It made me want to get away from there as soon as I could.

*

At Christmas 1964 the Mutations played the Christmas dance at the girls' school. There were five hundred girls there, with us four guys, which was an eye-opener because we felt like rock stars for the first time. I realized at that moment that being in a band – a good band, anyway – could be pretty cool if you were interested in girls, as we all were.

My performance was hardly stellar, though: my drum kit was so rickety that the tom-tom fell off, and the cymbal stands weren't stable so the cymbals kept sinking closer to the floor. I fell backwards off the stool too. Everybody had to wait until my kit was put back together before we could play on. It was dreadfully embarrassing. I didn't know it at the time but a girl called June was there watching us on our first ill-fated performance. She later asked me if it had been me doing my Keith Moon impersonation.

Not long after that, the local authority merged the Driffield boys' and girls' secondary schools. One Monday morning, half of my class were moved to another room, and then a load of girls came in carrying their satchels. One of them was a pretty brunette with a Sixties Helen Shapiro-type hairstyle. She was wearing a mini skirt (just within the school regulations) with white knee-length socks! Needless to say, she got my attention all through that first morning. In fact, as she walked in, I saw her and I thought, 'I'm going to marry her', even though I wasn't even looking for a girlfriend at the time. It was very strange, because I'd never seen her before in my life. I found out her name, and that she was from Middleton on the Wolds, a village not far away, but it took me a while to pluck up the courage to make a move.

In fact, I got John Flintoff to ask June out for me, although

I later found out that before he approached her she'd put a Valentine's card in my school desk. She lost her nerve, though, and took it out before I saw it. Our first date was sweet: I took her to the cinema but, a bit unromantically, I don't remember the film.

I still went and watched the Roadrunners every time they rehearsed at the Cave or played a gig – I think I was the only one there who wasn't connected to the band. They were about five years older than me, which is a lot at that age. I was still at school and they were working men. I used to sit there and watch Johnny intently; for me, he was just as good as Bobby Elliott of the Hollies, who I really admired. Johnny had great style, he never messed a beat up and he was also a nice guy on top of that. He and I are still in touch to this day.

I watched every move Johnny made when he played the drums at the Cave, and I remembered it, and then I went home and practised those exact things on my own kit. I listened to a lot of LPs all the way through, too. If I wanted to analyse a particular drum beat, I'd play the record and rest my finger on the vinyl: that slowed it down enough so that I could hear what tom-tom was being played, and so on.

I had fallen utterly in love with the drums, and, with them, the dream of being a star. It was all downhill from there . . .

2

RATTED OUT

A turning point came in early 1965 when I got a really bad report, which with hindsight I deserved. The teachers wrote that I was disrupting the class with my wise-guy comments, and they also noted that I'd never once made it to school on time that year. This didn't go down well with my parents, and I felt pretty bad about it, so for the next six months I knuckled down and worked really hard.

I did my mock O levels that summer, which I thought went well, but when I got the results the teachers had marked me down for my previous bad behaviour – even though all that had been six months earlier – and given me E grades in some of the subjects. An E grade was a pretty bad fail at O level. I assumed there had been a mistake, so I went to a teacher and explained that I was top of the class in those subjects and therefore the E grades couldn't be correct.

The teacher told me to go and see the headmaster, John Harrison.

'We know how well you did in the exams – but six months ago you were messing about every single day,' he told me.

'That's true,' I admitted, 'but surely I've behaved better since then? You can't give me an E if I'm at the top of the class.'

'We can write anything we want about you, Woodmansey,' he said, looking squarely at me.

I told him that wasn't fair, but he wasn't about to back down. He told me that all the teachers had talked about me in the staff room, saying what a troublemaker I was. The fact that I'd behaved myself for the previous six months meant nothing, because I'd been so bad before that point.

This conversation all came as a bit of a shock. I thought about my situation and realized that if I stayed on to do the actual O levels in the summer of 1966, it would be a pointless exercise if the teachers weren't willing to teach me. What the headmaster said next made all that irrelevant.

'Either you leave,' he said, 'or we'll kick you out. It's up to you.'

I told him I was leaving. What else could I do?

'And what are you going to do when you leave school, Woodmansey?'

'I'm going to be a pop star, sir, and be on *Top of the Pops*.'

'You're a moron, Woodmansey – and you always will be. Get out.'

Some years later, in 1972, after *The Rise and Fall of Ziggy Stardust* had been released and I had indeed played *Top of the Pops*, I considered driving up to the school in a limo and sticking two fingers up at his office, but I never did it. Perhaps I should have. John Harrison retired in 1991 and died in 2013, but I bear him no ill will all these years later. After all, being kicked out of school helped me focus on my drumming.

As I walked out of the school gates that July, the thought

of never having to go back and do lessons that I wasn't interested in filled me with excitement. The elation didn't last: a moment later, that feeling was replaced by terror. I clearly remember thinking to myself, 'Oh shit. What am I going to do with the rest of my life?' I'd been unable to answer that question when the careers officers had asked it of me, and I was no nearer to answering it now.

I didn't have a clue what being a working person was all about. Although kids could legally leave school at my age back then, I'd planned to stay on; I thought that I'd get smarter and wiser if I did that, and things would fall into place. I hadn't planned on walking out of the school gates, aged fifteen, straight into real life.

So now I had to face my parents. I knew my mum would be disappointed and my dad would be angry, and I had to find a way to sell it to them.

'Look, I've decided to leave school,' I told them at the dinner table, trying to hide how scared I felt. 'I really want to get a job. You know, learn a trade and make a decent living for myself.'

This was a lie, of course – I still wanted to be a drummer in a band – but I couldn't think of another way out of my predicament.

Fortunately, my dad nodded. 'All right then, son. It's about time you did something with your life.'

My mother was less easy to convince; she obviously thought that I'd thrown away my education – and with it my potential. But she had to accept it. I didn't want to go back to school, my father wanted me to learn a trade and that was that.

In essence, I'd been let down by the education system, but on the other hand it was entirely my own doing. I suppose I was different from most of the other students who understood why they were studying logarithms or technical drawing, or whatever the subject might be. I didn't; I only wanted to do something that I enjoyed so much I'd happily get out of bed in the morning every day to go and do it. School certainly wasn't that something. Music might well be but, in the meantime, I had to get a job.

My father got me an apprenticeship as a plumber and an electrician with a local firm in Driffield. As part of the apprenticeship I was supposed to study at college, but the firm didn't want to pay for it, so that didn't happen.

More importantly for me, the Mutations got their first proper gig (I don't count that awful June-witnessed Christmas performance the previous year). It was at the Buck Hotel in Driffield, which is still there. We were talking music with the landlord one night and he asked us if we'd play there for a fiver between us. Our band – Frank and Paul on guitar, John on bass, Michael on vocals and me on drums – got a pound each to play six songs, including 'Green Onions' by Booker T & the MGs and '(I Can't Get No) Satisfaction' by the Stones, which had been a hit that summer.

There's a repeated part in 'Satisfaction' which is just a drum beat with no other instruments going on, and I was absolutely petrified when it came along, even though it's only two bars long. Those two bars felt like an hour to me; every time we played that song I thought to myself, 'Will I get through this without cocking it up?' I managed it each time, though, and, believe me, that was the high point of my career up to then.

We also did an original song called 'Swan Lake', which was embarrassingly bad. I can't remember how it went, but put it this way: I'm glad YouTube didn't exist back then. We didn't have stage clothes and just wore regular gear like polo-neck sweaters and camel-coloured trousers because we hadn't got as far as thinking about an image; we didn't even know if we could get through a single song in front of an audience, who were mainly just locals.

After that, we started playing regularly at the Buck Hotel, earning £5 each for the night. That fiver was a big deal, because it meant that I was a professional musician. Not only that, there's nothing so good for improving your musical skills as some kind of residency, because you have to get it right, night after night. More gigs came along after that: there were quite a few rich farmers in the area and we'd play for their daughters' birthday parties.

My dad used to drive me to gigs in his van, which was good of him, but a bit odd given that he disliked me being in a band more and more as time passed. He probably thought it would be a short-lived hobby for me. Instead, it was my apprenticeship that was short-lived. I didn't understand the electrician part, and I really hated the plumbing work. I'd be in the middle of Driffield High Street, pulling drain rods through the drains while all the girls from the offices and factories were leaving work. You'd be trying to look cool while wearing rough jeans and an old jacket and pulling shit out of the ground – tricky to say the least.

The older guys generally ignored me: they'd been doing the

job for years and they didn't want an apprentice hanging around. They only ever talked about football, so I never really got into conversation with them. In the end, after about a year, the company sacked me, and it was deserved, because I was more interested in smoking than working.

After that Mum took me shopping because my parents wanted me to have some appropriate, hard-wearing clothes when I was looking for work. But by now I was devoted to fashion and was mostly to be found in narrow-legged hipster trousers and double-breasted jackets – all made by June who had left school and was working as a clothes designer. I also wore sand-coloured desert boots and had a long Army & Navy coat in navy blue. You couldn't wear those clothes in a blue-collar job. Mum was steering me towards a working man's donkey jacket which Dad wanted me to have, which was the exact opposite of what I was about.

'I'm really sorry,' I said to Mum, 'but I can't wear this. You can buy it if you want, but I'll never wear it.'

There was a real stigma attached to being out of work, so I asked my mates if they knew of any jobs going. It turned out that four of them were working in the Vertex spectacle factory. They told me it was cushy and they had a good laugh, and the money was good, so I went for an interview there. Luckily for me, the foreman who interviewed me was a pub singer. He knew I was a drummer and we hit it off; in fact, we talked about music most of the time rather than work-related stuff. I got the job.

My job consisted of taking a square piece of plastic with two holes in it, shaping it into spectacles, drilling holes in it, putting sides on it . . . and repeat. It sounds dull, but it wasn't bad, actually. I enjoyed it and the money was really good. We were on bonus schemes, and we had a game going on about who could be the fastest. Then the management bought time and motion people in to make us quicker, and we actually slowed down a bit, because they were useless – but we were still faster than anybody else who'd done it before.

As talented as I was at making spectacles, music was still my obsession. A bunch of us would travel twelve miles to Bridlington Spa to see major bands like the Small Faces, the Kinks, the Who – you name it. It was brilliant, like seeing creatures from another world. I'd sit and watch, my eyes glued on the drummers. And I was still with the Mutations. By now we'd played at the Driffield Town Hall and supported the Roadrunners several times on their gigs. That was all about to change.

It was 1968 and revolution was in the air. In America people were protesting against the Vietnam War. In Driffield we were protesting . . . about a fish and chip shop. One of the coffee bars in Driffield was going to be turned into a chippie, and the teenagers in the town were not happy about losing a popular hangout, so about eighty of us went down in a sort of procession and stopped all the traffic. I don't know who organized it, but word must have spread pretty fast because the local police were there – all two of them! – watching us chanting and shouting. For Driffield, it was a major event.

I was standing there holding a banner that read 'We want a coffee bar' when the Roadrunners' old Mother's Pride bread van pulled up in front of me and they leaned out and shouted,

'Woody, get in!' I didn't need to be asked twice, because they were the coolest musicians I knew, so I threw somebody the banner and jumped in the van. Inside I saw the singer Dave 'Les' Westaway, the guitarist Dave 'Feet' Lawson and Brian Wheeldon (now the bass player), all grinning at me.

'Listen, Woody,' said Dave. 'Johnny's leaving the band because he can't play any more. We want you to be our drummer.'

My mind raced. Playing with them would be a challenge, but also the best thing that ever happened to me. Now I'd be in a real band.

'Yeah, definitely,' I muttered, in my usual quiet way. Faced with a band of musicians who were all older and better than me, I was crippled with shyness. But inside, I was happier than I think I'd ever been. When I told the Mutations about the offer they all agreed I was right to take the job.

It turned out that Johnny, who was only in his early twenties, had developed arthritis in his arms. He'd only found out when he was riding his bike one day, couldn't turn the corner and crashed. When he was getting checked up they told him that he shouldn't make too many movements with his arms or he'd lose the use of them. That meant drumming was out. Everybody was gutted for him.

I played my first gig with the Roadrunners the following week, which was terrifying, because they were good musicians with several years more experience of professional gigs. Fortunately, I was a quick learner, and I knew a lot of the cover versions they wanted me to play. As a bonus they gave me Johnny's Premier drum kit, which was a vast improvement on the crappy Salvation Army kit which I'd been playing with the Mutations. The gig was at a church hall in Barton-upon-Humber and we played covers of songs by the Beatles, the Small Faces, the Who, the Stones and Tommy James and the Shondells.

Now I was in a real band for the first time, which felt great – like the next step on an important journey. The Roadrunners were good musicians and they were organized, with gigs lined up, and their own instruments and transport. June started making stage clothes for us, and we'd head to gigs dressed in beige, red and even purple suits, worn with black or white polo-neck sweaters.

I got on really well with the other guys. We had the same sense of humour: we'd recite entire *Goon Show* programmes in the back of the van. We did some pretty stupid things to amuse ourselves. Once, when we were driving to York, we saw a farm shop with a number of signs outside saying 'Potatoes, peas, carrots' in ornate lettering. We stole the signs, but we didn't just throw them away like a bunch of morons, we kept them in the back of the van. Then when we were heading back that way a week later, in the early hours of the morning, we hung them back up again, to surprise the farmer who probably thought his signs were gone for good.

We had a lot of laughs in that band. One of our favourite places was a club in York called the Enterprise, and when we were playing nearby we'd go there for a few beers after the gig. A guy called Guppy ran the club, although perhaps it's a bit generous to call it that: it was basically a dank cellar that played cool music like Tamla and early soul.

It was pitch-dark in that place, apart from a single red light at the far end of the dance floor. The other end was completely dark, so when you danced with a chick at that end you had to manoeuvre your way down to the light to see what she looked like. Guppy had a special room upstairs, where we'd listen to the Goons albums. That was fantastic, because we loved all that stuff, and we'd hang out there all night, laughing our arses off.

If we were going into a pub with two entrances, we had a sure-fire way to unnerve the clientele. Dave would go in one door, I'd go in another, we'd catch sight of each other and dramatically shout out 'Mick!' and 'Dave!' Then we'd run together into the middle of the pub and pretend to kiss, with a hand pressed between our mouths. Pint glasses would smash all around us, with people even more unnerved when they saw our long hair.

We weren't really trying to shock people; we just thought this was hilarious. But in retrospect, antics such as this one were an early, milder version of the gender-bending stuff that bands would be getting up to a few years later, not least the band I was in. Perhaps change was in the air, even at that stage.

Despite all the fooling about, the Roadrunners were a highly professional band and I travelled all over the county for the first time with them. We still didn't have a manager, but the guitarist used to call the booking agent each week and see what gigs he had for us. At one point we supported the Herd, Peter Frampton's band, at Leeds University. They were a big deal, and really dominated the crowd when they played live; Frampton had been the 'Face of 1968' in a magazine called *Rave*.

He was a good guy, and really validated me by coming into our dressing room and saying, 'What's your name? I'll see you at the top', a hell of a compliment from a musician as talented as he was. I never forgot that, and made a point of encouraging younger musicians when I'd made my own mark a few years later.

We looked shit-hot, by the way. There was a shop in Driffield called Alec Hall's, which was a 'gentlemen's outfitters'. A couple of young guys worked there who would buy in weird stuff from London, all the way through the mod period. They'd show us their new collections when we popped in on a Saturday and we'd buy clothes on credit, paying a bit off each week. That way we had a good flow of new clothes coming in. We wore things like hipsters, two-tone shirts, kaftans and long black Army & Navy coats.

Of course, my dad didn't understand any of this obsession with wearing the right clothes and playing rock 'n' roll. How could he? Our generation didn't want to look like their parents, but he would never have grasped that, even if he'd been prepared to make the effort. Back then you were supposed to toe the line, get a trade and be a proper grown-up like your parents were, but that's never happened to me, and it never will, so that was a losing battle for him. It's like that old joke: a kid says to his mother, 'When I grow up, I want to be a drummer,' and she says, 'You can't do both, son.'

With hindsight, I can imagine what all this was like for my dad. Back then, his generation had come through the Second World War as teenagers and been aware of some truly terrible things – things that kids like me, who had escaped all that, couldn't possibly imagine. He hadn't fought in the war himself, but he'd been in some nasty skirmishes in Hong Kong. I remember he told me that he was on guard duty one night when Chinese snipers were about. He was shitting himself all night, because they could kill you at any moment from their position up in the hills. That doesn't exactly make you the most tolerant person afterwards.

My dad's generation just wanted to settle down, look after their families and encourage their kids to get a trade and do well in life. When we rebelled against all that, it must have been a real shock for them. You can imagine just how much worse it was when we started growing our hair long and wearing the most outrageous clothes imaginable, especially in Yorkshire.

Pretty soon my father and I were in a war of our own. He didn't like me coming home late after playing gigs with the Roadrunners. He'd lock the front door, so I had to sit in the outside toilet for a couple of hours with only a little paraffin lamp for company. In the winter that was bloody cold. Sometimes my mum would wake up in the night, take pity and come down and let me in. I'd creep up quietly to my bedroom without waking up my dad. None of this was going to stop me playing in the band, but it wasn't exactly good for my morale.

My parents thought I'd thrown my talents away by becoming a musician. I know that they just wanted the best for me, but to their generation the idea of me becoming successful as an entertainer or a performer was no more than a dream. In those days you were pushed towards having a trade. I remember that if anyone was out of work in our town, you knew who they were. Nobody stayed out of work for long, because everybody wanted a job, no matter what it was. That was the attitude around me.

After a fight with my father he'd kick me out and I'd say,

'It's OK, I'll go and live with June', because she had her own flat by then. That didn't go down well, of course: men and women weren't supposed to live together unless they were married. After a day or two, my dad would send my mother over to get me back, saying, 'He's forgiven you!'

It seems trivial now, but we were still arguing about how I looked, with my long hair and jeans covered in satin patches of different colours and leather trim around the pockets. I certainly looked pretty weird by Driffield standards, but in comparison to what I'd be wearing a couple of years down the line it was fairly sedate.

One day I was searching for my jeans, but I couldn't find them anywhere. I asked my mum if she'd washed them and she said no, they were in the dustbin. I went and looked – and there they were, covered in eggshells and potato peelings. My dad had thrown them in there because he hated them so much. 'Thanks, Dad,' I thought, and got them out and put them on, filthy as they were, because I didn't give a damn.

Meanwhile, things weren't going too smoothly with the Road-runners. There'd been a bit of trouble in the band between one of the members and his girlfriend: she'd caught him playing around with other women, and so she gave him an ultimatum – her or the band. He quit, and the rest of the members quit shortly afterwards, so there was no more Roadrunners and I was out of a gig for about three months.

I wasn't going to stop playing the drums, though, and I auditioned for a few bands. Some of them were pretty talented: one of them was psychedelic rockers Iron Butterfly, who were best known for their song 'In-A-Gadda-Da-Vida', although I had no idea why an American band would be auditioning in London. When I got there, I found about a hundred and fifty other drummers all playing their kits in a big hall. It was an almighty racket, and the band wasn't as musical at that point as it later became, so I decided I didn't want that gig, even if I got through the audition. I was also invited to try out for a group whose singer went on to join Sharks, who were successful in the seventies. Their bass player was a guy called John Bentley, who later joined Squeeze. They were playing a form of West Coast Americana, which was a bit trippy for me and not really my thing, so I decided not to bother.

At the time, the coolest band in Yorkshire were the Rats. Their guitarist, Mick Ronson, had a great reputation, which I realized was fully deserved when I saw the band at an open-air festival in 1969. I was blown away by his presence on stage and his guitar playing; he was four years older than me and had been playing with bands since 1963, when I was just a kid. It later turned out he'd seen me drum with the Roadrunners at the same event.

The Rats had experience, having spent time in London doing gigs, but they had never quite got the attention they deserved from the record companies. The music they made varied from blues to rock covers and even psychedelia – they'd been known as Treacle for a while. They were one of the first bands from our area to get really big amplifiers – their stage was filled with gear and it looked really impressive.

A few months after I saw Mick play at that outdoor event I was at Vertex doing overtime on a Sunday when I looked up from the glazing wheel at my workbench and the Rats were standing there. They'd sneaked through security and asked people where I was.

'We're the Rats, and my name is Mick Ronson,' Mick told me, before introducing their singer, Benny Marshall, and their bassist, Keith 'Ched' Cheeseman.

Mick looked very cool: he had long blond hair and was wearing a crisp white shirt, a long black coat and neatly pressed black trousers with black slip-on shoes, almost like a young English Tom Petty.

'Pleased to meet you,' I said. 'How did you get in here?'

'We sneaked in,' he smiled. 'We needed to talk to you.'

It turned out that the Rats had come all the way over from Hull to ask me to join them. That was quite a compliment, and they were all really nice guys, so of course I took it seriously.

Mick said their drummer, John Cambridge, had left and that they wanted me to join the Rats. He added that I'd have to come to the audition and pretend I hadn't got the job yet, as they'd promised an audition to six other drummers who had insisted on having one.

'No problem,' I replied. Inside, I was delighted. This was the break I needed. I'd liked being in the Roadrunners, but the Rats were a much more professional band – and I knew that I'd fit in with a guitar player as good as Mick.

I did the audition, joined the band and we started gigging that week. It was clubs and pubs once more, just like the ones I'd been playing with the Roadrunners – but the Rats travelled more widely because they'd been going longer. I remember we did a lot of town halls. It was semi-professional gigging, because we were all still working and we didn't make much money from the band.

Later I found out that the Rats had wanted me, probably after seeing me play, because Mick hoped to move the band on to a more professional level and thought I would help with that. John knew some people in London and we heard that he went down there to join a band called Junior's Eyes, which played original material as well as backing other musicians. One of these was a guy called David Bowie, but I knew very little about him so Junior's Eyes barely crossed my mind. I was too busy concentrating on the Rats.

In retrospect, both Mick and I owe Johnny a nod of gratitude: if he hadn't had the guts to move to London, Ziggy and the Spiders would never have happened in the way they did.

Mick was the focus on stage, of course, but the Rats didn't have a leader as such – we all pitched in. I liked him a lot: he was funny, shared my sense of humour, and we dressed the same way. He had learned to play the piano and the violin, and to read and write music up to a certain level, before he jumped to the guitar, but that wasn't something he bragged about. He probably thought we'd take the piss out of him if he admitted he played the violin. Later on, he'd draw on those other talents to create musical arrangements on songs that are loved the world over. He told me once that he was always striving to achieve the same tonal qualities in his guitar playing as he did on the violin.

I'd had some laughs with the Roadrunners, but it was another level of enjoyment with the Rats – because they literally didn't give a shit about anything or anybody. When we took on a new roadie, for example, he had to undergo an initiation where we stripped him naked in the middle of a city, and then we'd fuck off and leave him there for twenty minutes. We did this to one guy in the outskirts of Leeds, leaving him in nothing but his boots, and then drove off for a coffee. Half an hour later we went back and he was hiding in a doorway, as well he might.

On paper all this stuff might sound a bit harsh, but I can assure you that it was all in good humour and a big part of our bonding process. Anything went in that band. We had a stupid rule where if the van drove around a roundabout and one of us shouted, 'That was nice, Daddy! Can we do it again?' the driver had to go round the roundabout again. The rule was cast-iron: even if we were running late for the gig, because we'd got there late from work. Sometimes, the driver had to go round eight or nine times, because it was funny, to us anyway.

I remember we did one gig in a gymnasium, run by these massive bodybuilders and bouncers and other heavies. These blokes were telling us that some arseholes had been nicking weights from their gym, and that if they ever found out who the culprits were they'd tear them limb from limb. Our singer, Benny Marshall, was a bit lazy when it came to helping clear up the equipment, so to get our revenge we secretly took some weights and stuffed them in his bag.

We packed up the gear, without any help from him as usual, and came to get him when it was time to leave. 'Come on, Benny!' we shouted, as he stood talking to some of the bodybuilders. He went to pick up his bag, but it wouldn't move. Trying to behave like everything was normal, he kept talking to them but he couldn't hide the look of terror on his face. He got away unscathed, though. Another time we piled all the equipment that we had on his bed and went home. He cursed the hell out of us because he had to shift it all himself. Any trick like that which one of us dreamed up, we did it.

I had my first experience with drugs in the Rats after a roadie of ours went down to London and brought back some grass. The idea of drugs was quite shocking to us back then, because they weren't easily obtainable and did not really come up in conversation. Even Mick, who had been around a bit, didn't know about drugs because he was raised a Mormon. He didn't even drink alcohol.

It probably wasn't the best idea to smoke my first joint right before a gig. Billed as 'The Rats Reform', the show in Hornsea was sold out because we had quite a reputation in those parts, and also because the band had been in a hiatus for a while and it was a comeback gig of sorts. We were nervous because about four hundred people were coming to see us, so the roadie said, 'Have a pull on this, it'll help.' We did and he was right: our nerves disappeared.

We kicked the gig off with 'Crossroads' by Cream, playing it in every style you can imagine: calypso, blues, reggae, skiffle . . . everything. At the end of the set we came off saying, 'That was fantastic!' We didn't realize that we'd been playing the same number for forty-five minutes. We were out of our minds, just from that bit of grass. I never even noticed the crowd's reaction but it can't have been good.

The roadies looked at us in disgust and said, 'You can pack your own fucking equipment up. We've never been so embarrassed!' So they pissed off, and we howled with laughter. That taught me and Mick not to do drugs when we were working.

People were so innocent about all that stuff back then. It's hard to believe, but one night we got an old shoebox, wrote

'Drugs' in big letters on it and stuck it on top of Mick's amp while we played. It really freaked people out, but it was just a joke. That's how naive the audiences were back then – people genuinely believed that if you had drugs, which you obviously would if you were a degenerate rock band, you'd keep them in a special, clearly labelled box.

Drugs didn't play a major part in my life at any point, partly because their effects scared me. After that first experience, we went to a dealer's house in Hull for more grass, and I was shitting myself. There was a guy there on acid and it freaked me out, so I knew right away I would never do anything like that. That helped me later when drugs were more readily available, in that I was never interested in doing more than smoking grass.

Again, despite all our fooling about, the Rats were a serious band. We covered songs from Jeff Beck, Hendrix, Cream and many old blues tracks. We once played a gig supporting Jon Hiseman's Colosseum. Part of our set included a drum solo, which I had to perform before Hiseman himself, who was a world-famous drummer. Talk about pressure – but I did it anyway, and his roadies told me that Hiseman thought it was great that I had the balls to do it, and he enjoyed it.

Mick, Ched and I had another project going at the same time as the Rats: a band which initially featured Mick singing and playing guitar. He couldn't do both at the same time, though, and he couldn't really sing anyway, so we asked a guy called Alan Palmer to join us. At the time, Alan was the singer in a band called the Mandrakes, and our project never really took off, although he later changed his name to Robert Palmer and went on to enormous success in the eighties and nineties with hits like 'Addicted to Love'.

I was generally moving along in a directionless way, I suppose, working at Vertex in the daytime and gigging all night, to the general irritation of my parents. I could have gone on like that for some years, I suppose, but in late 1969 the Rats unexpectedly split up.

'Woods, mate,' Mick told me, 'I'm going down to London, because Johnny reckons I'd fit in with this singer he knows down there. I'm sorry, I really am, but don't worry – we'll sort something out'.

Johnny was John Cambridge, and when Mick told me the singer was called David Bowie I immediately remembered seeing a flyer for his single 'Space Oddity', which had been released in July 1969, around the time of the first moon landing. I'd heard the song on the radio, but it hadn't really made an impression on me. I thought it was a folk tune with some flowery production, and I didn't like folk music because there were no heavy drums in it. I was a bit of a snob: if music wasn't progressive, and it didn't have a tough edge or demand skill from you, I looked down on it.

It was a blow when Mick left to join Bowie's group, but at least he and I had an understanding that we'd play together again. Still, I had no band for about three months, and after playing with musicians as good as the Rats, I couldn't find a local group that I even wanted to be a part of. It was a depressing time. At this point, music as a career was starting to seem like an impossible option – so when I was offered a really good job at the factory where I worked, I seriously considered it.

In previous months I had begun to excel at the Vertex job. I knew a lot of people on the other machines, so I learned how to use those as well as mine. When those machines broke down, the operators would ask me to fix them because the guy who was supposed to fix them was running behind. I wasn't trying to get promoted or anything; I was just bored, and wanted to do things to pass the time.

The people in charge noticed this, called me in and asked me to be the second-in-command to the foreman – even though I was a young kid and there were thirty-five-year-old men there who had been waiting years for that job to come their way. I was uncomfortable with this and said, 'This can't be right. The other blokes aren't going to like this,' but they said, 'We don't care. You're the only one who knows how to set all the machinery up.'

This was in spite of the fact that for the past year or so I never got to work on time, because I was gigging with the Rats every night and didn't get home until five most mornings. They warned me that I'd need to be at work by a quarter to eight every day to get everything set up. If I did join another band, that would be tricky, but it wasn't an insurmountable problem.

The money they were offering was really good. You got holiday pay, and they said there'd be a car and that they would help you get a house, too. It was essentially an offer of a career for life, if I kept my nose clean. So I told my parents, and of course they thought it was wonderful, and they told my relatives, who all said how great it was, too.

I was probably going to take the factory job – it was too good not to. For that area, it was a really great job. The offer came on a Friday, so I told them I'd give them my answer on Monday, when I'd had the weekend to think about it.

On the Saturday, I got a phone call from David Bowie, asking me to join his band.

3

ALL THE MADMEN

'Is that Woody?' said the voice on the phone.

I said it was.

'I'm David Bowie.'

'Hello there,' I replied, surprised.

'Mick Ronson gave me your number,' he told me. 'I've got a band down in London – I believe you know my drummer, John Cambridge?'

'Yes, I know John,' I said.

'Well, John's leaving the band,' he continued. 'Mick says you're a really great drummer and that you'd fit in perfectly, as a player and as a person, so we want you to come down and join us in London. You don't have to audition – the job's yours if you want it – and I've got a place where you can live. I also have Tony Visconti on bass and he's my producer.'

He sounded polite, and Mick had taken the trouble to recommend me to him, so I didn't want to be rude to the guy. I said, 'Sounds good to me, David – but I just need to look at a few things.'

He was keen to get an answer from me, so I said I'd call him back on Monday.

It might be difficult to imagine now, but in early 1970 Bowie seemed like a one-hit wonder. His single 'Space Oddity', which got to Number 5 in the charts, had come and gone, and the follow-up, 'The Prettiest Star', had flopped. His first album, *David Bowie*, had been released in 1967 and included whimsical songs like 'The Laughing Gnome' and 'Love You Till Tuesday'. It hadn't worked and neither had the second album – also called *David Bowie*, bizarrely – which came out in autumn 1969. Not that I'd listened to it. I'd been listening to bands such as Led Zeppelin and Cream over the previous couple of years; Bowie's influences were obviously completely different. My friends wouldn't even know who Bowie was if I asked them about him.

On the other hand, Bowie's band – who were now called the Hype – were obviously talented, which appealed to me. The four musicians had made a bit of progress, but not much: they'd played a *John Peel Show* on 5 February, and done some gigs around London. One of these was unusual because they'd dressed up as superheroes. Bowie was Rainbowman, Tony Visconti was Hypeman, Mick was Gangsterman and John Cambridge was Cowboyman. That show, with its theatricality, has been seen since as one of the moments that inspired the UK glam scene.

Most importantly as I saw it, Mick and I were like brothers. We'd travelled the length and breadth of England in the Rats, and when you spend that much time cooped up in a van with someone, you get to know them pretty well. I was very close to Mick. He wasn't the saint that he's been made out to be since he died in 1993, but he was a good man whose word I always trusted, so if he thought Bowie had potential, that was important to me.

Of course, I'd have to move to London, which didn't immediately appeal. It would be a big jump to go to a new city with new people on a career path that I didn't have much experience of, apart from a couple of years of playing in semi-professional bands. I knew it had to be done, though. Nowadays you can live in Manchester, for example, and still be in a big band, but it just wasn't possible to do that back then. London was where you had to go if you wanted to make it as a rock musician, just like the Beatles had a few years before. The door to rock 'n' roll success was slightly open if you wanted to go through it, but you couldn't go through it from Hull, and the Rats were never going to be big in any case. We just didn't have the right connections to anyone else, or any connections at all come to think of it.

My problem was that I'd been offered a great job which could potentially set me up for life, and that kind of offer didn't come along very often to twenty-year-olds in my part of the world. The Vertex job might sound unattractive to you, reading this forty-five years later, but it might well have taken me to the comfortable standard of living that my parents dreamed about for me. All my mates worked there, and I really liked it.

I sat on the sofa on Friday and Saturday, going backwards and forwards, getting nowhere. The TV was on but I wasn't paying attention to what was on it. I knew my parents wouldn't want me to say no to the factory job, and I knew that June and my friends wouldn't want me to leave Driffield either. I sat there and tried to picture what my life would be like in either scenario.

I couldn't do it. I was stumped, so I sat there, numbly, for hours. Mick knew that Bowie had called me and rang to see what I thought of the offer to go down to London – but it didn't help.

'Come on, Woods,' he urged. 'We'll have a laugh, and David's a good songwriter. He's a good frontman too, and we're not gonna do fuck all up in Hull. He's got a big place down in London. You'll love it.'

After he rang off, I stared at the TV. In my head I imagined being sixty-five years old, about to retire, with my grand-children around me. I'd just had my annual holiday. We were doing all right for money, and we had a nice house and every-thing was fine. Then a band came on the TV; I didn't know who it was, but they fitted in with the scene that was going on in my head. I was talking to my grandkids, pointing at the TV and saying to them, 'When I was twenty, I could have done that!' – and the whole thing went on pause.

Suddenly I opened my eyes wide, and I knew that was the truth. If I took the factory job, that would be my future, and I'd be looking back with regret. I would have rejected my one chance to see if I could make it as a musician, which was the only thing I ever wanted to do anyway. I didn't want to work in a factory for the rest of my life, after all.

I realized that even if I came back from playing with Bowie, and I was in the gutter with rags on, and all my mates and relatives were saying to me, 'Ha ha, you wanker – we told you not to go!', I could stick two fingers up at them and say, 'Fuck you. At least I tried.'

And that was it. I called Bowie on Sunday morning and said, 'I'm in. I've got to give a week's notice but after that I can come as soon as you want me.'

'Great. I'll see you a week on Monday. You can come down with Mick, who's in Hull at the moment.'

I went to the factory the next morning and told my boss that I didn't want the job, and also that I was leaving. Of course, he thought I was an idiot.

'So you're going to be a pop star, are you?' he said.

I knew he was taking the piss, so I said nothing. Also, I could see his point. In an agricultural town like Driffield, no one went off and became a rock star. No one had ever done it, and there was no reason why anyone ever would. In his eyes it just wasn't going to happen.

My parents' reaction was twice as bad. They went completely mad. My mum burst into tears and my dad shouted at me, 'Are you bloody mad? You've just been offered a foreman's job at Vertex!'

'I really think this is going to work out, Dad,' I said lamely. I knew I would never convince him. I had been nervous about his reaction, of course, but I was expecting it because, as I've already said, I'd only ever had negativity from my parents when it came to music.

'Well, let's see how long this band lasts!' yelled my dad, and stormed out.

I can't blame him for that, but I was adamant that, win or lose, this was what I was going to do. A fundamental truth that I've always held is that you have to be able to handle winning or losing with the same attitude. If you win, great; if you lose, deal with it. You simply say, 'I didn't get that one,' and move on. I had no idea if it would work out for me in Bowie's band. I didn't particularly like his music, and I didn't know if he had talent. But I did know that I needed to get to London if I was going to make it as a musician.

It was a lot of blind faith on my part. The odds were stacked against me in every single way. I was an ordinary guy from a country town in a conservative part of the world, with parents who wanted me to get a proper job, at a time when rock music definitely wasn't seen as a viable career option.

My mates didn't really want me to go to London either, because we were a close bunch. When I told June about it she didn't quite know how to react, because she didn't know how long I'd be away. She was the only one who really understood what I wanted to achieve and the two of us had talked about the possibility of leaving our small town for London someday to further our careers. Even though that day had arrived a little earlier than planned, she understood I had to do it.

I left home a week later, on a rainy Monday in March 1970. I'd only been to London briefly a couple of times, once on a school day trip and once for an uneventful audition; I didn't know the city at all. I was being totally uprooted from my home town to a completely new environment. It was fortunate that Mick was making the journey down with me, because he'd been up in Hull that weekend. I got a train from Driffield to Hull and met Mick at the station, and we went down to London together. Bowie sent up a roadie to fetch my drum kit from Driffield, which seemed quite grand to me.

On the train I asked Mick what kind of music we'd be playing. He said it was a bit folky and that Bowie was a good frontman, but that was about it. He had no idea what Bowie had in mind either.

'He's a good bloke, though, Woods,' he assured me. 'We'll be sleeping on mattresses at the top of the stairs, but you don't mind that, do you?'

When we got to London, Mick had to go off to see someone – he was going to join us the next day – so I went out to Beckenham, the suburb where Bowie lived, on my own. It was a nice part of London; actually, it didn't feel like London at all. The streets were clean and leafy; the houses were large and distinguished; and while it wasn't as affluent an area as Chelsea or Kensington by any means, it was definitely a nice part of the world.

I remember walking with my two bags, which contained pretty much everything I owned, up to Haddon Hall, a massive Victorian house at 42 Southend Road. I was surprisingly nervous as I knocked on the door.

I recollect exactly what Bowie looked like when he opened it. He had light brown curly shoulder-length hair and he was wearing a rainbow T-shirt, a necklace, bangles, tight red corduroy trousers with a sparkly belt; and blue slip-on shoes with red stars that he'd sprayed on to the top of each one. I thought, 'Whoa – he definitely looks the part.'

As for me, I had curly hair halfway down my back, a denim shirt, a pink tie-dyed vest, frayed jeans and moccasins. It was the progressive rock look.

'Pleased to meet you,' Bowie said. 'It's nice of you to come down.'

He invited me in, asking me how my trip had been and all

the usual polite bollocks. Then we sat in his lounge and immediately started talking about music.

'I'm writing songs for a new record,' he told me. 'Have you
heard my albums?'

I told him I hadn't, trying not to make it obvious that I
didn't think much of his work to date.

'The music might be a bit different this time,' he went on,
perhaps sensing what I was thinking. 'Tony Visconti's going to
produce the new album and he's got some great ideas.'

The vibe was relaxed, and Bowie was confident and intelligent. In that very first conversation I found myself testing
him as we sat there, just as he was testing me. I wanted to
know what he could do, musically, because I'd come a long
way and I needed him to be good.

'What direction do you think you'll take with the new
songs?' I asked.

'I'm not sure yet,' he replied, 'but I know they need to be
different from my older songs, and stronger. I want to make
an impact, and I need to move on from where I was before.'

He then played me some of his older songs on an acoustic
guitar, and, to my relief, I really liked his singing voice. It
was different from what I was used to – very clear and very
English. It was obvious that the singer Anthony Newley was
an influence, and although I wasn't the biggest Newley fan I
liked Bowie's voice because it was pure. I was used to blues
wailing from heavy rock singers – Robert Plant, Paul Rogers
and so on – but Bowie didn't have that kind of voice at all. He
had a completely different approach: he'd express emotions
in his vocals but just enough to put his point across to you,
which I understood immediately. He could reach high notes,

and hold them, and he never, ever sang out of tune. I never once heard him hit a bum note in all the years we played together.

To my surprise, I found myself thinking, 'Fuck, these songs are good', even though I'd previously dismissed them as being too lightweight for me. I particularly liked 'Wild Eyed Boy From Freecloud', which had been the B-side of 'Space Oddity'. Perhaps I'd been wrong about him. (I must admit I grew to really like 'Space Oddity' too.)

Then Bowie played me his two albums. Some of the songs were a bit too 'novelty' for my liking, but there was depth in some of the others. The viewpoint from which those songs were written was unique, even back then. It felt as if only he could have written them. I'd never heard anything like them before, and they really got my attention.

What was most important to me was that Bowie could write songs. I needed him to be a good songwriter. We'd tried to do our own songs up in Yorkshire with the Rats, but we'd failed miserably, because we just didn't have those skills even though we were good musicians. So I had a checklist in my head of things that I wanted from Bowie: I wanted him to be able to write, and to be a confident musician, which I could tell he was, just from seeing him sitting there and playing the guitar.

It wasn't obvious what his songs were about, but that didn't matter to me; the important thing, as I saw it, was that I had a story written in my head by the time he finished playing one of his compositions. That story was true for me, and it took me on a journey that I enjoyed. Good songs are supposed to do that and that, to me, was the sign of a good songwriter.

After we'd been talking for an hour or so, a pretty blonde woman came in, walked over to me and said, 'Hi, I'm Angie Bowie. I'm David's wife, and I'm a lesbian.'

I stuttered, 'Oh . . . It's nice to meet you. I'm Woody.'

I couldn't look Angie in the eye. I knew what a lesbian was, but I'd never spoken to one, so I didn't really know what to do with that information. I wasn't a homophobe by the way, just confused. It was a weird thing to say to someone the first time you met them and, also, why would Bowie and Angie have got married if she was a lesbian? I needed some time to think about it!

Angie was quite something: loud and vivacious, with her American accent, moving her arms and body all the time. She was twenty and I found out later she had been born in Cyprus to American parents, and had been a student at Kingston Poly when she met Bowie. As Bowie and I chatted that evening she flew in and out of the room like a mosquito on speed, interrupting whatever we were talking about. If she liked what she heard, she'd throw in a loud, unsolicited opinion.

Bowie would gaze at her with affection at those times. They'd got married just before I came down to live with them, and they seemed very much in love. They cuddled and kissed, frequently and passionately.

My first evening with Bowie was amazing. Although he was only twenty-three – which seems very young now – he appeared self-assured and sophisticated. Occasionally he would be open and warm, like one of my mates from Yorkshire: you could crack jokes with him and talk about *Monty Python's Flying*

Circus, which had appeared on TV a few months before. He loved the Pythons' surreal sense of humour, and so did I.

'And what is the name of your ravishing wife?' he'd say, quoting from the 'Marriage Guidance Counsellor' sketch.

'It's Deirdre!' I'd reply, in a high, simpering voice.

'Deirdre . . .' he continued, lasciviously. 'What a beautiful, beautiful name!'

And so on.

At the same time, even while we were throwing jokes around, I noticed that there was a certain detachment about him. Bowie seemed like an artist in preparation: he looked as though he was planning things in his head, even while he was talking to you and looking directly at you. You couldn't help but feel a distance from him when that happened.

As we talked, it became obvious that when Bowie's career had failed to take off after 'Space Oddity', he'd taken a bit of a knock and was struggling to find a new way to express himself. Although he'd done a certain amount of recording by then, he was going through a period of significant change. I noticed something handwritten on the wall at Haddon Hall. It read 'Not conformity but radical', with the name 'Ken Pitt' – who was soon to be Bowie's ex-manager – written above the word 'conformity' in establishment-type writing, and the word 'radical' had the word 'rebel' written after it in different, more aggressive lettering. That summed up the period of chaos he was in when I joined him, to an extent at least.

Tony Visconti arrived later that evening, accompanied by his then girlfriend Liz Hartley, and I liked him immediately. He was twenty-six, so a few years older than the rest of us. He was an American musician and producer from New York who had moved to London in 1968 and had had some success working with Georgie Fame, Procol Harum, the Moody Blues, the Move and Tyrannosaurus Rex, Marc Bolan's band. Then, in 1969, he was asked to produce Bowie's second album and they'd hit it off straight away. I knew he'd worked with a load of successful people, and as the five of us sat down for dinner at the Bowies' dining table, I asked him what he had in mind for Bowie's new album.

'We're going to put together the songs over the next few months,' said Visconti. 'Have you seen the rehearsal room yet? No? Let's go down there after dinner.'

Visconti was assured, confident and very upbeat in the way that Americans often are, compared to us cautious Brits. His presence made me feel as if I'd taken a real professional leap forward by coming down to be in Bowie's band. What I also loved about him was that he understood the English sense of humour completely, which was unusual back then for anyone who wasn't from this country. He could hold his own in a conversation about Monty Python or the Goons as well as any of the rest of us.

After dinner, Bowie showed me around. Haddon Hall was divided into eight flats. He rented most of the ground floor, and he had the main entrance as part of his flat, so the entire building looked like it was his, when he did photo shoots and so on there. You walked through the front door and there was a little kitchen on the left, a bathroom on the right and then the main living room in front of you. At the other end of the room a huge staircase led up to a stained-glass window on the landing, where the doors to the other flats had originally been.

It looked exactly like the massive staircase at Tara in *Gone with the Wind*.

At the top there was an area on the other side of the banisters where Mick and I shared a mattress. Tony and Liz had a room downstairs; Bowie and Angie also had their room downstairs; and there was a lounge. The other person living there was Roger Fry, an Australian who was Bowie's driver and roadie. He had a mattress under the stairs.

The flat was sparsely furnished, perhaps because the Bowies, Visconti and Liz had only moved into it the previous December. There was nothing but a chest in the hall, and a bed and some drawers in Bowie's room, the ceiling of which he'd sprayed silver. He had also bought a really nice antique dining table and chairs, which he'd painted red, adding gold to the carved details. The first time we sat down to dinner at the table, I noticed how artistic it looked. This was to be my home for the next year and a half.

The domestic arrangements were simple. Mick and I were paid seven pounds a week each. Angie would be the one to hand me, Mick and Tony our cash. Bowie paid the rent for the place, and we all chipped in to a household kitty for food. It was a bit like a hippie commune, which was fine by me: the progressive aesthetic of it suited how I was feeling at the time.

Bowie didn't seem like a wealthy man by any means. He was getting royalties from 'Space Oddity', so he had a bit of money, although not a lot by the look of it. I didn't sign a contract with him at that stage; it was all done by verbal agreement. Money didn't cross my mind as long as we were housed, clothed and fed – that was all that mattered. I was just happy to be a professional musician, in London, with a chance of making it.

Bowie and Angie were obviously used to a slightly more luxurious level of living than Mick and I were, especially when it came to food. This became slightly irritating within a few weeks of my arrival. We'd put our money into the kitty, and they'd spend it all on a single meal, so we'd have fuck all to eat for the rest of the week. For instance, they'd buy luxury food items, sometimes just enough for one meal, and then we'd ask where the potatoes were, and there weren't any – because they hadn't bought any.

In retrospect, they weren't really cut out for running the house. When the food ran out Angie would complain, 'You get nothing for your money these days.'

I'd say, 'I know. There's not even any potatoes!'

We'd eat toast and whatever else we could scrape together, and no one starved, but when you've got five hungry people in a household, arguments are inevitable.

One day Tony, Mick and I had a massive row with Bowie and Angie, and we ended up saying, 'We'll buy the fucking food!' But then Angie would try to cook what we'd bought, and she'd burn it. She was a shit cook; perhaps that's why Bowie was so thin. He never cooked, and rarely ate. After a while Mick and I decided to make meals for ourselves and leave them to it.

But none of this really mattered, because we had music to make. Bowie's plans to record an album and tour it afterwards were basic, but they sounded achievable. He had a deal with the progressive rock label Vertigo for his new album, and Tony was going to play bass and produce it. Vertigo was a great choice for the album: the label, a subsidiary of Phonogram, had been set up the previous year and had released albums by Rod Stewart and Manfred Mann. They were all about pushing boundaries, and we had high hopes for the new LP.

As Bowie came up with his new songs we rehearsed them, in Haddon Hall's old wine cellar. Tony, Mick and I turned the cellar into a soundproofed rehearsal room. We constructed a wooden frame within the ceiling and walls, and covered this with a soundproof board made of compressed straw. We then filled the gaps between the wall and the board with sand. It was solid, which was good, because it was deafeningly loud inside.

It was a really small room, the width of my drum kit, and perhaps three drum kits long. It was dark and smelled of damp, as all cellars do, but we didn't care because we loved playing down there. We spent a lot of time playing various bits of music, just trying things out. It was good. I really enjoyed the vibe that Bowie, Mick, Tony and I created. We were feeling each other out, musically, and on the occasions when Bowie wasn't there the three of us would embark on long, improvised jams that flowed on endlessly.

We three backing musicians were all equally good at what we did, and there were no instructions from Bowie, apart from things like, 'There's three bars of this here, and then this other part comes in; drums come in here', and so on. We'd learn the arrangement and get on with it.

Occasionally Bowie would say he liked the beat I was playing, or the groove, but he obviously just expected me to be good, so he usually said nothing at all. He was clearly the band leader, but he never really called the shots, if that makes sense. He basically left things up to us: we were expected to figure out what was needed to make the songs as good as they could possibly be. If we hadn't been able to do that, we wouldn't have been in the band in the first place.

Bowie and Tony were good at what they did, but as we rehearsed I was reminded once again that Mick could play literally anything on the guitar. The man was a genius. When he played a Jeff Beck song, for example, he didn't just get close to Jeff's playing; he played it exactly as Jeff did. It was the same with Jimi Hendrix or Paul Kossoff of Free, or anyone else whose guitar parts he chose to play; there wasn't really a Mick Ronson sound as such back then, because he could do anything. Whoever he was copying, he nailed it, and he had a reputation for being able to do that.

Without meaning to sound boastful, I was the same: I could play every fill that Ginger Baker did on certain Cream tracks, because he was one of my idols and I'd studied what he did down to the last detail. People would come up to me and say, 'Man, if I closed my eyes, I could swear I was at a Cream gig, you sound so much like Ginger.' That was a compliment, of course, but after a while I began to want my own sound rather than someone else's, as did Mick, and we both worked hard to achieve that goal.

Sometimes during rehearsals Bowie would tell us, 'Come on, let's have a break and go to a club', and of course we said yes. He'd take us to a place called El Sombrero, at 142 Kensington High Street. The first time Mick, Bowie, Angie and I went in there I was blown away. It had a star-shaped dance floor lit from beneath, and the music was fantastic: soul, old R&B and rock. The place was full of beautiful people, dressed to the nines, and the women were gorgeous. Mick and I had no idea such places existed.

We were standing having a drink when a guy walked up and slipped a note in my hand.

'What's that?' Mick asked.

'It's probably a note from a girl that he's been asked to pass me,' I said, a bit smugly. I'd had a lot of attention from girls by this point, being in a band. Then someone gave a note to Mick, and another guy came and put one in my top pocket.

This kept happening until we had about ten notes each. It looked a bit crass to just open them up while we were standing there, so we went into a dark corner and read them. They all said things like, 'I'm at the bar next to the blonde, come on over. My name's John and I think you're really cool.'

'They're all blokes!' Mick said. We were stunned, because we'd assumed these guys had been running errands for all the gorgeous chicks around.

Angie came up to us. 'What's happening?' she asked. We told her and she started laughing.

'Don't you know this is a gay club?' she asked.

'No!' we replied. What a disappointment. But there was style and creativity there, in the music and the clothes. That club attracted a very talented crowd.

We had a pretty civilized existence at Haddon Hall. There wasn't much debauchery until we went to America in 1972. I never saw Bowie do any drugs, or even drink much. He might have had the odd lager, but that was it. The rest of us were the same. As I mentioned before, Mick was raised as a

Mormon so when I first met him in Hull he didn't drink or smoke, or even touch tea and coffee. In London, though, that gradually changed: one weekend I saw him rolling a cigarette and then he actually had some coffee. Next thing I knew, he was trying a lager. Eventually we smoked a bit of grass, but that was it. We knew that drugs like cocaine existed, and that a lot of rock bands took them, but they seemed very distant from where we were and we had no plans to make them part of our lives.

We all smoked cigarettes with enthusiasm, though. Mick often used to wake me up in the middle of the night and say 'Woods! Are you awake? Do you want a rollie?' I obviously didn't want a rollie, so I'd pretend to be asleep, but he wouldn't stop until I got up, smoked a cigarette, drank a cup of tea and had a chat with him about our plans for the future.

Gigs came along slowly, more slowly than I would have liked, having played a lot live with the Rats and the Roadrunners before that. We didn't do an actual, scheduled tour at all in 1970, but initially Bowie and I did a bunch of odd pub gigs, just for fun really. I wasn't paid for those; I was living on my retainer of seven quid a week, but I didn't care. Sometimes Bowie would call upstairs and say, 'Woody, we're doing a set at the Three Tuns tonight.'

The Three Tuns was a pub on Beckenham High Street. Bowie had set up a short-lived Sunday night folk club there with his then girlfriend Mary Finnigan in 1969, which they'd turned into a local Arts Lab. He'd been inspired by the influential Arts Lab in Drury Lane – where you could watch all sorts of avant-garde performances, including mime. We did

very little preparation for our gigs there. I didn't even know
what we were going to play, because we didn't have songs finished yet, but I took a goatskin mat with me and we'd jump in
the car. Once in the pub I'd sit on the mat and play bongos,
totally improvised, while Bowie played acoustic guitar and
sang. Sometimes Mick would come along and play a bass that
he'd borrowed from Tony. Often it would be just Bowie and
me. Sometimes we'd do two or three of these pub gigs a night.

Bowie said a particular line every night: 'We've ripped off
the goatskin idea from Marc Bolan!' because Bolan's percus-
sionist Mickey Finn would also sit on a goatskin next to his
boss. But I left it at a gig one time, so when Bowie next made
the joke, there I was, with no goatskin, looking like a twat.

Bowie was good at playing gigs with an acoustic guitar
and reading bits of poetry, but when I joined him there was
really no identity in what he was doing. He was just somebody
who could sing and write and put it across, and, as I saw it,
it wasn't likely to attract tons of interest. But within a few
weeks of playing with him I began to understand his viewpoint on music more clearly. He wasn't the archetypal rock 'n'
roll musician at all. Most musicians can jam, for example; he
either couldn't or didn't want to do that. He was a good guitar
player, though, and incredible at putting unusual chords together; there are guitar players around today who say, 'What
the fuck is he playing there?' when they look at his songs.

Bowie wasn't just a skilled musician: he could sing, he
could act, he could mime, he could paint, he could design
. . . there were so many options for him that at first he had
difficulty assembling all his ideas and choosing the right path.

He would often adopt different accents; sometimes he used to talk to us in a Yorkshire accent, but he wasn't taking the piss. He would speak in an Australian accent if an Australian was there. Nobody pulled him up on it; that's just how he was. He couldn't help it – different characters seemed to flow through him. He was like that with everything: he'd see something he liked and try it on. He seemed to be able to take on a persona – Neil Young or whoever – and then write songs better in that style than that person did, and be totally authentic about it in an unforced way.

It became obvious after a while, though, that even if Bowie hadn't settled on the path he was going to take, he believed that he would ultimately make it in the music business. He acted like a star, and he looked like one, and he talked like one, although we could still have a laugh with him. It sounds weird, I know, but back then I saw him as a kind of Marilyn Monroe or James Dean character. He was much more than a rock star; he wasn't like Paul Rodgers or Robert Plant or Roger Daltrey or any of the rockers that I'd grown up listening to. He didn't fit that mould in any way. His songs genuinely were not like anybody else's, and they were good – really good.

I quickly found out that Angie was an important catalyst when it came to Bowie making up his mind to do something. She pushed him in directions that she thought he should go, and he obviously valued her opinions.

You'd hear where Bowie's influences came from; some songs had an early sixties flavour but when you stepped back and thought about it, you realized that giving people something familiar was the right thing to do. He had the ability to duplicate things and say them in a way that was uniquely his.

That's the correct way for an artist to operate. Later, for the presentation of his songs, he pulled from fashion, he pulled from theatre and he pulled from elements of everything that he'd come across until that point.

Our chance to take a step up came when we recorded our first album together. *The Man Who Sold the World* was recorded at Trident and Advision Studios in London in April and May 1970. There've been a lot of conflicting reports about how the songs were written, so let me set the record straight.

Bowie wrote all the songs, but we three musicians – Mick, Tony and I – arranged most of them. Some of the songs were just chord sequences when Bowie brought them to us. He'd say, 'This is the verse' and 'Here's the chorus' and 'Maybe we'll do this for the middle eight' and so on, so we would take what Bowie had written on a twelve-string acoustic guitar and adapt it for a rock band, while rehearsing in the cellar at Haddon Hall.

On the later albums it wasn't done that way: Bowie nearly always brought completed songs to us, with at least a sequence of verse, chorus, middle eight and so on. On *The Man Who Sold the World*, the basic structures of the individual sections were there, but they didn't always join up, so Tony and Mick did some work on that.

During the recording of *The Man Who Sold the World*, Tony became Mick's mentor. Mick was really interested in how to record, and how to arrange strings, and he'd help Tony write the arrangements out. After all, Tony was a fully-fledged, successful producer so Mick followed a lot of his instructions.

We all benefited hugely from Tony's experience and willing-
ness to share it with us. Bowie was lucky to have him on
board, and I wasn't surprised that they remained friends and
colleagues for the rest of Bowie's life.

Tony had some great ideas, and used them to make *The
Man Who Sold the World* sound the way it needed to sound
– although he also asked Mick for some advice. He'd say,
'What kind of bass playing should I do on this album?' and
Mick would tell him, 'Learn how to play like Jack Bruce
and we'll be all right!'

I remember the day Tony brought me a guiro, a Latin
American percussion instrument that he wanted me to play.
He obviously assumed that I knew about percussion, but I
looked at this hollow cylinder, with ridges down one side and
a hole at the end, and thought, 'What the fuck do I do with
this?'

'Do I blow across the hole?' I asked.

He said, 'No, you prat!' and gave me a stick to rub across
the ridges, producing a ratchet sound. You can hear it on the
title track. Then he gave me wood blocks, castanets, timpani
and other things I'd never played before and showed me how
to use them; he really expanded my vocabulary, and I began
to feel like a genuine musician.

While all this was going on, Bowie spent a lot of time with
Angie. When he showed up at the studio, he usually just sat
on a sofa in reception with her. The fact that Bowie was out
there doing that was frustrating Tony no end, because he
didn't work like that; he wanted the principal artist on board
the whole time. I think they had a bit of a bust-up about it.

When Bowie came in and completed the songs with his vocals, the argument dissipated, though.

It wasn't too difficult for us to play the songs, complex as some of them were. Some of the drum parts on the album were fairly tricky, though. When I was getting ready to record, I tried out the parts in my head, thinking, 'I've got to play this particular drum roll somewhere.' I listen back to some of the parts now and I think, 'How the hell did I play that?'

We jammed a lot of the album; we knew what the songs were about, so we played around until we found something that worked. It was really loose, like all the music that I liked in the seventies, such as Zeppelin and King Crimson. People say Zep were so tight, but if you listen you can hear John Bonham going out of time. It doesn't matter, though; that's what rock 'n' roll always was for me. Nowadays there are more rules, which to me have screwed up what rock is supposed to be about.

When the three of us were recording those tracks, it was fun working as a team to find the right parts. We set up our equipment in the studio like we would for a live concert: drums in the middle, Mick on my left, Tony on the right and Bowie out front. As we had a lot of parts to create for the songs, it seemed the best position to do this from. We had a collective mission to make all the songs as exciting as we could. This was, after all, my first time recording in a major studio, so it was a big deal for me and there was a lot to learn. It was great having Tony to work with, with all his experience.

During the recording of the album, we mostly drank tea and coffee. Maybe Mick would have an occasional lager. It was totally disciplined and very work-oriented. After the album was finished, back at Haddon Hall, it was totally different: there were parties every weekend.

Marc Bolan was there quite a bit. He was the same age as Bowie, and they had been friends since 1964, when they'd been hired to paint the walls at an office owned by their then manager, Les Conn. Like Bowie, he was undergoing a period of transition. Tyrannosaurus Rex had had minor hits with singles 'Debora' and 'One Inch Rock' and his fourth album, *A Beard of Stars*, had been released just before I joined Bowie's band, getting to 21 in the charts. Now Marc was also switching from acoustic hippy folk to a rockier sound and Visconti was going to produce and play bass on their next album that summer.

Bolan behaved like a pop star in that he loved being the centre of attention, but he didn't do this in an annoying way, I should add. He was similar to Bowie in that sense, although he was a lot more precious about everything. I remember once he came around wearing a black cape, a floppy hat and ballet shoes.

I once asked him about his songwriting methods, and he told me, 'I have a tape recorder in every room, so I don't forget any ideas. I even have one in the toilet.'

I thought that was a touch excessive, but I was impressed when he told me he'd had guitar lessons from Eric Clapton.

Bolan and Bowie were good friends, although they were rivals underneath their friendship, but it wasn't a hindrance in any way. In their heads, they were both going to be the next big thing.

I also met Arthur Brown that year, although he seemed a bit lost to me. His band, the Crazy World of Arthur Brown, had had a massive hit two years before with 'Fire', but when I asked him what he was up to, he didn't seem to know.

'My band split up last year,' he told me.

'So what are you going to do now?' I asked.

He just shrugged, and that was it from him.

I got on better with the singer-songwriter Roy Harper, who played at Haddon Hall once. His fourth album, *Flat Baroque and Berserk*, had come out a couple of months before I met him and had been his most successful so far, getting to 20 in the charts. The night he played, Mick and I got stoned in the basement flat, where Bowie's friend Tony Frost lived. I think he worked as a bodyguard and bouncer at a London club but that's as much as I gleaned from him. He had the same sound system in his basement that you'd have in a club, so we used to go down there and listen to music. Frost also had the best grass in London, so we'd get stoned while listening to reggae.

So we had a joint with him, and then we came upstairs because a party was on, with the Bowies' set of friends in attendance, and we knew that Roy Harper was going to get up and play. This wasn't a particularly easy thing to do. Around the main hall there were flats with pensioners and families living in them, and we had to keep the music fairly quiet as a result, especially late at night. Roy had been told to keep the volume down, so at first he played quietly. The crowd sat silently, listening and passing joints around.

At one point, though, Roy really let rip and started playing unexpectedly loudly – at full blast. Me and Mick instantly lost it, laughing our heads off, and ended up crawling under the table because we couldn't handle it. People thought we were laughing at Roy, and told us to shut the fuck up, but we weren't being disrespectful; it was just that we were stoned and at any second we expected people to burst out of the upstairs flats and kick everybody out.

On other occasions, Bowie played us reel-to-reel films of Lindsay Kemp, the mime artist and dancer who had taught him to mime. I thought Kemp's image was a bit strange, although I could see that he was interesting from an artistic point of view, even at this early stage. I just couldn't see how his art was relevant to anything that we were going to do. Of course, I evolved from that position as time passed and my horizons broadened.

All I really knew at this time was that I wanted our band to succeed, because I was pretty ambitious. I realized that I wanted to be in the next big band – and not just in any big band, but the biggest band. I hoped Bowie would choose the right way to make this happen, and I wanted to help him succeed.

I remember when *The Man Who Sold the World* was finished and the mix completed, Bowie put it on at Haddon Hall and as we sat around and listened to it we were all really excited. As I mentioned before, it had been our first time in the studio with a proper producer, and now we had the chance to hear what we'd created. I had no idea what my drumming was going to sound like, and Mick didn't know how his guitar playing would come across.

As I listened, I thought we'd done a great job. My skills were still coming along at the time, but I had a good feel for when to sit back and when to step up with the drums. A lot of the bands we'd grown up with would often have improvised sections in their songs that gave a feeling of freedom, even though they still followed a structured arrangement, and that was what we did on *The Man Who Sold the World*. Cream and Zeppelin were particularly good at that. It was a natural way for us to think; we weren't thinking of the songs as especially structured.

Bowie had already written most of the first song, 'Width of a Circle', before we went into the studio. It was one of the few songs that was almost complete when we went in. Drums-wise, it was just a case of me finding the right beat. The second part of the song, which has a different tempo, didn't exist until we came up with it through jamming in the studio. Bowie added a melody and vocals to that part later.

On 'All the Madmen', Tony had the idea of having a bolero section, where he encouraged me to play on the bell of the ride cymbal, and make a little tune out of the cymbals. As for 'Black Country Rock', I never knew what this song was about. I just knew that once you'd heard that riff it would stick in your head for days. Some good music had come out of the Midlands; maybe that's what the song was about.

'After All' was one of the first examples of Bowie's odd take on life. The idea behind the song was that we all grow old, but that we still remain children at heart. For a gentle song like this one, my drums had to be subtle; it was mainly a hi-hat, just keeping it together, and occasionally a bit of ride cymbal and floor toms.

On 'Running Gun Blues', there are floor toms with echo on at the beginning, and you can hear me playing the tambourine. It was a dark subject: a soldier who has returned from war and he still has his gun, and he wants to kill people. It seems more relevant today than ever. 'Saviour Machine' is a sci-fi song about a president who had invented a machine that controlled everything in the world, from the weather to disease. Unfortunately the machine got bored and was begging to be disconnected, thinking of starting wars or creating a plague to relieve the tedium. It had some really cool time changes in it, and musically was quite challenging to play. It is also relevant, because the world's getting a bit like that, isn't it? More and more control being handed over to machines.

There are some big drums in 'She Shook Me Cold'. In this song we were being out-and-out raw and sexual – well, at least I was! I still think Mick's guitar intro on this song is probably the rudest, dirtiest guitar ever recorded. 'The Man Who Sold the World' is such a cool song and probably the best-known recorded track on the album, later covered by Lulu and Nirvana. I'm also playing the guiro and the maracas in this one. Finally, the theme of 'The Supermen' comes from Friedrich Nietzsche; I wanted to feel like a superman when I played it, almost like Thor with his war hammer. I did feel that way, too. I also backed up the drums with tuned timpani, which I loved playing.

Those subjects – Nietzsche among them – would come up in conversation with Bowie, but we didn't really dwell on them. He'd say that this song was about the future of man, where machines have developed their own consciousness. These were wild concepts.

The Man Who Sold the World is an interesting album because it didn't have a commercial attitude behind it. We played whatever we were inspired to play, as opposed to someone telling us that a song was going to be a single so it needed to be three and a half minutes long. That wasn't part of the game on this album, so I really expressed myself.

It was our *Sgt. Pepper*, if you like, at least in progressive rock terms. I'm making that comparison because on these songs we were able to open up and do whatever we felt was right. The three of us let it all out on our instruments, and then came back together and clicked on certain sections. We had a Moog synth as well, played by the Bowies' friend Ralph Mace, which was about the size of a room with what looked like a thousand leads!

This was a big album, and pretty bizarre in some ways, but we all trusted Tony to know what he was doing so we could step up and let rip if we wanted to. That's a great feeling to have when you're recording – a sense of security because the producer knows what he's up to. If it ever got too weird or too far from the point, Tony would say something. He'd occasionally give me some instructions about the drums, but he was going by the feel of it because he was also new to this kind of music. If he heard something he liked, he'd ask us to repeat it.

So much of *The Man Who Sold the World* was guided by feel. When I look back at it I can see that Bowie was experimenting with a new sound. For me, this album was Bowie jumping into rock 'n' roll with both feet.

It's incredible that he could still write such great songs among all the confusion. In some ways the whole year of 1970 was a mess. Our band was new, and firing on all cylinders, but none of us – least of all Bowie – knew what direction was right for us. We were having fun, but fun wasn't enough.

4

OH! YOU PRETTY THINGS

After recording *The Man Who Sold the World*, all four of us wanted to go out and tour the songs live, but that didn't work because there was no money to buy a van and equipment. There was no booking agent that I know of, Bowie was in the process of splitting with his manager Ken Pitt, and his champion at Vertigo, Olav Wyper, had left the company. It seemed as if there was nobody on his side.

We started to miss playing gigs. There's only so much rehearsing you can do, after all. Maybe Bowie wouldn't even have got booked to play live at the time, despite the fact that 'Space Oddity' had reached Number 5 the previous summer. By now it seemed that hardly anyone knew who he was, proved by the fact that he and I had been playing as a duo in front of small pub crowds.

So nothing was really happening in the summer of that year, and living on seven pounds a week was becoming difficult, with no gig money coming in. Mick and I were getting a bit disillusioned, and Bowie had pissed us off a bit when he sang 'Black Country Rock'. That's a great song, but for some reason he felt he had to sing it like a caricature of Marc Bolan. We weren't fans of Bolan's 'oh-ow-oww' singing voice, so when he started singing it like that, Mick and I said to each other, 'Fucking hell. I can't go out on stage if he's going to sing like that!' Even though it was just one song, it really grated with us for some reason.

We knew Bowie had plans for us, because he told us that he wanted two musical entities to exist – us as the Hype, and himself as a solo artist. Angie went to Phonogram and persuaded them to give the Hype a £4,000 album deal, and so we now began thinking about having not one but two possible careers ahead of us.

That August, Bowie had a gig at Leeds University. He was going up there in his car, a Riley – we'd demoed a song about it, actually, called 'Rupert the Riley' – and Mick and I were in another car with the gear. On the way up there we came to a crossroads with signs pointing to Hull or Leeds, and we just looked at each other.

'What are you thinking, mate?'

We both started laughing and said to the driver, 'Take us to Hull!'

So that was it: we went back to Hull and left Bowie to his own devices. He did the show that night solo, on an acoustic guitar. I suppose he must have been a bit pissed off with us, but he never said anything. The following year, Angie did mention in passing 'the famous gig that you guys didn't show up to', but it was said in good humour and clearly it was all water under the bridge at that point.

I stayed with June, who was now renting her own house in Hull. I didn't go back to Driffield; in fact, I barely even spoke with my parents at this point. I knew they'd think my career as a musician had failed, but I had no intention of giving up on the Hype. We got our old singer Benny Marshall back from our previous band the Rats, renamed the Hype Ronno – after Mick's nickname – and found an agent. He got us gigs, so now we needed a bass player. Geoff Appleby of the Rats helped us out for a few gigs, but we needed someone who could commit to us permanently.

The obvious choice was a guy called Trevor Bolder who had stepped up once, when the Rats' then bass player Keith Cheeseman kept getting electrocuted at a gig, which was at a youth club. There had been something wrong with the wiring and it kept giving him shocks, so he wouldn't play. Trevor was a mate of Keith's and had come along to watch. We knew he played bass so we asked if he'd take over and he bravely did! We saw then that he had tons of presence and playing ability. Now we asked him if he would come and play bass with us in Ronno, and he agreed to.

Trevor had a beard when I first met him; it was later that he grew his sideburns long, when we adopted the glamorous image.

So now, in Ronno, we had two bass players, because Visconti was still playing bass with us. There are photos of us with both him and Trevor, but we never played live with both of them. The record deal enabled us to buy equipment and record with Tony as our producer, but none of us were real songwriters and we didn't really have enough material for a full album. In January 1971 we did release a single called '4th Hour of My Sleep', which was written by an American called Tucker Zimmerman who was signed to Fly, Bolan's label. Tony had produced his 1969 album *Ten Songs*. The B-side was called 'Powers of Darkness', which is a pretty heavy, Black Sabbath-type song. We even shot a promotional film at the Marquee, although it was only shown in Scandinavia, and the single didn't get anywhere.

Tony had much more success with Marc Bolan, whose single 'Ride a White Swan' had come out in October and by late January had reached number 2 in the charts. The album *T. Rex* was also a hit and it seemed that Bolan was going to find stardom before Bowie. *The Man Who Sold the World* was released in April 1971 in the UK and, after all the hard work we'd put into it, didn't sell many copies in the UK, although it was reasonably popular in America (where it came out in November 1970). It didn't make the charts in either country until it was reissued two years later. Maybe it was too obscure for its time, with its lyrics about soldiers going mad and Nietzschean themes. Perhaps the public wanted to hear blues-rock bands like Led Zeppelin more than this kind of heavy, arty approach. I still love it, though.

A lot of attention was focused on the cover, which featured Bowie in a dress made for him by the fashion designer Michael Fish. I remember him coming downstairs in that dress one day at Haddon Hall, and telling me that he had a photo shoot. I was a little surprised, because I was still fairly new to Bowie's ideas. A man wearing a dress just wasn't normal, as I saw it back then, so I asked myself if he was serious. But when I realized that he was, I adjusted my expectations and started to try and appreciate what he was doing. I was definitely changing as time passed . . . It was more like a robe than a dress anyway; long, flowing and rather beautiful. In my mind it was like something from a Renaissance painting.

Although I thought Bowie looked pretty good in that dress, I also think that with a different cover *The Man Who Sold the World* might have done better. I can't imagine many Led Zeppelin fans carrying the album under their arms – it doesn't quite go, does it? Then again, the American cover was a picture of a cowboy with a gun, pictured outside a mental institution, and it wasn't as effective, I thought.

Meanwhile, Ronno carried on gigging, doing covers at universities. Our set included a Bowie track, 'Queen Bitch', which he'd written when we were at Haddon Hall, and after we left he said, 'Take that one, you can have it.' That was good of him, now I come to think of it. We liked the song, but the problem was that Benny looked like a Hell's Angel. His image fitted most of our set, but when he sang lines like 'In her frock coat and bipperty-bopperty hat' it didn't quite work, although the song went down well on stage and it was great to play.

On 14 May 1971 Ronno played the Cavern Club in Liverpool, which was a real high point for me. I remember thinking, 'I'm setting my kit up where Ringo Starr set his up!' It was sweaty and packed out. There were shelves all down one side of a curved wall, and I noticed that, as the night went on, pint glasses were stacking up there. Some of them were full, or nearly full, which seemed weird, because people apparently weren't drinking their beer. But then I realized that you couldn't get out of the club, so if you needed to piss you had to piss in the pint glasses and then put them on the shelves. The place fucking stank as a result.

That night we were supporting a band called Tear Gas,

who later went on to form the Sensational Alex Harvey Band.
I remember the drummer Ted McKenna played a drum fill,
and my head spun around. I was like, 'What the fuck was
that?' because it was truly unbelievable. I met Ted afterwards
and asked him about that fill. When he answered, it was as if
he was speaking a foreign language.

'I'm just using basic drum rudiments, Woody,' he told me.

I had no idea what he was talking about.

'What the hell are rudiments?'

'Techniques, man – the building blocks of drums,' he went
on. 'Did you never learn them when you were a kid?'

It was obvious that I hadn't, so Ted showed me some of
them and explained why they're useful. That was my introduction to drum theory. I'd learned everything by ear before then,
from listening to Hendrix and Cream and the Stones and so
on. It really opened up the technical side for me, although it
took me ages to figure out how to read and play the rudiments, as I didn't read music. My drumming improved a hell
of a lot with Ronno, and my future playing on the Bowie
albums was more effective as a result.

Not long afterwards. Mick got a call from Bowie, saying
that he had new management, and asking if Mick would come
back and join him again and bring a bassist and drummer
with him.

Mick's first choices were apparently Rick Kemp and
Ritchie Dharma from the Michael Chapman Band, who he'd
played with before. I didn't find out about Mick auditioning
them until many years later. He could have picked them
because Bowie had started writing some of the *Hunky Dory*
songs and maybe Bowie had explained to Mick that they

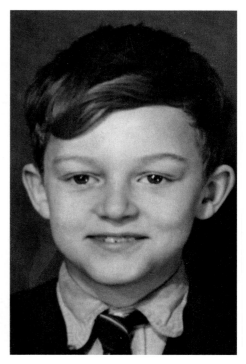

About two years old and
such a cutie!

A well-behaved schoolboy.

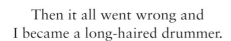

Then it all went wrong and
I became a long-haired drummer.

The Roadrunners.
From left to right:
Les Westaway,
Brian Wheeldon,
me and
Dave Lawson.

Above. The Rats at
Burton Constable,
supporting Free
and The Nice.
Left to right:
Keith (Ched)
Cheeseman, me
and Mick Ronson.

Left. On stage
at the Hull Arts
Centre.

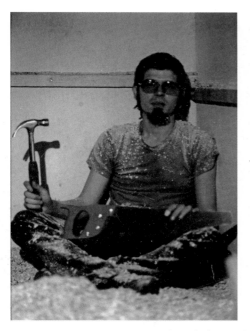 

Tony Visconti (left) and myself at Haddon Hall,
building the rehearsal room.

Mick in the gardens at
Haddon Hall.

Bowie at Trident studios,
during the recording of *The Man
Who Sold the World*.

A rare 1970 gig with Mick and Bowie on guitar and myself on bongos!

Bowie in Haddon Hall in 1970. Mick and I were sleeping on a mattress at the top of the stairs.

Introducing Ziggy
to the world at
Friars Aylesbury,
29 January 1972.

Trevor Bolder
and myself early
on the Ziggy tour,
1972.

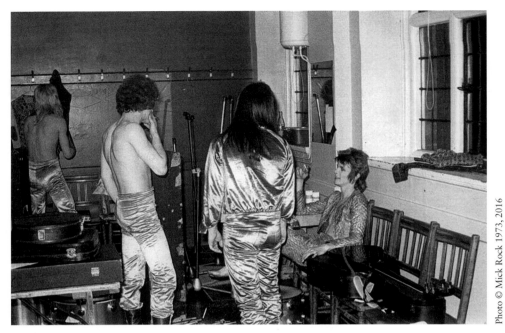

Legendary photographer Mick Rock captured us getting ready for a gig.

Performing 'Starman' on ITV's *Lift Off With Ayshea* on 16 June 1972 – and wearing some make-up for the first time.

On holiday in Cyprus in autumn 1972, with Bowie, Angie and Trevor.

Bowie at our
first American gig
– Cleveland,
22 September.

Mick trying to ignore my attempts
to learn guitar, in one of our
identical hotel rooms on the
US tour in 1972.

Mick, somewhere in America!
December 1972.

Trevor getting made up by
Suzie Fussey.

Tony Frost demonstrating
a move on Trevor.

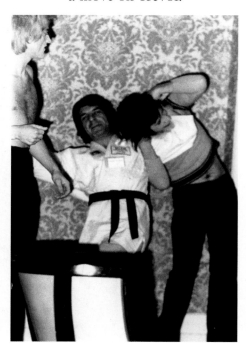

weren't as 'rocky' as the ones on *The Man Who Sold the World*, but that's just my guess. Apparently the audition didn't work out, though. Also, Bowie wasn't too keen on the fact that they were 'lacking in the hair department', according to Mick.

Shortly after this Mick asked if I would go back to London with him.

'What do you reckon, Woods? Bowie's got a new album in the pipeline.'

I shrugged. 'Seems like a good idea to me. Ronno's not doing that great, is it?'

So the two of us went back to Haddon Hall, nine months or so after we'd left. Ronno's Phonogram contract expired at some point, although there was a bank account that had some money in it. We couldn't get hold of it because we three signatories were never in the same place to withdraw it. It's still there, as far as I know.

This time we were without Tony Visconti, who had gone off to produce other artists; his career producing T. Rex was taking off, and I think he'd received a lot of other offers. He recently told me that he was fired by Bowie's new manager Tony Defries, but Mick and I knew nothing about that at the time. Tony and his girlfriend Liz had moved to Penge, in south London, and Mick and I took their room in Haddon Hall. By this time Bowie had written some songs for *Hunky Dory* and we were going to debut them on John Peel's radio show, because Peel liked Bowie and had done sessions with him for his earlier albums. We threw ourselves into rehearsals, once again in the old wine cellar.

Bowie's whole vibe was different this time: he was more dynamic and more focused. He was full of new ideas and couldn't stop talking about the plans he'd made for us. A lot of this stemmed from Tony Defries, who had been advising Bowie for a while, and had recently gone into business with Laurence Myers at GEM. Defries was the opposite of Bowie's old manager, Ken Pitt, who as I understand it had been trying to push Bowie in directions that he didn't want to go in – towards musicals, for example, or perhaps into light entertainment, which is funny to think of now. Bowie had said, 'No, I'm more radical than that', and they'd parted ways.

Defries wasn't exactly what you'd call a warm guy. I didn't really interact with him; he'd come along during the recording sessions, and listen and nod at you and talk socially, but he wasn't on our wavelength. In fact, I found out later that Defries told Visconti he had wanted to get rid of me and Mick after we'd finished recording *The Man Who Sold the World*. To Defries it was all about business, and indeed he was a sharp-talking, dynamic kind of guy. Bowie obviously thought that Defries was going to be a useful business partner – and it's true that Defries ended up doing a lot of good things for him, including arranging the funding of the recording of *Hunky Dory* and getting Bowie a new record deal.

Most importantly, though, Bowie had been to America in early 1971 to promote *The Man Who Sold the World*, while we'd been off playing with Ronno. While there he'd seen Velvet Underground play live and discovered The Stooges. The trip had completely revolutionized his thinking. Magpie that he was, Bowie had taken these influences and was incorporating them into his new songs. The songwriting was different when he came back – some of it darker, some more decadent, but it was all more lyrically expressive. Bowie's previous approach to songwriting before *The Man Who Sold the World* and now *Hunky Dory* seemed quite quaint and English in comparison. Now it started to have shape and form. I think that seeing how Lou Reed and Iggy Pop were writing from their own viewpoint, whether people liked it or not, really helped him. Lou sang about heroin and S&M, for example, which was something of an eye-opener for us.

Bowie played us a reel-to-reel projection of Iggy Pop and The Stooges playing live in Cincinnati which nobody had yet seen in this country. In the film, Iggy walked bare-chested and feral on the shoulders of his audience, throwing peanut butter at people. It sounds innocent, but it was quite impressive because it showed the power he had over people, and that he was unafraid to use it. Bowie played us music by the Velvet Underground, too, and we got off on the decadence of it. We also listened to Neil Young and Crazy Horse, which became another definite influence on the new album.

The musicianship in the bands whose songs he was showing us was sometimes a little primitive and often very simple, but the point was that there was definitely a spirit there – and that spirit influenced us profoundly.

Back at Haddon Hall, Bowie talked to us at length about his new direction. In his opinion the rock 'n' roll business had become dull; what the kids wanted and needed was excitement. He'd talk about seeing James Brown and other sixties artists who had a real, thought-out production when they played live; even if the production was a bit rubbish and vaudeville, it was still creative and exciting. He'd throw out these ideas and we'd tell him what we thought, based on the experiences we'd had.

I'd always admired an R&B band called the Artwoods, who had had a three-year career in the mid-sixties, splitting in 1967. They included Jon Lord, who had gone on to form Deep Purple, plus Ronnie Wood's brother Art, and Keef Hartley on drums. They weren't really big or well known, but they had a certain something. I mentioned to Bowie that the Artwoods did a fight scene as part of their show, which looked real: the singer pretended to be pissed off at the guitarist and the guitarist would smash into him and knock him off the stage. It was exciting, and fairly punk rock in nature. I talked about this with Bowie; he and I went through lots of conversations along those lines. It turned out he was a fan of the Artwoods, too.

The other major change when Mick and I returned to Haddon Hall was that Angie was heavily pregnant. Bowie was looking forward to being a father, and perhaps this contributed to his renewed energy at the time. I'm not sure he was what you'd call a particularly considerate husband, though: at times, Angie would be lying on their bed, in serious discomfort because she was so close to giving birth, and I'd be the only one in the place who took care of her. I didn't do much, I admit, but at least I'd take her a cup of tea and check that she was OK.

Although she obviously had other things on her mind, Angie was a big supporter of Bowie's new self-confidence. She was constantly urging him to continue with these ideas, and I don't think he had many other people of that kind around him. They were intellectuals in the way they discussed these things.

As we watched him write more songs for *Hunky Dory*, we noticed the change in him. The songs were more commercial, and definitely better. You heard them once and remembered them, because they were more immediate. In a sense, this period was Bowie saying, 'Fuck you, I can write songs! Give me a ukulele, give me a trumpet, give me anything – I'll write you a song.' He'd grabbed that cult American scene feel and added it to the equation. The result was good music.

I look back now and I realize that Bowie was breaking away from what was supposed to happen in rock 'n' roll. Other bands were sticking to the way that rock music had been in the fifties and the sixties, and the dream of the sixties had fallen on its arse because those bands thought the whole world was going to change, and it didn't. It just went into a slump. All the enthusiasm for life that the sixties bands had had, and all their messages about how good life was going to be for a new, enlightened generation, had vanished by 1971. That's how we saw it anyway.

There was a period when it did look possible that my generation – the first kids after the war, who wanted nothing to do with what had come before – would change the world for the better. Drugs clouded that impulse to improve the world, though, among other things.

In response, our attitude was 'We'll do it then: we'll fucking take it somewhere.' We weren't going to take this apathy lying down, but it was risky, because we were going out there with something different, with baggage that had not been in rock 'n' roll before. You might as well stick your neck out and see what happens. Good music was always behind our attitude, and when you have that you can't fail, we believed.

We knew that *Hunky Dory* was going to be different from the albums that Bowie had recorded before – more accessible and definitely more immediate. He'd sit writing songs in his lounge with his guitar, or in his bedroom, where there was a piano.

He would shout, 'Woody, I've finished a song!' and I'd go in and he'd play it for me, and I'd usually say, 'That's good, I like that', if I liked it, which I almost always did at this point because he was writing such good songs. Rarely, he'd play something less good, and I'd say, 'It might be tricky to turn that into a rock song.' But most of the time, the songs stunned me, they were so good.

When Bowie was writing a song on the keyboard, the music would reverberate around the house because it was so loud, so you'd get to know the songs a little that way. You'd be walking around Haddon Hall singing them before you even played them downstairs in the cellar. This time, unlike the previous album, the songs were mostly complete when Bowie brought them to us, although we'd add our own parts, of course.

On 30 May Zowie Bowie – who now goes by the name Duncan Jones – was born. Bowie wasn't there at the birth (at that time men were not usually present); he was back at Haddon Hall with us. When Angie brought Zowie back, he was looked after by his nanny Susie Frost, Tony's wife, in the basement flat, so we didn't see much of him. Life carried on as normal, at least for Mick and me, but for David the birth of his son was obviously a prominent moment in his life.

*

We still needed a bass player, so we asked Trevor Bolder to come down. He arrived the day before a pre-arranged radio session, John Peel's *In Concert* on BBC Radio 1, on 3 June 1971. It was a live show and Bowie didn't want it to only feature him singing – he wanted it quite loose and a little theatrical. He brought in Mark Carr-Pritchard on guitar and three of his friends, Geoffrey MacCormack, George Underwood and Dana Gillespie, who'd been a teenage sweetheart of Bowie's and was also one of Tony Defries' clients. Poor Trevor had twelve tracks to learn – overnight. I don't think he ever recovered from the ordeal. Whenever the red light went on in the studio after that, it reminded him of that time. He admitted that it always put him on edge.

The songs featured on the show included 'Queen Bitch', 'Bombers', 'Supermen', 'Looking For a Friend', 'Almost Grown', 'Oh! You Pretty Things', 'Kooks', 'Song For Bob Dylan', 'Andy Warhol' and 'It Ain't Easy'. The lead vocals were shared on some of these songs with David's friends. That show was the first broadcast we'd done in front of a live audience, and the first time Trev, Mick and I had played together as Bowie's band. It was an exciting moment and I rang June and told her we were on and to listen, which she did.

At Haddon Hall Trev slept on the landing – obviously that was what the new apprentice had to do. His bass playing was excellent, and unusual: he played more melodically than most bassists at the time, and he was really powerful when we played the rockier tracks.

Trevor really fitted in with the rest of us; he was a nice, quiet guy, although when he'd had a few drinks he'd talk a lot, really loudly. I remember when he visited the Sombrero for the first time. Mick and I were at Haddon Hall that night and Bowie was having a party where a lot of the guests happened to be gay. When Trev arrived back at the flat he came up to Mick and me and in a voice like a foghorn said, 'I've been to this club, and you won't believe this, but everyone there was fuckin' gay!'

'Come and have a drink, mate,' I said, taking him to one side before he embarrassed himself any more in front of Bowie's crowd. Bowie had overheard, but he thought it was hilarious.

Bowie was working on a side project around the time we rejoined him, a band called Arnold Corns, whose name was inspired by Pink Floyd's 'Arnold Layne'. It was fronted by a clothes designer and gay friend of Bowie's called Freddie Burretti. In hindsight, Freddie was supposed to be a sort of proto-Ziggy Stardust. The B&C label had released Arnold Corns' awful single – versions of 'Moonage Daydream' and 'Hang On To Yourself' – in May 1971, and it disappeared without trace. That track had been recorded in February. Now Bowie wanted us to play on the new single. Mick and I were sceptical, but we'd met Freddie a few times and thought he was OK – if a bit naive – and he was certainly extremely good-looking, like a Greek god in fact! So we agreed and on 17 June, me, Mick and Trevor recorded 'Man in the Middle' and (the B-side) 'Looking For a Friend'. That was when we realized that although Freddie looked like the ultimate rock frontman, he couldn't sing a note. The guy had no voice what-soever. He tried to sing while Bowie sang along with him, but the recordings were terrible.

Essentially, Bowie was attempting to create a rock star

while standing outside the concept, but he decided to do it himself when it didn't work out. The rock star character he'd created gave him a viewpoint to operate from, as I understand it, although he had no idea how far it would evolve.

At the same time, Tony Defries had arranged to demo a new Bowie song to attract RCA into a record deal, so we recorded a cover of 'It Ain't Easy' by Ron Davies down at Trident. Dana Gillespie did backing vocals on that song, and we also recorded a rocked-up version of 'Andy Warhol' with her. Defries had Bowie on one side of the demo tape and Dana on the other because he was shopping for deals for both.

But these were distractions from the main issue, recording the new album. It was a lot of fun; Tony Defries did introduce us to good food, I'll give him that. After the recording sessions we'd go to this little restaurant that was behind a door on Oxford Street. You'd never think there was a restaurant there, but it was a family place, upstairs in someone's home. You'd go up and there'd be about eight tables with white tablecloths. We'd start with a massive bowl of king prawns on ice, and then we'd have spare ribs to die for. Defries knew his wine, too. We'd be there until three or four in the morning; it used to be a great night out.

Mick and Bowie did most of the arrangements this time, and Bowie and Ken Scott shared the production credits. Mick had worked closely with Tony Visconti on *The Man Who Sold the World* and it sparked a real desire in him to be a producer and strings arranger. He'd watch his mentor, Tony, like a hawk and say, 'What's that you're doing?', 'How do you do that . . . how do you do this?' During those sessions he'd help Tony write out string parts.

We were learning fast as musicians. Mick, Trevor and I listened back to the songs on *The Man Who Sold the World* and discussed them in great detail; from the drummer's perspective I started to think about less being more. Later, 'less is more' became a catchphrase in the business, but back then it really wasn't common to put it into practice. Compare the drum parts on the two albums, recorded less than a year apart, and the differences are like night and day.

Any recording drummer's job is to find a beat that makes sense within a given song. After all, the first thing that people hear when they listen to a piece of music is generally the beat. They're tapping their foot to it before they even know the song has started. That was the approach that I took.

My job was to find the drum parts that integrated with the song's meaning, and that made me concentrate more on what I was doing and what Bowie needed. I noticed that some drummers would only hit a cymbal once, right at the end of a song – and the effect would be so right, and so spot on, that it twisted my head around about playing drums. It made me put the emphasis back on what a song sounds like on piano or guitar, when it has a clear rhythm running through it but no actual drum beat as yet.

Bowie never told me what he wanted when we were recording *Hunky Dory*; the one time I went a bit too hard rock on him he let me know straight away. That was understood. I didn't need his direction, and he willingly let me do my job and trusted me to do it.

That sounds funny, maybe even arrogant, although that's not the intention – but you ask a person what they want and they tell you, and then you decide, based on your knowledge of rhythm, if they're right or not. If you record what they ask you to record, and it's not right for the song, you can't blame anyone else afterwards, can you? That's exactly how it was with Bowie. I made my own decisions about what was needed and what was right for the songs. The same principles apply to life in general.

What Bowie's songs really needed was a groove that didn't detract from the melodies and the vocals, and which had exactly the right drum sound. If I could figure out some cool drum fills that would end up being hooks for the songs, so much the better – and then my job would be done.

When I was recording songs with Bowie, I was sometimes tempted to go a bit mental and overplay, but that would have been unnecessary, and perhaps destructive to the tone of the album, even if Bowie had permitted it. I could have fitted in some more extravagant parts here and there, but they wouldn't have contributed to the song, and that's what counts. It would have just been me showing what I could do, so I discarded that viewpoint all together for *Hunky Dory*.

Mick and Trevor completely understood what I was saying about ensuring that everything was right for the feel of the song. Bowie wasn't usually part of those conversations: he got bored quickly in the studio, so we didn't have long to record our parts or to work them out. He was flighty, and he wasn't into long discussions about the songs, so we had to nail our parts quickly.

I don't mean to imply that Bowie wasn't focused on the music; he certainly was. Angie wasn't around much for these sessions, and Bowie was very into getting everything right. He and Mick would arrange the songs. They'd say, 'Let's do intro, verse, chorus, verse, verse, middle eight, verse, outro', and that would be it. Putting the songs in order was simple, although someone had to do it, and I'm not diminishing the importance of doing it. When it came to the actual notes we played, that was our job.

We spent a lot of time getting everything right. Trevor and I spent many hours practising together as a rhythm section, so that the bass and drums would be locked in as one. You can feel the groove lock down when that happens. As musicians, we really loved that feeling. In the studio it might be a few takes before that locking in happened and we were settled into the right groove – but we never had that luxury with Bowie.

It was close enough most of the time, and in fact we got used to his way of operating later on, and were able to lock in with each other quickly, but in the early days we were required to get it by a certain take, which made the early sessions dif-ficult. We'd play a song together twice, and he'd say, 'OK, that's done. Next song!' and we'd say 'What?'

I'd say, 'We've only played it twice, and only once correctly, so if we do it again, we can probably get a better one' – but he'd say, 'No, it's perfect.' When this first started happening, Mick, Trevor and I would say to each other, 'He's mental – maybe he doesn't realize how good we can get it?' But then Bowie would record a vocal on a song, and then re-record his twelve-string guitar, and we'd say, 'Fucking hell, he was right.'

I started to realize that while Bowie wanted the parts played correctly, more importantly he wanted them to sound fresh. If you record multiple takes of a song, you automatically end up playing from memory of what worked on a previous take and so the recording loses that freshness and spontaneity.

You end up copying yourself rather than creating something new.

Bowie knew his own mind, and tolerated no other opinions apart from ours. I remember during one of the sessions, one of the apprentice tape operators ventured an opinion of a song part we were discussing. The room went deadly quiet; nobody acknowledged his opinion and ten minutes later he was replaced.

Hunky Dory was a new approach for all of us; we all went through a growing process to a certain extent, not just Bowie. Mick was a master at finding hooks that would stick in your head, and Trevor was an unusual bass player in that he never played obvious lines. His bass parts would give Mick ideas for guitar parts, so we all had a real rapport. My approach, as I've said, was to play totally for the song; a lot of musicians say that, but we did it better than most.

Nearly every Sunday morning through this period Bowie's mother, Peggy Jones, would come over to Haddon Hall. She was very normal – not what you'd expect David Bowie's mother to be like at all. She looked like any other woman in her late fifties, with carefully arranged hair and a long coat. Bowie's father, John, had died of pneumonia in 1969, just two years before; his Riley was the car that Bowie drove.

I remember once Peggy came up to the landing where Mick and I were sleeping and brought us a cup of tea and a biscuit. Mick woke up suddenly, thinking it was the day of a recording session.

'What time is it?'

'It's ten past nine,' she said.

The session the following day was due to start at nine,
so Mick leapt out of his sleeping bag, bollock-naked. Peggy
screamed, dropped the tray and ran downstairs.

'Mick, it's Sunday, not fucking Monday!' I shouted but he
was so stressed he didn't understand what I was saying. We
called him 'Flasher Ronson' for the next two months.

Peggy was great; she'd tell Bowie off for this, that and the
other.

'Are you eating enough?' she'd ask him every time she
came over. 'You're ever so thin.'

'Yes, Mother,' he said, like an obedient son. 'Angie looks
after me.'

We all exchanged glances. It was funny to see him feeling
uncomfortable for a change.

We'd all sit at the table for a Sunday roast cooked by Peggy
and Angie, band and family mixed together. Bowie's half-
brother, Terry Burns, who was ten years older than him, would
sometimes come too. He had suffered from schizophrenia and
had no filter on what he said. You'd ask, 'What have you been
up to, Terry?' and he'd reply, 'I've been wanking.' His mother
would say, 'I don't think people want to hear about that at the
dinner table', while we tried not to laugh.

Poor Terry killed himself in 1985, but in a way I always
thought his influence on Bowie brought him a certain immor-
tality. All the songs about madmen and madness that Bowie
wrote in the years when I was with him – they definitely had
their roots in Terry's schizophrenia.

After our Sunday with the Joneses it was back to work on
Hunky Dory. Ken Scott, who had become famous for working as an engineer on the Beatles' *Magical Mystery Tour* and

'White Album', and had also engineered Bowie's previous two albums, was a stickler for detail when it came to getting sounds. He had it all to prove, because *Hunky Dory* was his first full production gig.

Years later, Ken told me he had taken on the job with David thinking it wouldn't matter if his first album production wasn't very good, as it probably wouldn't be that successful anyway. When David played him the songs for the album, Ken thought to himself, 'Oh shit. These are great songs. This guy's really got something.'

Ken would often spend half a day getting a drum sound. Sometimes a tom-tom might be ringing or buzzing a bit, so he'd stick ciggie packets on the skins to get them to sound perfect. The result was terrific. Ken wanted the sounds to integrate and belong together, and he put real quality in there. He definitely had the right pedigree. He was a nice guy, and what was most important was that Bowie respected him and listened to his suggestions. He admired Ken's attitude, which was that producers could bring some personality and charisma of their own to recordings, rather than merely tweaking the faders on the console.

I think Ken's contributions played a major part in the success of these albums, not only because of the quality of the sound and his impeccable mixing ability, but because he managed to make the tracks timeless. Ken and I got on well. We'd go round to his house for dinner and the occasional party. They were always great nights. I enjoyed my first fondue at Ken's house, the new thing for dinner parties at the time.

We'd worked on some of the songs in our rehearsal room at Haddon Hall. This was mainly to give Bowie and Mick a chance to get ideas for the arrangements. The recording itself didn't always go perfectly smoothly. Bowie would tell us on a given Friday which songs we were going to record the following Monday and we'd work on those over the weekend. But then he'd often ask us to do completely different ones when Monday came, so all that time was wasted. We'd tell him we didn't know those tunes, so he'd play them to us twice, and roll the tape. Just before the red light came on, I'd be desperately asking, 'How does this end?' You really had to nail it by the third take because Bowie got bored so quickly and the atmosphere would get pretty dark if that happened. We made sure we always got it down by then.

As a result, we were all on a knife edge in the studio, and it could be stressful. You had to work out how to pull off what was needed, because, as I've said, Bowie rarely gave you any direction. He didn't really know how to discuss specific notes and feels, so you had to find it yourself – and quickly – which made you play with a lot of attention to getting it right.

We played with feeling on the *Hunky Dory* songs. For example, we'd heard Bowie playing 'Oh! You Pretty Things' at Haddon Hall when he was first writing it, and Mick said then that we needed a lift in the choruses from the drums. I worked out a quirky snare, bass drum and hi-hat pattern that worked and didn't get in the way.

There was a lot of that going on. 'Quicksand' is a good example of what I'm saying here, because the whole feel of that song was apathy. Everything was hopeless, and we had to go there with the right emotion.

We'd learned our craft playing blues, and you can't play blues properly unless you can feel it. You have to concentrate on the emotional side of the music, and when I played with Bowie the music pulled on that side of me. He wasn't a blues musician, but I had to back up the emotion that was going on lyrically and musically. He revisited those emotions on all the records I played on, from *The Man Who Sold the World* to *Aladdin Sane*. He was trying to say similar things each time, but in a more immediate or different way.

By the time we recorded *Hunky Dory* I thought Bowie's voice had improved a huge amount from *The Man Who Sold the World*. When he did the vocals, he did them quickly because he wanted to keep them fresh and uncomplicated. He was keen to lay down the music and get the song done, so he'd sing a vocal and it would be note-perfect in the first take. He'd ask Ken, 'Was that OK?' and Ken would nod.

'I'll sing another one and you can mix them together,' Bowie would say.

After he was done there'd be a stunned silence from Ken, because doing two note-perfect takes like that is practically impossible. But David would do it, and Ken would be fiddling with his moustache, saying, 'Fucking hell . . . that is spot on.' He'd play back both takes simultaneously, but you couldn't hear the two separate vocal tracks, just a thickened version of the first one.

What impressed me so much was all this musical ability was just the tip of Bowie's talent. There was so much else going on there, and it all tied together in a way that hadn't been completely obvious the first time I saw it. For instance, the first time I saw Bowie doing mime, I thought, 'What the fuck has that got to do with rock 'n' roll?' But then I realized that he was coming at it from outside music, so to speak. He was standing on the outside, looking in, and using whatever he needed for his intended effect.

The opening cut on the album was 'Changes'. I've always thought the line 'Every time I thought I'd got it made, it seemed the taste was not so sweet' was about 'Space Oddity'. He thought he'd made it with that song; then he found out that he hadn't made it after all. He was almost admitting it had been a false start. The song encapsulated the ups and downs he'd experienced, and made it clear that he was going to keep on changing until he got it right.

Musically, *Hunky Dory* is a step forward, too. With 'Changes' you can hear that we have more experience as players, thanks to everything that we'd been through. At the same time, Bowie's songs were more understandable while still putting across his points of view. He seemed more certain of how to express himself now.

I was particularly pleased with the drums on 'Changes', because I managed to pull off a balance of economy and expression on that song. My aim was to find a feel that allowed Bowie's vocal to breathe. He needed enough space and time to express himself, and my drums had to make that happen. For that reason there's a lot of space in this song where I don't play anything.

With a lot of his songs I would ask myself what the pulse needed to be to drive the song along. One of the keys to a successful piece of music is the beat. I don't care what kind of music it is; the rhythmic pulse is the carrier wave for the song, while the lyrics carry the message. Whether that song impinges on a person or not, that remains true. You can depress people with drums, too: play a little slower and you'll have them on the floor. You can do both in the same song; in fact, you can create whatever emotion you want in your groove.

On 'Oh! You Pretty Things' the drums don't come in until the chorus. That was planned. When it came to the arrangements this time, either David would have done them already, or he and Mick would work on them together. I had to serve the song, stay on the money and not be brash. For example, we tried recording drums for 'Eight Line Poem', but they were too much for it. It was all about giving the songs what they needed.

The highlight of *Hunky Dory* for me, and indeed of all the songs I recorded with Bowie, is 'Life on Mars?', which I think is magnificent. We got Rick Wakeman in to play the piano. Rick, who is an absolute virtuoso, had worked with Bowie on 'Space Oddity' as he was the only session player around who had a Mellotron at the time. This time, Bowie said to him, 'Do your thing as a keyboard player, but treat it as a piano piece.'

We'd only previously heard 'Life on Mars?' with Bowie plinking away on the piano; he could change chords, but he didn't add any flourishes or embellishments, so when Rick started playing it we were gobsmacked. Incidentally, the piano at Trident that Rick used was the same one as used on the Beatles' 'Hey Jude' and later by Freddie Mercury on Queen's 'Bohemian Rhapsody'.

Rick's playing on 'Life on Mars?' is the best piano recording on a rock song ever, in my opinion, and it's the track I'm most proud of from the whole of my career. The song totally came to life in the studio. Mick and I worked out beforehand how the drums had to be, as Bowie wanted quite a lavish string arrangement. Mick played me the outline of the arrangement on guitar, so I could work out how the drums would fit. At the time I remember approaching it with the concept of 'John Bonham plays classical music'.

This was Mick's first big string arrangement and it was unbelievably stressful for him. He was quite a nervous person; sometimes his hands would shake. He really wasn't the confident showman that you saw on stage. It was even more difficult because in those days you used the BBC's string players as session musicians, and they were very conservative. They were good players, but it was impossible to build any kind of rapport with them because we inhabited such different worlds.

Mick knew that he was going to have to deal with them – and even conduct them. On the day, the string players came to Trident and took their seats, ready for the session. Bowie and I were looking through the large glass window in the control room at the scene below. We watched Mick walk into the studio and introduce himself.

They didn't look that impressed; in fact, they seemed almost resentful.

Mick then stood in front of them and carefully rolled a cigarette. As a way of taking charge of the scene I thought this was a stroke of genius. The musicians then played the arrangement twice, which Bowie and I thought was amazing; we gave Mick the thumbs up. The leader of the string section then said to Mick, 'We love the arrangement, but we'd like to do another one. I think we can do it better.' This was unheard of. String musicians usually want to get in and out of the studio as quickly as possible. The next take was the one that ended up on the album. All this was amazing to witness.

When we recorded the basic track for 'Life on Mars?', Ken didn't want to end up with a lot of takes that he'd have to sift through, so he would just record over old takes. We'd done one take, which was OK, and a second which was really good – but right at the end, as it was fading out, a phone rang while we were recording.

The phone was in a bathroom next to the studio. It was intended for session musicians, who used it to call out to find out if they had work lined up, but nobody ever called in on this phone. It was really weird that it rang during the fade-out of the song. Mick said, 'For fuck's sake!' We then did another take – and it was excellent.

When we listened back, the song faded out, and then the phone rang, and then the end of the earlier take could be heard after that, because the new take had started earlier on the tape. Bowie liked it, so we kept it. That was smart of him; I thought it was a really classy touch.

I remember Ken finishing the mix of 'Life on Mars?' and calling the four of us to come and listen to it in the mixing suite. The sound quality is really good in these places, and when he played it I remember saying, 'Holy shit!' It was the first time that I almost forgot that it was us playing. It was that good. We were the ones who the music was affecting; we were feeling the impact of what we'd caused. I almost forgot what was coming next, as we listened.

Bowie had told us earlier that the 'Life on Mars?' concept had originated with a 1968 song called 'Comme D'Habitude' by Claude François and Jacques Revaux. Bowie had been asked by his then manager Ken Pitt to write English lyrics for it. However, his version – called 'Even a Fool Learns to

Love' – was rejected. Paul Anka's English-language version was released a year later by Frank Sinatra. It was called 'My Way'.

This had pissed David off, so he had decided to write his own version, not ripping it off but using similar chord sequences. He said it was about a young girl's view of the modern world and how confusing it was. In the song she's watching a film and unable to relate to either reality or the film. The film tells her there's a better life somewhere – but she doesn't have access to it.

The fans loved 'Life on Mars?' when it was released as a single in July 1973, when it charted at Number 3 in the UK and stayed there for thirteen weeks. By that time Bowie had become a huge star. Back in December 1971 hardly anyone seemed to give a damn about us or *Hunky Dory*. Funny how things ch-ch-change . . .

'Kooks' is obviously about Bowie's son, Zowie. I thought it was a really modern way of a couple singing about their kid, just as John Lennon had sung about his son. There was a cuteness about it that didn't need embellishing; it just required a simple beat.

Conversely, 'Quicksand' was a pretty dark song. Lines like 'I'm sinking in the quicksand of my thoughts' took it to places that I hadn't heard many other artists go to, at least in a personal message from themselves. It was a bit unnerving, actually. The drums come in and out all the way; it's a pretty tricky arrangement, because we don't bring the parts in where you'd expect. We deliberately made the flow as oblique as possible, because that was what the song needed.

The more introspective sound of this song was inspired, at least as I see it, by artists such as Jacques Brel. Bowie had started listening to these singers, along with Scott Walker and other experimental songwriters, after his foray into American subcultural music such as the Velvet Underground. He'd play those records to us and we'd listen intently to what those guys were trying to say.

Hunky Dory then goes to 'Fill Your Heart', with an arrangement that is similar to Biff Rose and Paul Williams' original; there were brushes on the original. I don't usually use brushes, but I did on this occasion. 'Andy Warhol' is acoustic, and there are no drums on this track. Then there's 'Song For Bob Dylan'.

Dylan had obviously influenced David a bit as a folk singer. To me, that song was David saying, 'You've dropped everybody in the shit, Dylan; you're not doing what you're supposed to be doing. You've stirred everything up. You've said, this is wrong and that is wrong, but you've got no solutions.' I think that helped him to become the solution himself; to say, 'I'll tell everyone where to go, then.' It was a bit cheeky of Bowie, mind, because Dylan had been a massive influence on our generation.

Bowie wrote 'Queen Bitch' after being influenced by the Lou Reed and Andy Warhol crowd. The version we'd done in Ronno had a different guitar part, but of course it was familiar because we'd played it a lot. To me he was saying in this song that he could sum up their attitude in a single song that was better than fifty of theirs. We wanted to capture that American feel without losing our Englishness.

And at the end of the album there's 'The Bewlay Brothers', which I think is amazing. David recorded it while the rest of

us went out for a meal; he stayed behind and had finished it
by the time we came back, and I thought it was mind-blowing.

'What's that song about?' Ken asked him.

'I have no idea,' David said, 'but you wait – when the
Americans get hold of it, they'll go apeshit. They'll call me
the Messiah. They'll read so much into it about what I am'.

And that's what happened. The pictures in our minds that
those lyrics summon up are amazing, and the song seems
full of knowledge. Bowie later referred to the song as a
'palimpsest', in other words a manuscript of writing beneath
which older writing can just be faintly seen. That sums it up
very well.

Hunky Dory is a classic album; it has been included in
many best albums lists over the decades. It's just what it is:
beautifully played and recorded, and absolutely full of ideas.
While Bowie was writing it, he'd come up with new ideas and
say, 'We're going to add strings to "Life on Mars?"', or 'Let's
end "Changes" with a slow, saxophone outro', and we'd be
like 'Fucking hell, this is amazing!' He was changing all the
time, and although he didn't know it that was to be his *modus
operandi* for the rest of his life. He survived that way.

So *Hunky Dory* was in the can by August, but we didn't know
when it would be released. Defries had used some of the tracks
to help secure a deal from the big American label RCA but we
weren't involved with that. We, the band, still hadn't signed
any form of contract. Recording good songs, playing good
gigs and not having to worry about the rent was enough for
us; we were still young and naive.

The month was memorable for another reason, as it introduced Bowie to an outrageous cast of characters who would become part of all our lives. In August 1971 Andy Warhol's infamous show *Pork* arrived in London. Apparently the show was based on conversations and activities recorded at Warhol's place in New York, the Factory, and although I didn't get to see it myself, it was later described to me by one of the cast as an 'orgy with arty dialogue'. From pictures I saw of it, that seemed like a good description to me. Bowie, Angie and Defries did go and see the show and met the Warhol actors/superstars, discovering that they had connections to the New York underground art/music scene. Tony Zanetta, who played the Warhol character in the show, introduced Bowie to Warhol himself in September, while Bowie was in New York to sign his RCA contract. On the same trip Bowie also finally met Lou Reed and Iggy Pop.

Once the contract was signed and Bowie was back in London, we discovered RCA wanted three albums out of him. I can't imagine they had any idea how quickly those albums would arrive.

5

HANG ON TO YOURSELF

There's a list of attributes that any good album has to have; you can tick them off, one by one. Did *Hunky Dory* have good songs? Yes. Did the songs have a message? Yes. Did the vocalist communicate with the listener? Yes. Could the musicians play? Yes. Did they play with feeling rather than just accuracy? Yes. Was the album mixed and balanced correctly? Yes. And so on.

But we couldn't play those songs live, or not all of them anyway. Apart from 'Queen Bitch' and 'Life on Mars?' they just didn't translate to the rock band format. Mick, Trevor and I looked at the songs on *Hunky Dory* and realized that you couldn't really tour the album, which was where we were supposed to be going next. We needed new songs if we were going to head out on tour, and build our audience that way. As it happened, Bowie had written so much material throughout 1971 that he'd stockpiled another album's worth of songs, and with RCA behind him and Defries demanding another album to comply with RCA's contract we would soon be back in the studio to record the follow-up to *Hunky Dory*.

One day Bowie said to us, 'I've got a title for the new album. It's called *The Rise and Fall of Ziggy Stardust and the Spiders From Mars.*'

I thought, 'Fuck me – that's a long name.'

But before we started rehearsing for the new album, we had two weeks off and Bowie said, 'Do you want to come to Cyprus on holiday?' We were all knackered, and Bowie especially needed a break, so he, Angie, Trevor and I jumped on a plane. Zowie stayed back at Haddon Hall with his nanny, and Mick had a production job to do in Canada with a band called Pure Prairie League, so it was just the four of us.

A friend of Angie's lent us a house which was sparsely furnished but comfortable and someone Angie knew came in and cooked for us. We had a bedroom each, and it took us a while to get used to having lizards crawling on the ceilings in the rooms. The house also had a private beach – or at least I hope it was private, because I walked around naked some of the time. I got up earlier than everybody else, so I could take my clothes off without feeling embarrassed, and go for a swim. Being in Bowie's band must have been making an impact on me: I never would have done that a couple of years before.

Cyprus was a beautiful place. The island was completely unspoiled, and it was a couple of years before it was split into Turkish and Greek territories, so you could go anywhere. There weren't many other tourists there.

I hired a car, although I'd never passed my driving test. I'd previously had lessons from my dad and so had a provisional licence, but, guess what, the lessons didn't go very well. The car hire place was next to the police station and the two policemen knew I didn't have a proper licence and they were fine with that. There wasn't much in the way of traffic in the area where we were staying, though some of the roads had a steep 200-foot drop to the sea below. After one look over the edge, Trevor said, 'Fuck off, Woods, let me drive this bit.'

We visited the markets and bought fabrics for clothes, as well as going snorkelling and taking out high-powered speed-boats, which belonged to some of Angie's friends. We drank the local ouzo and retsina and went out to eat in the evenings, smashing the plates afterwards in typical Greek style. It was a great holiday.

The whole time we were there Bowie was writing new songs; he didn't rest that much. I never heard some of those songs again, ever, which is a shame because I thought they were really good. He was a pretty normal guy in a relaxed environment like this, although he wouldn't talk about foot-ball, or cars, or politics, or any of that casual stuff that most people chat about; he liked to talk with a purpose. He was a good listener, too.

On the flight back from Cyprus to England, about halfway through the trip, lightning hit the tips of the wings of the plane, bouncing from one to the other, and Bowie was terri-fied. In fact, the plane was shaking so badly, we all thought it might be all over. It was a real kiss-your-arse-goodbye moment.

I looked at him and I could see all the blood vessels in his face, because he had gone so pale. He wasn't a fit, healthy person back then, because he hardly ever ate, and he almost passed out on that plane. That was too close for comfort for him, and he didn't fly again until the late seventies because it was too traumatic.

Where Bowie was most normal was when we'd go out clubbing to the Sombrero or the Speakeasy, which we frequented back in London. He loved dancing to Tamla Motown and to the soul and R&B music that clubs played before disco. He was a great dancer – unique, perhaps, but still good. He definitely stood out on the dance floor.

It was a weird relationship between Bowie and me, I suppose, because he was my boss but also a friend. He introduced me to a view on art that I hadn't considered before. Bowie would say to Mick and me, 'Shall we go and see such-and-such an exhibition?' and Mick's usual reply was, 'No, what do I want to go and see that for?' whereas I'd say yes, generally, because I was interested in some of these things.

We spent some of October rehearsing the new tracks for *Ziggy* in our basement studio, then in November we went back to Trident and recorded most of the tracks. It's funny now to think that most of the album was in the can before *Hunky Dory* even came out, especially because we'd come a long way in a short time – Bowie as a songwriter and the rest of us as musicians.

Ken Scott was producing again; he was one of the best at getting the right sounds and making a particular part sound like it belonged. Once again all the arrangements were done by Mick and Bowie.

As ever, if things were going well in the studio, Bowie was very easy to work with. If they weren't, it would get a bit dark, because he couldn't explain in musical terms if something wasn't working for him. He lacked the vocabulary. He knew when I hit the right beat, or if Mick played something that was correct, but he didn't know how to explain it to us if those things weren't right. In that situation, he'd either sulk or just leave.

That would create tension for all of us, so each of us would think, 'Fuck! Is it me who's doing something wrong?' When that happened, the three of us would keep playing, and work on different things, until we came up with something that he liked.

On those occasions Bowie really was like a child. He rarely raised his voice, though, apart from one occasion at the beginning of the *Ziggy* sessions when we were playing something in a way that he didn't like.

'You haven't fucking learned this!' he shouted.

There was a horrible silence. No one knew what to say, and none of us – even Ken Scott – were any good at diffusing tension, so we just scrapped what we'd done and started again. Maybe he was just having a bad day, or maybe we were. None of that is important, really. We were all prone to the usual frustrations that creative people have. Bowie may have known nothing about what you could do in the studio, or what the controls did, but he was always right in his judgement.

'Let's play this chorus twice here,' he'd say to Ken.

'You're sure?' Ken would ask.

'Yes, just try it.'

Bowie would always be proved right. Not sometimes; *always*. It was uncanny. After several takes of a guitar solo he'd say, 'That take is the right one', and he'd be spot on.

Trident was on two levels, so if you were recording your part you'd have to go out of the control room, down some stairs and across the floor in the lower studio to where your gear was set up. Ken and I would watch Mick recording his solo, knowing there was always a chance that he would go into uncharted territory and we were willing to give him a chance as we knew what he was capable of. Mick himself never really knew when he'd got it. He just took it as a matter of fact that he could play the guitar. He was very modest.

So Mick would go down there and get his sound right while Bowie was reading *Melody Maker*. He would record a few takes, and Bowie would say, 'Ken, use the first one' without even looking up. Mick would do another six takes, trying to outdo that first one, and technically they'd be better but they wouldn't be as good, because they wouldn't have the right feel. He wouldn't even remember recording the first one by then, but Bowie knew the first one was the best. That happened many times. He had incredible instincts that way, which impressed all of us.

It's funny: Ken Scott said that it took him about a year to realize that *Ziggy* wasn't a concept album, but it was the right thing to spin it that way, so that people could contribute to the concept themselves. We never talked about it having a concept. Bowie never mentioned one, and perhaps he didn't know if it needed one or not, because when we'd finished recording the album he hadn't written or recorded 'Starman' yet. That song was the catalyst for the whole concept of the album, which became the story of Ziggy, the alien who came to save the earth only to be destroyed by rock 'n' roll excess.

Ziggy Stardust begins with my solo drum intro on 'Five Years', a song about the world ending. Ken got a fantastic drum sound for me; he was Bowie's George Martin. There were little nuances here and there that you thought probably wouldn't add much to the songs, but they did. They helped to build the dynamic and kept the listener glued to it.

When we first started recording I wasn't happy with my drum sound. I told Ken that my tom-toms sounded like me hitting cornflake packets and my snare sounded like a big packet of crisps. When I came into the studio the next day, Ken glanced up at me casually.

'Can you check your drums, before we get started,' he said.

'Yeah, OK.'

As I got to the drum room I glanced through the window but couldn't see any equipment. Puzzled, I opened the door and there on the floor, in place of my drums, were two Kellogg's corn flakes packets, a bag of crisps and plastic coffee cups in place of my cymbals. They were all mic'd up just as my kit had been. As I gaped at them I heard roars of laughter behind me. Everyone had crept down the stairs to see my reaction! They were pissing themselves. This stuff kept us sane, or relatively sane anyway.

After this episode we brought the drums back into the room and Ken and I worked on getting the rockier sound needed for the *Ziggy* songs. On *Hunky Dory* I'd used low tuning on all the drums and lots of gaffer tape, pieces of sponge and so on taped to the skins to create the fairly dead drum sound that was needed. On *Ziggy* we needed a more open, live drum sound, so I tuned them higher and hardly any damping was used.

Ken was also an excellent mixer. Perfection in a mix makes it soulless, although it's achievable if you persevere, but perfection is not the right target. It never is, when you're making art. The aim is to convey the right emotions at the right time and in the right way. If we spend another hour on it, will it improve the communication and the emotional impact? If so, go for it. If not, leave it as it is. That was how everything was done.

It sounds so simple to say it, but a lot of recording bands don't grasp it, and seek perfection rather than communication. If a shit snare sound does something wonderful to a song, you don't send out for a better snare drum and tune it up and record it again, because you'll kill the special thing that you had.

'Soul Love' is next. The concept of these alien songs was important, so when I picked a drum beat I didn't want it to be too unfamiliar; I wanted it to have a futuristic edge without being gimmicky. I tried to find that in all the tracks. I knew how John Bonham or Deep Purple's Ian Paice would do it, but that wasn't the point. As I've said, I followed the maxim that less was more, and avoided making everything too busy.

The new version of 'Moonage Daydream', which we'd recorded before with Arnold Corns, blew our heads off when we finished it. It was a dirty, sexy, rock 'n' roll track from the future, and I had to communicate that, so I had to find a beat that not only rocked but was a stable rhythmical pulse that would work even through the far-out solo sections.

And then there's 'Starman', which might be Bowie's best-known song, alongside 'Heroes' or 'Space Oddity', perhaps. It's funny to think that when we finished recording the *Ziggy* album, it wasn't on it.

I remember how this went. *Ziggy Stardust* was done as far as we were concerned, but Defries came to Bowie and told him that RCA needed a single. They liked the album, but they didn't feel that it had a song that would grab people instantly.

'I'm going to write my own "Somewhere Over the Rainbow",' said Bowie, sitting down to write a song on his acoustic guitar. We went back to Trident between Christmas and January and recorded 'Starman'. Without that one track, the album might not have come out at all.

'It Ain't Easy' was hard to play because there's a bass drum and the jangling guitars, but no hi-hat to help me keep time. Getting that to feel good and be on time was tricky. 'Lady Stardust' is dead straight when it comes to the drums, and 'Star' is a steal from Mitch Mitchell's beat in Jimi Hendrix's 'I Don't Live Today', but speeded up, because it kicks. As a future rock band, we thought, you would be influenced by the great rock artists of the past, hence the Jimi reference.

'Hang On To Yourself' was partly 'borrowed' by the Sex Pistols. Glen Matlock came to a talk I gave and told me, 'You know I ripped off the bass part, note for note, for "God Save the Queen"?' That had never occurred to me before. We were full of youthful arrogance when we played this. We were saying, 'Pin back your fucking ears and listen!'

The drum beat in 'Ziggy Stardust' is influenced by King Crimson, believe it or not. I love '21st Century Schizoid Man' because of the way that Michael Giles starts and ends the rolls in unusual places. I thought the whole feel of this song would suit that approach.

'Suffragette City' was just balls to the wall and go for it. It's one of those funny grooves: you listen to it and you think 'Is that all there is to it?', but when I tried different beats the song was diminished. Somehow the beat that is on there keeps the listener involved and doesn't let up. You are in there until the end. Talking of endings, 'Rock 'n' Roll Suicide' almost ends the *Ziggy* album on a downer, but by the end it takes everything up a notch again.

As we were recording *Ziggy*, we gradually realized that we were capturing something that was modern, fresh and in the right creative spirit. There's an immediacy, a nowness, that gets onto the vinyl, which bands that do thirty takes nowadays and join six of them up in Pro-Tools never achieve. The playing might be superlative, but there's no life to it. That happened in later years: rock went up its own arse and everybody lost out. Kids nowadays are used to hearing empty, lifeless music made with digital technology.

We were starting to think of our music as something special at that point. But while I knew the music was good, and I was incredibly proud of it, I was concerned that it might be a bit much for the public. Was it too weird? Would anybody understand it? Possibly, and possibly not. A cheesy song called 'Knock Three Times' by Tony Orlando & Dawn was Number 1 at the time, and there was lots of average music of that sort in the charts.

Bowie was determined. He was really going for it, 24/7, which was impressive. He didn't have any 'ifs' – 'if' we make it, or 'if' we do this or that – even though he didn't have it all together yet. He was trying everything to make it work.

Like him, we were in this for a reason: we wanted to kick the music business up the arse. Every now and then the business needs to be shocked by somebody approaching it from a new angle – something that hasn't been done before – and that's where we felt we came in. We wanted to make it more entertaining, create some great rock music and tour the world. The artist is often a rebel against the status quo, because he or she sees that something needs to be said, or improved, or changed. That impulse is there, and is one of the reasons I became an artist, a peaceful way of making things better.

Mick, Trevor and I moved out of Haddon Hall in late 1971. It had been a fun place to be, of course; at one point, I saw half a dozen naked girls who turned out to be models from various fashion magazines dancing around downstairs, giggling and screaming. I recognized one of them from a shampoo ad on TV. This happened when Mick and I were still sleeping on the landing. I woke up, peered through the banisters and couldn't believe my eyes.

'Mick!' I hissed. 'Wake up!'

It was early afternoon, so we hadn't got up yet.

Mick opened an eye and groaned, 'What is it, Woods?'

'Look down there!'

He crawled over to the banisters, looked down at what was going on and started to laugh. So did I.

Angie, who was down there with the dancing girls, saw us and shouted up, 'Put your hard-ons away, boys, they're all lesbians.'

Mick said, 'I'm hungry – aren't you?'

I said, 'Yeah.'

And down we went. It was the best tea and toast we'd ever had.

It wasn't always like this: sorry to disappoint you. Over the years, there have been rumours about the orgies that supposedly took place at Haddon Hall when we were there. There were certainly odd times where I'd meet people I hadn't seen before at breakfast, and I'd think, 'I wonder where they slept last night?', but if there were any orgies our invitations must have been lost in the post.

Anyway, after a year and a half or so, Haddon Hall was getting a bit overcrowded with all the Bowies' friends coming over and hanging about. We had a bit of money by now because our weekly wage had gone up to £50, so we wanted a flat of our own and moved down to a place at 6 Beckenham Road, about a mile away.

We still went over and rehearsed at Haddon Hall, though.

Hunky Dory was released on 17 December 1971, which was an exciting time for us. We could hear ourselves on the radio at last and it started to feel as if we were on our way.

The album has that amazing cover image, with Bowie in a sexually ambiguous pose and long blond hair. He had taken a Marlene Dietrich photo book to the photo session, so the pose was definitely influenced by her look. Bowie's school friend George Underwood contributed to the artwork – the same George who infamously, and accidentally, gave Bowie an enlarged pupil during a fight when they were both about fifteen. It left Bowie looking as if he had different coloured eyes.

The album did moderately well, compared to Bowie's previous releases. The songs are great and it was clear that we as a band were moving up to another level, somehow. The four of us had been giving it everything we'd got. Even though *Hunky Dory* wasn't a big hit, and 'Changes' didn't chart when it was released as a single in January 1972, it did receive plenty of airplay and it felt as if major developments were around the corner.

We couldn't have imagined just how major . . .

6

STARMAN

The year 1972 was shaping up to be an insane one for us. An English tour was booked from January until September; *The Rise and Fall of Ziggy Stardust and the Spiders From Mars* was set to come out in June on RCA, even though we were still flying high because *Hunky Dory* had just been released; and, in the autumn, we were going to America for the very first time as a band.

What could possibly go wrong?

It's hard to imagine now, but ridicule and career suicide were very real concerns. We knew our music was brilliant, but our look . . . Our 'education' on showmanship and image had started back in Haddon Hall around the time we were recording *Ziggy*. We always had weekends off and David used them.

'There's a play in London that I'd like us all to go and see,' he announced one day.

'What's it called?' I asked.

'I don't give a shit what it's called,' he said. 'The lighting director there is really good and I want you to get an idea of what can be done with lights.'

Looking back, I suppose that, at the time, bands would use red, green and yellow lights and possibly a strobe light. It was very basic. So he more or less asked us to watch the lighting, not the play. It was quite an eye-opener when we saw how the lights integrated with the music and the scene on the stage, and helped create more impact.

Once we even went to see a ballet – I think it was *The Nutcracker* – which was funny because we all thought it was just a night out and we bought popcorn, crisps and Cokes before we went in. When the performance started we had to very gently place these things on the floor as they were too noisy to devour! I actually enjoyed the ballet, which surprised me. And once again we saw how the lighting added so much to the performance.

David was tackling us on the clothes front too. We had a bit of a clothes allowance now and so we started to shop on the fashionable King's Road in Chelsea. We particularly liked Alkasura – which was a favourite of Marc Bolan – and Mr Fish (owned by Michael Fish, who'd designed the dress Bowie wore on the front of *The Man Who Sold the World*). Freddie Burretti, David's friend and clothes designer, had also intro-duced us to Stirling Cooper clothes, which we liked because of the cut of the jackets and the trousers, which were more like jeans and fitted well around the crutch. Very rock 'n' roll.

I remember the first time we went to these chic clothes shops, Bowie bought a black and green striped satin suit. I bought a brown velvet jacket with a peplum and embroidery down the front, and a mustard-yellow canvas jacket. Mick got a suede jacket that had multicoloured snakeskin lapels. We also bought t-shirts with unique designs.

The femininity and sheer outrageousness of the offstage clothes, let alone the soon to come onstage gear, was a stretch for us at first, I admit. But after a while, we calmed down and got used to the idea. We knew we couldn't just wear jeans and t-shirts any more, on or offstage. It wouldn't have worked. Plus we got used to standing out in a crowd, pretty quickly I might add. So it definitely appealed to our rebellious artistic instincts.

For shoes, more prosaically we went to Russell & Bromley. I remember the sales assistant looking at our selection and saying, 'You do know these are girls' shoes?' We did! They looked better and more stylish than any men's shoes and complemented our new clothes. It's quite ironic that Mick, Trevor and I chose these ourselves, considering our initial reaction to what we'd be wearing on stage in a short while.

So we had started to look more like a rock 'n' roll band. At least, we thought we did.

One weekend at Haddon Hall Bowie started to talk about our stage clothes. He mentioned the films *A Clockwork Orange* and *2001, A Space Odyssey* which we all loved. He said he liked the look of the 'Droogs' in *A Clockwork Orange* – who were dressed the same, all in white, their trousers tucked into black ankle boots – and thought we should look like a gang. He then showed us some drawings he'd done, of collarless bomber jackets with zip-up fronts and lace-up boots which almost came up to the knee. I think at the time we just shrugged it off as an 'idea', although we did like the concept of being a gang.

A week later we found ourselves in the fabrics department of Liberty of London, following David and Angie as they sorted through the shelves. Occasionally they'd ask us, 'What do you think to this?' We hadn't really joined up the dots at this point so we'd answer dismissively, 'It's all right.' Between ourselves we'd be saying, 'This isn't really rock 'n' roll, is it!'

Having said that, the four of us had been to see Alice Cooper at the Rainbow, Finsbury Park, when he toured the UK in 1971 and his band wore very similar outfits to the ones we eventually had made, although I think theirs were less stylish and less well made, and they didn't have the boots. (Funnily enough his band was originally called the Spiders, before becoming the Nazz and then simply Alice Cooper.)

Back in Beckenham swatches of the fabrics they'd chosen were brought out. Freddie Burretti had helped refine Bowie's concept and it was he who'd suggested the outfits should be different colours – pink, blue and gold – so we had the gang image but it was less menacing than the 'all white' of the Droogs. It was decided that Trev would look best in blue as he had dark brown hair. Angie suggested that Mick would look best in gold as he had blond hair. That only left one colour!

'I'm not too sure about pink!' I said.

'I know what you mean,' Bowie said thoughtfully, 'but it takes a real man to wear pink and pull it off.'

I obviously fell for this line as that's what I ended up wearing.

The Droogs also wore a codpiece and Freddie used an idea from the Stirling Cooper jeans to simulate this idea, adding a separate piece of fabric cut in a zigzag from the waist down to the crotch on either side. (The influence of *A Clockwork Orange* was also heard in the live show, because we used the electronic version of Beethoven's Ninth Symphony from the film's soundtrack to open every gig.)

We had a second set of outfits that were just as outrageous. Mine was a brown and gold top with gold lamé trousers. Trev had another blue outfit but the top was made from a flock material. Mick's was a sequined maroon jacket and black trousers. Bowie had a black and white flock top with white satin trousers. They were all made in the same style: collarless bomber jackets and tucked-in trousers. All these clothes were made by Susie Frost, Zowie's nanny. Freddie may have helped make some of Bowie's outfits, too.

The boots were a kind of trendy looking wrestling boot, flat and laced up the front and made of coloured patent leather. Mick's were green, Trev's were blue and mine were dark pink. We all also had a pair of black patent leather boots while Bowie had his red ones.

During this deep discussion on who was wearing what, which went on for some time, Angie burst into the room and in a panicky voice said, 'You've got a problem, boys. Ronson's just packed his case and headed for the station. He said it's all too much for him, he's quit the band!'

Bowie said to me, 'Go find him and talk to him, do whatever you have to do to get him back.'

So I made my way to Beckenham station to find Mick sitting on the platform looking very pissed off.

'Where are you going?' I asked.

'Back to Hull,' he said. 'I've had enough. I can't go on stage wearing clothes like that. I have friends who'll see me. It's all too much, I just wanna play guitar.'

'I understand what you're saying,' I said, 'but it's not going to work wearing jeans and t-shirts, is it? I remember when we were in the Rats you wore Apache boots and a long tasselled waistcoat and wristbands. That was over the top for the time, plus I've seen pictures of you wearing a real girlie frilly shirt so it's not that much of a leap, is it?'

We then talked about how it would either work brilliantly or not at all and there was always the possibility that we could be laughed off the stage, but it was worth the risk, wasn't it?

Eventually, after much talking it through, he said, 'I suppose you're right', and we headed back to Haddon Hall.

Quite a few people have claimed that I'm the one who said, 'Fuck off, I'm not wearing that', but this time it wasn't me.

As well as the clothes, the shoes, the lighting, etc., what was still needed to complete the transformation of us all, Bowie concluded, was the hair.

A young woman called Suzi Fussey worked in a local Beckenham hair salon where she did Bowie's mother's hair. Mrs Jones would talk to Suzi about her son and eventually Suzi was asked to come up to Haddon Hall to do Angie's hair. While she was there Bowie asked her, 'What would you do with my hair?', which was shoulder-length and brown at the time.

'I'd cut it short,' Suzi replied, which she did.

So he had the start of what would become the Ziggy haircut. The colouring of it would come later. I don't remember exactly when.

Daniella Parmar, a muse of Freddie Burretti's, often came over to Haddon Hall with him. She would regularly have different coloured hair; once it was very short, peroxide blonde with an ice-cream-cone shape cut into the back and dyed in three colours! This inspired Bowie to look for a more synthetic hairstyle for Ziggy. He found a girls' magazine with a model on the cover who had red hair (apparently she was a Kansai Yamamoto model, though I didn't know that then). He copied the cut and colour and had Suzi carry it out. When his hair was finally completed he asked, 'What do you think?'

'It looks amazing,' I said. 'I've never seen anything like it, especially on a guy.'

My hair was now shorter, and styled, but it was still brown. A couple of months into the tour, I decided I would have the Ziggy cut and also have it bleached blond. It made me look a bit unearthly, perhaps like a member of Ziggy's family.

Back then there wasn't the range of hair products we have today; in fact, the trick to the Ziggy hairstyle, which stood up on end, was a ladies' setting lotion called Gard, which you spread over your hair before blow-drying it straight. We needed Suzi to join us on that tour so she could do all our hair, and she also became wardrobe mistress.

Later again on the tour, Trevor would have his long brown hair dyed jet black and Angie worked on those incredible sideburns by spraying them silver. Mick's blond hair was styled and highlighted.

The transformation was complete.

On 11 January we unveiled Ziggy on a pre-recorded session for BBC Radio's *Sounds of the Seventies* with John Peel. It wasn't broadcast until 28 January, though. We went back on 18 January to record another session for the same programme, this time with Bob Harris, to be aired on 7 February. Both were recorded at the BBC Maida Vale studios.

The set list was 'Hang On To Yourself', 'Ziggy Stardust' 'Queen Bitch' and 'I'm Waiting For the Man', for both shows. On the Bob Harris show we did 'Five Years' as an extra number. This was just the four of us with Nicky Graham on piano.

After that, on 19 January, we began a week of rehearsals for the British dates at the Royal Ballroom on Tottenham High Road, driving up there from Beckenham at lunchtime and going through the whole set, twice each day, non-stop. As I sat at the back of the stage I could see the three other guys interacting up front so I'd suggest things to them, like standing back to back for the beginning of 'Queen Bitch', and then kicking away from each other when the heavy chords began, because it looked exciting that way. We'd adjust the lighting as we went along, too.

Everybody threw in ideas, although you had to be pretty sure it was a good idea before you suggested it, or Bowie would ignore it. The show wasn't choreographed to within an inch of its life, but most of the major movements on stage were planned, along with the lights, to complement the music. I enjoyed being part of the creativity.

In the midst of rehearsals, we had our second shock to the system when we read an interview Bowie had done with the *Melody Maker* saying that he was gay and always had been.

This was completely new to us, despite the environment we'd lived in at Haddon Hall. He had his camp moments and effeminate poses but we assumed if he was gay he'd have mentioned it to us at some point. We'd got used to him doing things to get attention so we thought this was just another example. I must admit we never asked him outright as we'd never witnessed anything that made us think he was.

After the interview even Angie said, 'You could have thought of your wife and at least said you were bisexual!'

Attitudes towards homosexuality were different in those days as it had only been decriminalized five years before in Britain. So, true or false, it was a courageous statement to make. It definitely sent shock waves through the music world and focused a lot of attention on Bowie and the Spiders. Still, all this – the clothes, Bowie's statement – felt like a massive risk. When something outrageous hasn't been done before, you worry that you'll be a laughing stock and you'll never get another gig in your life – which was a consideration, believe me.

Mick did an interview with a magazine right after that. His first statement to the journalist was: 'Before you start, I'm not gay.' More comments like that would have blown everybody's cool, so Bowie stopped us doing interviews. Of course, with the way we dressed now, most people assumed we were gay anyway. This was tough for three northern boys like me, Mick and Trevor, but we had a down-to-earth sense of humour about it.

We saw that people were genuinely unnerved by us. We would go into studios dressed the same way as Bowie, and the engineers would look at us with unease. You could tell from their faces that they thought we were gay because Bowie had said that he was. There was a certain attitude towards you.

We thought it was funny, though. I remember Mick and me sitting on the sofa in one studio, while engineers were tweaking the mixing desk six feet away – and you could feel the atmosphere. They were uncomfortable, as if they didn't know what they were letting themselves in for. What were we, they wondered?

Mick nodded towards one of them and said to me, 'He's got really nice legs, hasn't he?'

'No, the other one's legs are better,' I said.

As the engineers cringed we cracked up laughing. They just looked at us, faces bright red.

'You think we're gay, don't you?' I said.

'Well, we weren't sure . . .' they answered.

We had that a lot, but we just played around with it.

At the beginning of February we recorded a session for *The Old Grey Whistle Test*, presented by Bob Harris, which was British TV's major music programme at the time. We performed 'Oh! You Pretty Things', 'Queen Bitch' and 'Five Years'. I've never forgotten what happened with 'Five Years'.

We'd done a run-through so we knew where the cameras were going to be and I felt fine. But on the final run-through someone had decided that, as 'Five Years' ends with just drums, it would be better to finish on a close-up of me. I wasn't aware of this until we were actually recording and at the end of the song the main camera started coming closer and closer to me . . . It was unexpected and I was absolutely terrified. All I could think was that millions of people were going to be watching me. I hope I managed to disguise my feelings but I'm not sure if I did. When June saw it on TV she spotted my suppressed terror.

And then, almost two years after I first came down to

London and met David Bowie, we were finally taking the music out on the road. After all the recording we'd done, I was really looking forward to playing the songs live although I still felt some reticence about how the look of the show would be received.

The first gig of the *Ziggy* tour was at the Toby Jug, a large, red-brick pub in Tolworth near Kingston, on 10 February. About sixty people were there and we came on around 9 p.m. Before the show we got changed into our stage gear in a tiny dressing room and we could hear the punters outside drinking and chatting. When we went on stage, we played that little pub as if it was a stadium. I watched Bowie, Mick and Trevor up front; they were full of energy, and made sure the crowd gave them their full attention. It was a great start to the tour.

We were optimistic, and we knew we'd build up momentum as time passed – but some of the early gigs were only half full. The girls usually liked it, but most of the guys didn't: the show was so over the top and outrageous, especially in small spaces like those.

I've no idea why we played such small gigs to start with, although I appreciate that we weren't really in a position to play bigger ones because it hadn't all taken off yet. The audience were right on top of us – in hindsight far too close.

We mixed up songs from *Hunky Dory* and *Ziggy Stardust*, with numbers like 'Space Oddity' and 'My Death' by Jacques Brel, which Bowie performed halfway through in an acoustic part of the show. Although a lot of the show had been worked out in rehearsals, playing every night is really the only opportunity a band has to fine-tune things and develop as a live act, and that's exactly what happened.

Ziggy was the cosmic yob . . . posing, pouting, high-kicking like Rudolph Nureyev one minute and a futuristic Elvis the next.

Bowie was finding his character night after night. From my view at the back of the stage he was trying things out and discarding them left, right and centre. At the same time the rapport between Bowie and Mick was taking on new dimensions. Mick was a natural hard-rocking macho man, stomping and posing around the stage, often making grotesque faces as he pulled off the ultimate guitar performance. He was the perfect counterpoint to Bowie's effeminate, androgynous alien alter ego, and soon to become rock god, Ziggy.

Trevor and I held down the rhythm section and never let up for a moment, driving it hard and heavy where needed and playing with as much feeling as we could muster between us.

The chemistry between the band was really working and it felt fantastic and so right. This was what rock 'n' roll was all about and what we'd all talked about creating months earlier. Exciting and ass-kicking.

Now, on those early shows on this tour we'd hang around with the crowd after the show, wearing all this finery, because we hadn't yet got into the mindset of leaving the stage and locking ourselves away in the dressing room after we played. We would chat to the fans, mainly girls, who tried to get very friendly with us, not realizing that the male members of the audience were becoming antagonistic.

'Queers!' shouted some bloke from across the room one night.

We ignored him, but there was a silence around us and we knew that trouble was brewing, so we took off.

After another show when the atmosphere got threatening again Bowie said to Mick, 'You said you had a roadie with the Rats who was pretty tough, right?'

'Yeah, Stuey George,' Mick replied. 'He lined up an entire audience against a wall once and made them shut up!'

This was true. Our mate Stuey was as hard as nails. The Rats played a gig at Cottingham Hall near Hull back in 1969, and there was some aggression from the audience. Stuey went out there and made every single one of them stand against the side wall of the venue until they'd calmed down.

'Why don't you ask him if he wants to come and work for us?' asked Bowie.

Stuey was a black ex-boxer and, that old chestnut, a lovable rogue. If I ever questioned him about his past, he would grin cheekily and say, 'It's all just rumours, Woody, just rumours!' He could always take a joke which, being around the Rats, was fortunate. I remember his girlfriend once banned him from coming with us to a gig in Leeds – a situation he took seriously. After ten minutes of our jibes – things like 'It's all right, Stuey, we understand', 'What's it like being under the thumb?' and, 'So now we know who wears the trousers' – he got in the back of the van with the equipment.

'My girlfriend could be waiting somewhere down the road,' he said. 'She'll probably flag you down but don't say fuck all, or I'll get killed.'

Half a mile down the road there she was. We pulled up alongside her and wound down the window.

'Have you seen Stuey?' she asked.

'Yeah, he's hiding in the back of the van,' we chorused.

She started to scream abuse at him from outside while Stuey banged on the partition. 'Just go, just drive'.

He later got in the front of the van with us and said, 'You lot are a bunch of bastards, you've got me in so much trouble.' But he could always take a joke.

So Stuey joined us from Hull, moving into a flat in Beckenham. He came to every gig we did on the *Ziggy* tour after that. Tony Frost joined him not long afterwards, because he'd done martial arts and was another tough guy. We were relieved, because in the end somebody would definitely have got hurt if we'd continued with no security. The mere presence of those two mean-looking dudes was enough to stop any potential trouble from then on.

Bowie seriously impressed me as this tour began. He had this opinion about shaking up the music business, and how the *Ziggy* album and tours were going to do just that. He kept hinting in the press that everything was about to go off the scale when it came to the live show. The whole idea of being subversive through rock music started with him, and he was the first musician with the guts to actually go out and do it.

The British tour rolled on. As Bowie said himself later on, Ziggy was all about small beginnings. He was right, too, but it didn't take long for us to move up to bigger venues. We went from London, to the Midlands, to Glasgow, and to Sunderland, among other places, in February alone, and then we went back down again to the West Country and the south coast in March.

Bowie was loving it. He gave his all every night, and from our perspective on stage with him we could see that the crowd were as excited as he was. Early on in the tour it would take a while for them to warm up, and I'd be worried that our look was too much for them to take on board. In fact, there were several gigs where there was hardly any applause until about the fifth song, which was a bit unnerving. After one such show Bowie seemed very anxious.

'What the fuck is wrong with them?' he asked. 'Don't they know they're supposed to clap? They just sit there open-mouthed, staring at us.'

One of the crew interjected: 'David, they're in awe. It's like they don't want to miss anything and they're not quite sure how to respond.'

But as time passed the audiences became consistently enthusiastic, even at the start of the show. We knew we were on to something.

As we were touring the UK, Tony Defries was delivering the finished album *The Rise and Fall of Ziggy Stardust and the Spiders From Mars* to RCA Records in the USA.

Then 'Starman', backed with 'Suffragette City', was released as a single on 28 April in the UK. Suddenly we were on the radio again, and when the *Ziggy Stardust* album itself came out on 6 June it went straight in at Number 7, peaking at Number 5. Finally we were headline news.

The promotion continued with us performing 'Starman' on a show for Granada TV called *Lift Off With Ayshea* on 16 June. We were all getting changed in the dressing room before the show started when Bowie did something we hadn't seen him do before. He took out a bag containing make-up!

We watched in disbelief as he applied various strange substances to his face . . .

'Aren't you putting make-up on?' he asked.

The answers from us varied from 'Fuck no' to 'No fucking way'.

'It's a shame,' he said. 'You're going to be seen by hundreds of thousands of people and your faces are going to be green under these TV lights.'

He played us brilliantly: we looked at each other and we didn't even have to speak or discuss it. None of us wanted to look green!

He then asked us to get made up for the live shows, too, and we didn't like that at first – but as Bowie himself later put it, once we found out the effect the make-up had on the girls, we had no problem with it.

After all, Elvis had worn a bit of make-up on stage, so it wasn't like it had never been done before, and I remember seeing Paul Jones of Manfred Mann buying make-up from the chemist's in Bridlington once. But it quickly reached ridiculous levels.

'Who's nicked my fucking mascara?' Mick demanded as we got ready for a show one night.

'Don't look at me,' Bowie yawned in response.

'I haven't got it,' I said.

Mick stomped off to accuse Trevor. It was hilarious, and yet again I'd reflect on how far things had come since we were playing small clubs in Yorkshire.

A funny thing happened early on in the tour. Mick used to bend the strings on his guitar so much when he played that he'd go out of tune, and sometimes he would walk across the stage mid-song and try to tune Trevor's bass to his out-of-tune guitar.

Trevor hated this because to the audience it looked like he was the one out of tune. This occurred on a few nights until one night Trevor lost his cool and swung his guitar at Mick's head. Mick responded by doing the same.

In terms of pure theatre I thought this looked amazing, and I remembered the Artwoods doing a similar thing years before, so I suggested to Trevor and Mick that they have a fight with their guitar headstocks during the solo in 'Width of a Circle'. Mick arranged to give Trevor a nod when he was about to swing at him, and Trevor would back up. The idea was that they would just miss each other.

Then I told them that it would look even wilder if we put a strobe light on as well, although unfortunately they couldn't see each other as clearly, so they'd come off stage all scratched from being hit with each other's strings and occasionally they did hit each other on the head. Bowie loved all this, and it had the added benefit of giving him time to do a costume change.

We kept touring through June, playing shows in Sheffield, Middlesbrough, Leicester and elsewhere. These were middle-sized venues and universities, so we were making some progress.

Bowie fucked off to New York for a weekend in June to see Elvis Presley perform at Madison Square Garden. He later explained, 'I arrived late and our seats were right down the front and I'd made the mistake of wearing one of my Ziggy outfits. I was the only one there wearing glam clothes.' He added, 'I felt embarrassed.'

As an aside, the UK glam rock scene was fully established

at this time. Bolan had appeared on *Top of the Pops* performing 'Hot Love' with glitter under his eyes in March 1971 and
kick-started the movement, in the eyes of many. Bands like
Sweet and Slade followed suit. Bowie took it to another level,
though . . . Bowie's own views on glam came out in an interview in the *Telegraph* about five months later: 'I like Marc
Bolan's and Alice [Cooper's] work but I think we're in very
different fields. One does tend to get lumped in. But I think
glam rock is a lovely way to categorize me and it's even nicer
to be one of the leaders in it. I had been very much on my own.
There's security in being part of a trend. With a little bit of
luck, if I keep working hard, I can probably withstand it.'

Piano players came and went. Nicky Graham did the most
piano playing with us; he worked at GEM and later went on
to be a very successful producer and record company executive. He also worked as a gofer for us, but one night he failed
to get tickets to one of our shows for one of Angie's friends,
after which he suddenly wasn't in the band any more.

Around that time, Mick bought a car for his family up in
Hull, and it got vandalized. Some wanker wrote, 'Ronson is a
poof' on it. It didn't get any easier when we got to the famous
blow job moment at Oxford Town Hall on 17 June, a couple
of weeks after the *Ziggy* album came out.

Mick had been looking for some new tricks to do with his
guitar; he'd already incorporated playing his guitar with
his teeth during one of his solos. We'd been talking in the
dressing room that afternoon about how Chuck Berry did his
famous duck walk while playing, and Hendrix played guitar
with his teeth and also set fire to it. Dave Edmonds had played

his behind his back. Pete Townsend had 'windmilled' his and smashed his guitar to bits.

'We need something like that on stage,' said Bowie. 'All of those old ideas have been done. I've got an idea of what to do, but don't freak out and look surprised when it happens, Mick.'

None of us, Mick included, had any idea what he had in mind.

When Bowie got down on his knees in front of Mick that night and pretended to play his guitar with his teeth, Mick's back was to the crowd, so they assumed Bowie was pretending to give him a blow job. This was understandable, because he'd grabbed Mick's arse with both hands.

Some of the crowd laughed, some of them were speechless: none of them knew how to react.

I asked Mick what he felt about it after the show.

'I dunno, Woods,' he said. 'It's not really what I was expecting. People are going to give me lots of stick about it, aren't they?'

There wasn't much I could say to that, because he was right.

It became a regular part of the show and was definitely a press moment for us, one of a few that took place that year. We didn't even know that photographer Mick Rock had taken pictures of it happening, but it went on to be hailed as one of rock's classic moments, especially when it appeared on a full page in *Melody Maker* immediately afterwards. The journalists loved it, but I'm not sure the public were too keen; it was controversial stuff for 1972 but it made us infamous on both sides of the Atlantic.

As a result the band's profile was even further enhanced. A few shows later, we were playing at the Croydon Greyhound, with Roxy Music supporting us, and they had to turn away a thousand people who wanted to get in. A thousand! That's how popular we were getting. Along with this popularity came the girls. I'd like to sum this up by saying we worked hard, we played hard and we partied hard. After a show we would be pumped on the adrenalin and it was hard to come down. The groupies helped relieve us of the extra adrenalin! Bowie and Angie had an open relationship so I guess we all followed David's lead. Later on when I popped the question to my girlfriend June this was something I had to address. I did 'recover' from this conversation . . . more about that later.

On 6 July it got even crazier. We'd completed around fifty concerts and we had about another ten or so to do on the UK tour. To actually be able to perform night after night to packed audiences was amazing. All our fears about how we'd be received had been allayed; the audiences were amazing and wilder than we'd ever imagined. As we'd progressed through the tour we were continually tweaking elements of the performance to improve it. For instance, it seemed distracting during the show if, as very often happened, a couple of roadies had to walk on stage to fix something wearing their normal t-shirts and scruffy jeans. This definitely spoilt the illusion for the audience so it became policy for them to dress all in black. This was all part of the professionalism. We were all in high spirits, our confidence through the roof.

The single 'Starman' had been getting lots of airplay and was actually climbing the charts and we were asked to do *Top of the Pops*, which was recorded on 5 July, to broadcast the next day. You may remember how massive that programme was in the seventies: if you were on it, everyone saw you. It had a huge viewing audience of between ten and fifteen million. This was a real milestone moment for us.

Since deciding to be a musician at fourteen, this was the show I dreamed of appearing on – and now it was actually happening.

There were about six stages in the *TOTP*'s studio and there was an invited audience who were moved about between the various stages so as to be in camera shot for each particular artist.

We'd done a run-through, as had every other band that was on that day. The drums for some reason were out in front of Mick, Trev and Bowie, an unusual set-up, but nobody seemed to mind or even mention it.

I remember there was a corridor from our dressing room to the main stages. Status Quo were appearing that day, too, and we found ourselves standing opposite them waiting to go on. We were dressed in all our finery, including full make-up, and they were dressed in their trademark denim. We couldn't have looked more different. We gave each other nods and laughed when Francis Rossi said, 'Fuck me, you make us feel really old.'

Bowie played his part to the max, camping it up on stage, and at one point he threw an arm around Mick's shoulder. It was a bold move and quite a shocking gesture to make at this time, especially considering all the press concerning Bowie's sexuality.

During the line 'I had to phone someone so I picked on you' Bowie pointed directly into the camera and from reports at the time and ever since then this became a pivotal moment in his career. The impact of that performance was felt in millions of living rooms across the UK. It also landed the single in the top ten of the UK charts two weeks later.

Although we knew we'd done a good job, I have to admit at the time we didn't feel there was anything outstanding about that particular TV appearance. But it seems that a generation of future rock stars, too numerous to mention, were inspired and since then I've had the opportunity to speak to countless fans who told me of the buzz it created in the playgrounds and streets across the country the next day.

What we did realise was that we were now famous. From then on there were always fans camped outside the flat on the front doorstep, male and female, and we'd have to step over them to get to the shops. If there were too many, we sneaked out the back door and climbed over a wall.

Kids would bunk off school, arriving at some ungodly hour in the morning. By the time we got up and saw them they were obviously freezing. We'd tell them, 'You're supposed to be at school!' and they'd say, 'Yeah, but we had to come!' and so sometimes we'd invite them in. Mick would make them breakfast and we'd talk about music and school and so on.

Sometimes Bowie would come along and they'd gasp and then fawn over him. One group of kids told him that they were doing a project at school about him and his music, and wanted to ask him questions. He agreed, and he slipped into 'artist-being-interviewed' mode. Occasionally he'd say things to shock them, but, again, that was him attempting to create an effect.

In fact, even shopping took on a different perspective after this. Mick and I would be in a greengrocer's shop having selected our fruit and vegetables, and would take out money to pay for them only to be told, 'No we don't want paying. We saw you on *Top of the Pops*.'

Two days after *Top of the Pops* we played the Royal Festival Hall in London. It was a concert to raise funds for 'Save the Whale', one of the many causes espoused by Friends of the Earth. The poster for the event showed Bowie astride a whaling harpoon. Also appearing on the bill as support that night were Marmalade and the JSD Band.

Kenny Everett, the famously anarchic DJ, was the compere for the evening and introduced Bowie as 'the next biggest thing to God'. The reviews afterwards were amazing, *Record Mirror*, for instance, announcing that Bowie 'looks certain to become the most important person in pop music on both sides of the Atlantic'. But for us it was a special night as we had a surprise guest appearing with us. This was to be Lou Reed's first solo live appearance in this country. We had a short rehearsal with him during soundcheck; it didn't take too long as we had already been playing the tracks in our set at various times.

I thought Lou was cool. He definitely rose to the occasion and had been out and bought a black velvet suit decorated with diamond patterns of diamanté, like a glam Mexican. Towards the end of the seventy-minute set Bowie introduced Lou and we played 'I'm Waiting For the Man', 'Sweet Jane' and 'White Light/White Heat'. The two of them singing those songs together was amazing and, needless to say, it went down a storm.

Talking to Lou that night, he told me he'd had a great time. 'The British audience is very different to what I'm used to – they're more attentive. Playing places like Max's Kansas City, where everybody just freaks out and there are lots of drugs, is completely different.'

He asked me if I knew any of his music. I said, 'Yeah, all of it', which surprised and delighted him.

He also said he'd enjoyed performing with us because we'd played his stuff really solidly. I told him he reminded me of the early beat poets in NYC and I really liked the sense of decadence he managed to capture on his early albums. The conversation wasn't long; they never were with Lou as he seemed to have an ability to down a bottle of whisky in no time at all. I thought he was a sweet guy, though.

Lou Reed and the Velvet Underground were not that well known in UK at the time, and probably had a small following of a few thousand in the States. It was Bowie's intention to raise Lou's profile in the UK and to help him with a new album. In fact, Bowie and Mick would co-produce the recording, which would become *Transformer*. The original plan was for the Spiders to be Lou's band on the album, but this was later changed as it was considered a bit too confusing to have Lou Reed and the Spiders From Mars.

We had a reel-to-reel tape machine back at our Beckenham flat, so every night after the sessions, which started in August, Mick would play me rough mixes of what they'd done that day. I thought it was great, especially as day by day I'd hear the songs building up. 'Perfect Day' was beautiful and I loved

'Walk On the Wild Side'. Mick and Bowie's production was amazing. *Transformer* would go on to become a classic album.

Our next outing was to the Friars Club in Aylesbury. What made this unique, apart from a brilliant audience, was the fact that RCA had spent $25,000 to fly over a select group of American journalists to review the show. Defries had seen this as a perfect opportunity to create a media frenzy prior to our scheduled arrival in the US in September.

That night we did an impromptu version of the Beatles' 'This Boy'. We'd only ever done this once before, in Liverpool as a nod to the Fab Four. From reports at the time the reviews were very favourable.

Bowie had announced our next gig to the *NME* who were at Aylesbury: 'Hello, handsome, my name's David and I'm going to be at the Rainbow in lovely north London with the Spiders From Mars, some very pretty people called Roxy Music and a gorgeous butch blues singer called Lloyd Watson this Saturday and Sunday. It would be just too, too divine if you could make it there – and if you can't make it there, just be there, hmmm? It's going to be the most exquisite concert of the year.'

It was David's idea to put on a whole theatrical production for the show at the Rainbow Theatre on 19 August; a second show was added on 20 August when the first one sold out. We appeared on the poster as Ziggy Stardust and his band the Spiders – the first time, as far as I'm aware, that we were billed this way.

As I've mentioned, a major influence on Bowie as a performer was the mime artist Lindsay Kemp. Earlier in his career Bowie had joined Kemp's mime classes and had actually toured with him as part of his show on several occasions. Now Bowie wanted to include Kemp and his troupe at the Rainbow and the pair of them would choreograph a show that embellished the music we were playing.

The stage itself was designed with six ladders leading up to various scaffold platforms. On three of the platforms were screens and at different parts of the show shots of such rock icons as Elvis, Little Richard and Mark Bolan were projected onto these screens, giving the idea that Ziggy had already joined that august band. Other shots included Warhol's soup cans, Kellogg's corn flakes packets and Marilyn Monroe – it was all very pop art.

The stage was covered in sawdust so any dragging of the feet by band or dancers left a visible trail of movement.

Freddie Burretti made outfits for Lindsay and the troupe. There were about six dancers if I remember correctly; the outfits made them look like they were covered in spiders' webs. They all wore very ghoulish make-up. At one point Lindsay dropped down a rope from the ceiling dressed as a very freaky angel, smoking a three-foot-long joint.

One of the actors/dancers was a guy called Jack Birkett, who was almost blind – we watched him marking out the stage before the show so he would know where he was and didn't miss any lighting cues. During the show he would run to the front of the stage really fast and then stop near the edge. It was quite nerve-wracking watching him.

Throughout the whole set they performed choreographed scenes that from my vantage point, sitting beneath a scaffold section, helped create probably the most bizarre, theatrical performance ever – I doubt it has ever been equalled.

It was also the first time Bowie wore an outfit by renowned Japanese designer Kansai Yamamoto, whose model had influenced Suzi Fussey for David's hair. Bowie called it 'his bunny costume'; it was later known as his Woodland Creature outfit. It was a red leather playsuit or romper suit, and it didn't have legs! Mick, Trev and I wore the outfits from the second half of our normal show which were like our others but had collars, and were black/silver, giving a metallic appearance.

Aside from a couple of days at the Rainbow, once the full stage set was in place our rehearsals took place at the Stratford Royal Theatre, which is not really a rock 'n' roll rehearsal venue; it's for actors and theatrical performances. It was very 'proper' that we did it there.

There was a bar in the theatre that was frequented by actors, lighting technicians, etc., and during a break in rehearsals the four of us went there for a drink in our 'onstage' outfits. A guy who obviously had no idea who we were came up to us.

'Are you from the cast of *Star Trek*?' he said.

Without batting an eyelid, and in unison, the four of us answered, 'Yes.'

'Which episode? he asked.

'It's a new one, hasn't been shot yet,' Bowie told him.

'I'm not aware of that one,' he said.

What was funny was that later on that day we actually saw William Shatner, better known as Captain Kirk, in the bar.

The Rainbow shows were a resounding success. Once again Bowie had surprised us, demonstrating that he had more strings to his bow than we'd previously imagined.

The tour's official photographer, Mick Rock, was at the

show and videoed parts of it which were later included on the video for 'John, I'm Only Dancing', our next single.

The press got it. 'The whole evening could be judged a wondrous success,' wrote Chris Welch of *Melody Maker*, although he added, 'Eventually the faint suspicion grew that certain sections of the audience were slightly stunned and bemused by the jive David was laying on us.' He concluded, 'By God it has brought a little glamour into all our lives, and amen to that.'

'This was perhaps the most consciously theatrical rock show ever staged,' said Charles Shaar Murray at the *NME*. 'With perhaps the finest body of work of any contemporary songwriter, and the resources to perform this work to its utmost advantage, there really isn't anything going that tops the current *Ziggy* show,' he added. Murray also quoted Lou Reed as saying that the show was 'amazing, incredible, stupendous – the greatest thing I've ever seen'. Thanks, Lou, that was nice.

It turned out that to stage these two shows had been incredibly expensive so these were the only ones we did on that scale.

I met Mick Jagger at the Rainbow; he came to a rehearsal and was cool. He was mainly interested in my drum kit, for some reason. So was Paul McCartney:; they both commented on my drum sound. McCartney came to several rehearsals and sat and watched us with his wife, Linda. We had a whole piss-taking thing going on, where our roadie would continually wind us up about how he was well in with all the big stars. He wasn't, but he'd do this whole routine about 'Me, Paul and Linda are best mates'. He would stand behind Paul and Linda without them knowing, point at them and himself and give us a thumbs up.

I met Ringo, too, and we talked about drums. Elton John was also there. He is quoted as saying, 'What will I see tonight? I think I'll see an amazing show. I've followed him since he was doing gigs at the Marquee years ago. I remember him from The Lower Third and all that rubbish. I just think he's great.' I didn't speak to Elton that night but ran into him at the Beverly Hills Hotel during the US tour. More about that later. The interest we were getting was all a bit of an ego boost; after all, these were the rock hierarchy, and they'd come to see us play.

Incidentally, I found out several years later when attending Joe Elliott's (of Def Leppard) wedding, where I met Brian May, that Queen had come to see us play on many occasions and had based a lot of their image on Bowie and the Spiders.

And while I'm name-dropping, around this time I'd started to meet other musicians I liked, for instance Iggy Pop, who was around quite a bit as he and David had plans to work together. He was a bit alien to me, which I realize is a bit rich given that I was in a band with David Bowie. We had very little in common, but he knew what he was, and what he liked and didn't like – his opinions were very strong. His stage show at the time was intense: he thought nothing of ripping his chest open with a mic stand. Bowie and Iggy seemed to come from opposite ends of the spectrum both musically and as performers. But I did like The Stooges, we'd watch films of him with them and I was blown away by his performances. He had that unpredictable edge, a bit like Jim Morrison, where you never quite knew what he was going to do next. Maybe that's what they had in common.

I was fortunate to meet one of my heroes, Led Zeppelin's drummer John Bonham – one of the world's most famous musicians at that point; we went for a drink in the Ship on Wardour Street one night while we were recording at Trident. He was a big bloke, and he liked a pint. I thought he was a great guy, despite the fearsome reputation he had when he was drunk. Obviously we talked drums and we had a good time putting the world to rights.

I later met Jimmy Page and Robert Plant at the Crown in Tottenham. I was introduced to Robert Plant in the dressing room and he said, 'Woody Woodmansey, I know that name', and I said, 'Robert Plant, I know that name' . . . I'd just watched him perform from six feet away and was still blown away by his performance, so most of the conversation was me telling him why he was so good.

By now I was recognized in the street a lot, which I liked, unless I was trying to get some shopping done on Oxford Street or somewhere. I'd turn around and there'd be maybe fifty people behind me. I couldn't very well say, 'I've got shopping to do!' I'd chat with them and sign autographs until my arm was dropping off, and would often run out of time to get any shopping done. But I met some genuinely nice people who told me what the music meant to them. I had no problem with that.

So after all the time and hard work we'd put in over the last couple of years, we had a single and an album in the charts . . . we'd arrived and kicked some ass along the way, at least in the UK. The dream was becoming a reality.

7

LET YOURSELF GO

If we'd thought the British dates were big, we had our frame of reference completely reset when we went to America in mid-September 1972. It was the place we'd always dreamed of going to so we were hugely excited. I'd only seen it in movies. Up to then the extent of my overseas travel, aside from the trip to Cyprus, was a week's holiday in Belgium with June when we were both eighteen. The highlight of that was dancing in an Ostend nightclub into the early hours to a DJ playing music by Sly and the Family Stone! Bowie travelled to the USA with Angie on the *QE2* due to his fear of flying, while we flew to New York.

I still remember the looks the customs people gave us when we landed. We weren't wearing our full stage gear, obviously, but our hairstyles and glamorous street clothes definitely made us stand out from the crowd of business people and tourists who were waiting in the immigration queue alongside us. Mick had just got Suzi to add red, green and purple highlights to his already striking blond hair, which increased the impact.

A limousine was waiting to take us into the centre of New

York City. Staring out of the window, at first I thought yellow was the only colour Americans liked for their cars, until I realized these were taxis. I counted forty-two cabs sitting bumper to bumper in an uninterrupted yellow streak. All the streets were dead straight and seemed to stretch for miles in all directions. When the traffic stopped, twenty car horns immediately began honking, windows were wound down and abuse with an American accent added to the already chaotic scene. I remember thinking that New Yorkers didn't have much patience but it was exciting and this city was alive.

You had to get up to speed or you would get trampled in the rush – it was a long way from the polite London we'd left behind a few hours earlier. We felt as if we were in a movie but hadn't been handed the script, not yet anyway . . .

Looking up at the never-ending glass buildings that seemed to reach to the clouds, I couldn't believe how high they actually were and wondered who would want to live up at the top. Turned out it was me – my hotel room was up in the sky!

Nowadays the UK and America are much closer when it comes to things like culture, food and slang – but back then there was less crossover. We liked American music but we hadn't met many Americans, Tony Visconti and Angie being the obvious exceptions.

Attempting to recover from the aeroplane food the day before, Mick, Trev and I went to the hotel restaurant for breakfast. The menu offered 'full English breakfast' and I felt I needed a bit of home already. When it arrived it wasn't quite what I expected. Along with the eggs, bacon, sausage and tomatoes was a skewer filled with strawberries, melon pieces and grapes! Now maybe it was my northern roots showing themselves but to serve me fruit with my fried breakfast just insulted my senses. I had to remove the offending articles before I could tuck into my 'English breakfast'. That night we went back to the restaurant for an evening meal and I had a steak with all the trimmings, which was excellent. The dessert menu was exotic to say the least, and I just wanted some vanilla ice cream which wasn't on the menu as a single item.

I said to the waiter, 'Can I just have some vanilla ice cream, please.'

'Certainly, sir,' said he. 'What do you want on it?'

'Nothing,' I replied, 'just the vanilla ice cream.'

'I don't think I can do that, sir,' he said. 'You have to have at least one other item with it.'

I said, 'OK, stick a sausage in it. You may as well, you brought me strawberries and grapes with my eggs and bacon.'

He stormed off but did eventually return with just vanilla ice cream . . . It was my first rock star diva moment!

While we were in the US our new single, 'John, I'm Only Dancing', was slowly climbing the charts back in the UK. We'd spent a few days in Olympic Studios, London, back in June, recording it. I was particularly proud of my tom-tom fills which definitely added dynamics to the arrangement. We were all in the studio recording backing vocals for the song when Rod Stewart and the Faces burst in through one of the doors. They were dancing about and singing 'la, la, las' until everybody cracked up laughing. Then one of them said, 'See ya later', and they exited through one of the other doors as quickly as they'd arrived.

I remember the lyrics at the time seeming quite ambiguous to me. The song could be about a guy dancing with a girl and telling his boyfriend not to worry, he was 'only dancing', or he was talking to a friend whose girlfriend he was dancing with. Mick Rock had filmed us playing the track during rehearsals at the Rainbow and this footage became the video. RCA considered the song too risqué to release it in the US and *Top of the Pops* banned the video and refused to play it, the reason given that it wasn't to the BBC's taste . . . It was released on 1 September and by the time we'd got to New York it had reached Number 30 in the singles charts. It eventually peaked at Number 12 on 8 October. We were too busy in the US to think about the fact it wasn't performing quite as well as 'Starman'.

Meanwhile, Tony Defries had decided to set up his own management company, MainMan, which Bowie duly signed to. Since he'd first met the *Pork* actors and discovered their connections, Defries had been constantly phoning them up and asking how he should break Bowie and the Spiders in the US. He even gave them a box of *Hunky Dory* albums to distribute to DJs and underground artists that they knew in NY. Now he recruited Tony Zanetta to head up MainMan's US office and brought in some of the other cast members who would help organize our tour. There was Cherry Vanilla, who had played the title role of 'Pork', Jamie Andrews, who had played a character called Pall, and Leee Black Childers, who was the stage manager. It was comical because they were all extremely camp, the loudest people we'd ever come across and outrageous with it. This took a bit of getting used to for the Spiders. I'd met Cherry Vanilla earlier at the Sombrero club in London. She was sexy, outspoken but very easy to talk to on a one-to-one basis.

'Is Cherry Vanilla your real name?' I asked

'Yes,' she replied. 'Do you like it?'

'Yes,' I said, 'it sounds cool. But why Cherry?'

At this point she unbuttoned her blouse and exposed one of her very ample breasts which had a tattoo of cherries on it.

'I see,' I said, a bit lamely . . . If it wasn't for the subdued lighting in the Sombrero, she would have seen my blushing face.

We were rehearsing for the tour at RCA Studios in Manhattan and, having arrived in the US minus a keyboard player, we needed to find someone quickly as Bowie wanted to have the live performance as close to the recordings as possible. Mick suggested Mike Garson who had contributed piano to an album we'd all been listening to, *I'm The One* by an American left-field jazz artist called Annette Peacock. It had very cool jazz/funk beats and on some of the tracks she was singing through a synthesizer. We all thought it was amazing. There was some concern Mike Garson wouldn't be up for playing with a rock 'n' roll band, so Bowie had rung Annette to see if she would put in a good word for us. She agreed to and rang Mike and vouched for the musicality and credibility of the band. A few hours later Defries called him and he agreed to audition. He came down to RCA Studios and sat at the piano. Mick introduced himself and put the chord chart to 'Changes' in front of him.

'What can you do with this?' Mick asked

Mike began to play and immediately we knew were dealing with a highly competent musician who could handle tracks like 'Life on Mars?' He had the skills of Rick Wakeman but with a jazz slant, obviously. In Mike we had found a keyboard player who, although we didn't know at the time, would add so much to Bowie's future songs. I appreciated Bowie's vision here: in recruiting him to our band, he'd brought a really talented avant-garde musician to the rock music field.

Mike – who'd arrived for the audition in dungarees and a check shirt – was a bit freaked out by how we looked, as I recall. He got over it . . .

I found it a little hard to get to know him at first, because he didn't speak our language: he spoke jazz and we spoke rock. Also, we'd become a close-knit gang with our own sense of humour, so it took some time for us to open up to Mike, and for him to come out to us. At first he used to sit at the edge of the stage, in semi-darkness, but as time passed he came out of his shell and would take a more active part in the show.

So now we had our keyboardist. We also had our own tech crew with us, i.e. roadies, lighting, sound and security, some of whom had been with us since the Rats days. Suzi Fussey was handling hair and wardrobe. We had the Warhol additions of Tony Zanetta as tour manager, and Lee and Jamie juggling hats wherever needed. It seemed like everything was in place for the tour, albeit with a slightly bizarre twist. We were ready to kick some American ass!

As Bowie refused to fly we would be travelling throughout the tour by bus. His reflections on American life would inspire Bowie to start writing songs, many of which would be featured on the forthcoming album, *Aladdin Sane*.

The tour opened at the Cleveland Music Hall on 22 September. The venue held 3,000 and had sold out in two days thanks to Denny Sanders, musical director, and Billy Bass, programme director at WMMS Radio, who had played *Hunky Dory* and *Ziggy Stardust* tracks repeatedly, introducing the area to our music and creating an enthusiastic fan base. We were already the talk of the town by the time we got to Cleveland.

We began the show with 'Hang On To Yourself' and the crowd loved it. Bowie had done a press conference earlier that day and had been a bit withdrawn, but by stage time he'd shed any inhibitions and stalked the stage like a madman. We did more or less the same show as we'd done in the UK and if I remember correctly we included 'Lady Stardust', one of the few times we played this song live. The experience we'd gained on our UK tour, plus the addition of Mike Garson, really helped us find our feet and the sound of the band and the performance seemed to have moved up to another level. It was exciting and the audience let us know it was the same for them. At the end we received an ovation that lasted about ten minutes. We'd done our first US concert and it had gone down amazingly, the perfect start to the tour.

Bowie loved all this. He was still in control of the Ziggy persona at the start of the first US tour and was able to adopt and discard his onstage character with relative ease. He'd wanted to be famous for years, and had worked incredibly hard to achieve it – and here he was, the biggest star of the hour.

The next stop on the tour was Memphis, Elvis Presley's home town, which obviously made it even more exciting for us. It was another sold-out show and again the audience was at fever pitch and incredibly loud. This was another great confidence boost ahead of our debut gig at Carnegie Hall in New York a couple of days later. On the way to Memphis, during an impromptu guitar jam at the back of the bus, the seeds for what would become 'The Jean Genie' were sown. I think George Underwood was playing around with chords that were very similar to the Yardbirds' cover of Bo Diddley's 'I'm a Man'. Mick was also playing guitar. The whole bus was singing 'We're bus, bussing, bussing along', something banal like that, and it kind of summed up the general feeling. The melody and phrasing was not too dissimilar to the part of the chorus in 'The Jean Genie'.

The show at the prestigious Carnegie Hall was an important one for us. The Beatles had played there twice in 1964 and to succeed in the US rock market it was important we were a success in New York. We definitely needed to deliver the goods on the night. Working against us was the fact that Bowie had caught flu the day before and he had had a pretty sleepless night. He wasn't sure if he could muster the energy or even if his voice would hold out.

As our limo pulled up before the show we saw a giant searchlight outside the hall, which moved around lighting up the clouds and the tops of the skyscrapers, creating a Hollywood premiere feeling. It was a sold-out show and the guest list included Truman Capote, Todd Rundgren, Andy Warhol, Alan Bates, Tony Perkins and about a hundred British journalists plus US press.

We were all a little nervous before the show but we walked on after our usual *Clockwork Orange* intro tape to a standing ovation, which was a fantastic start. It looked like the biggest gig we'd done to date. This could have been due to the number of balconies, five in all, above the main seating area. We all rose to the occasion, including Bowie, despite his flu, though before one of the acoustic songs, Jacques Brel's 'My Death', he did warn the audience he might not make it to the end vocally. Suffice to say, he did a great version of it. The show really rocked and the audience were with us all the way. Before returning for an encore of 'Round and Round' we received a five-minute standing ovation. The reviews were all positive and, because of the success of this gig, more concerts were added to the tour.

We moved on through Washington and Boston and then slipped back to New York as we had a few days off to record 'The Jean Genie', which Bowie had now completed. We went into RCA Studios on 6 October. It took about a day to get the basic track down plus some overdubs, then a few more overdubs the next day. It's a great song, simple but full of energy with that huge guitar riff of Mick's, held in check by me and Trevor. I love the famous fuck-up in it where Trevor goes to the chorus too early. He pointed it out to Bowie at the time and Bowie said, 'Leave it in, I like it.' When we played that song live, Bowie told Trev to repeat the mistake. It was mixed in RCA Nashville, Studio B, and was to be our next single.

We felt like rock stars, but, now I look back on it, it hadn't really sunk in because while some gigs were phenomenal others would be only a third full. The phenomenal ones indicated what it could be like all the time, though, especially when we realized that on our next American tour all the venues would be full.

Every now and then I'd take a moment to consider how far we'd come since the Three Tuns, which looked packed out if it had forty-five people in it. Playing for venues full of thousands of people was like being on another planet. From New York we went to Chicago, then Detroit and over to California.

By now, we were getting cockier. Before this, we'd always gone on stage thinking, 'I hope they like us. I hope the music goes down well.' As time passed we thought to ourselves, 'This is fucking good! They *will* like it.' At the same time, all it took was a friend of the band, or a roadie, to say, 'You played that song better last night', or 'It didn't look so good when you did this tonight', and it fucked with our confidence and our understanding of how to play the show that night. As with any venture where there are lots of people involved, there were always opinions flying about. Bowie came up with the idea that no one should get near him or the band before a gig.

When we considered how to implement that, given that we had a road crew of forty or more, it was decided we would take on a chef whose job it was to find the best restaurant in each city, so that we could eat out and have time alone before the gig, with no distractions. This was a little extravagant but it gave us breathing space, so therefore was well worth it. We were totally separate and it really worked. Very occasionally Angie was there, but usually it was just the four of us in isolation. At those times we were the kings of our world; no one else could touch us. Occasionally we'd talk about the show and if anyone had any ideas on how to improve it we'd discuss it. In general, though, the conversation was just mates' banter with some dirty jokes thrown in.

One of the strange things about touring is that you begin to feel as if you're living in a bubble. This is mainly due to the fact that so much time is spent travelling the vast distances between cities, then, when you do finally arrive, you go through the same routine before every concert. Lunch, soundcheck, dinner, get dressed for gig, play gig, back to the hotel, sleep, wake up, more travel and on and on . . . What makes this even worse is that you're often booked into a chain of hotels like the Holiday Inn so you leave your room in the morning, go through the same old routine, open the door to your next hotel and the decor is the same as the one you just left the day before, right down to the pictures on the wall. It definitely feels like *Groundhog Day*! And in the seventies there were obviously no mobile phones, no laptops, no internet, so you were definitely cut off from the world for the length of the tour.

On top of all this, on the financial front no one carried cash . . . or very little anyway. There were no bank cards or credit cards back then either. Defries had arranged for RCA to book all the hotels for the tour; he then instructed the whole entourage to charge everything, including meals, to room service and told everyone to act like 'superstars' to give the impression that Bowie and the Spiders were already huge. Part of the Defries masterplan! Of course the crew soon mastered the art of spending and would use every service the hotels had to offer, including beauty salons, spas and boutiques.

We rocked St Louis on 11 October, even though it was not a 'Ziggy and Spiders' city; in fact, only a couple of hundred people showed up to a venue that held over 10,000, but Bowie turned it into a very intimate gig by inviting everyone down to the front. Then it was Kansas City where we did the show in our street clothes after the stage clothes failed to arrive on time. Then things changed again.

We rolled into Los Angeles for two sold-out shows on 20 and 21 October at the Santa Monica Civic Auditorium.

Legendary DJ and Anglophile Rodney Bingenheimer had a glam rock club on Sunset Boulevard called Rodney's English Disco. I first met him when he dropped in during the recording of *Hunky Dory* in Trident Studios. He was a very friendly guy and a total fan of Bowie and the band. He would continually say, 'You guys have got to come to the US, you'll be huge.' He'd done everything he could to create a buzz for us, so we did have a huge following by the time we got to LA. Without his help we certainly wouldn't have had the double sell-out shows.

The 20 October concert was broadcast on FM radio, the band's first live radio show in America. It became a quality bootleg album and, many years later, would eventually be officially released. A good mix of this concert was never done for either the bootleg or the official release but the recording did capture the energy and power of Bowie and the Spiders.

After playing so many shows on the tour we had really found our feet; we were on peak form that night and the feeling was particularly magical. Lucky, really, because we didn't actually know it was being recorded.

I still remember it clearly: the introduction, the version of Beethoven's 'Ode to Joy' from *A Clockwork Orange* was played with the house lights down, and it was spine-chilling, helped by the breeze blowing in off the ocean. The venue was a massive aircraft hangar that was jam-packed with people and the atmosphere was electric.

During the show there was some fuck-up with Bowie's microphone. I seem to remember that it kept slipping down, and wouldn't stay in place. Then a roadie came on with pliers to try and fix it, but it was taking too long, so Bowie just said, 'Give them here!' and the whole audience cheered. He took the pliers, fixed the mic and went into a stream-of-consciousness speech. The audience loved it, because he'd never said anything to them before, and I guess they didn't know what it was like to be talked to by David Bowie.

After Santa Monica, we had a couple of days off. Bowie went in to Western Sound Studios with Iggy Pop to re-mix The Stooges' album *Raw Power*. He managed to finish writing 'Panic in Detroit' while in LA, too.

We were staying at one of the world's most iconic and best-known hotels, the Beverly Hills Hotel on Sunset Boulevard. It had a couple of hundred rooms and more than twenty bungalows, which is where we were staying. Each of these was painted in the trademark colours of the hotel, peachy pink and green. (A silhouette of the hotel and surrounding palm trees would be featured on the cover of the Eagles' album *Hotel California* in 1976.) To us, feeling more and more like true rock stars by the day, this was the ultimate place to chill; we hung out by the pool, just drinking cocktails. We didn't feel out of place there because they were accustomed to dealing with musicians and movie stars. Some of the hotel's famous clientele had included Marlene Dietrich, Humphrey Bogart, Frank Sinatra and the Rat Pack. Marilyn Monroe's favourite bungalow was number 7 and John Lennon and May Pang had apparently hidden out in one of the bungalows for a week.

Mick, Trev and I shared a bungalow which was basically

a suite with three bedrooms, a lounge and a balcony. Elton John was in the bungalow next to us as I discovered when I walked out to have a cigarette and enjoy the view of the lush gardens. The first thing I saw was Elton on his own balcony.

'The British are coming,' he said, so I knew he recognized me. We then exchanged pleasantries about how different America was from the UK. He said he really loved *Hunky Dory* and *Ziggy* and how he'd been a fan of Bowie's since the beginning. I told him I loved *Madman Across the Water*, which had come out the previous year.

'You have to be careful when you're ordering room service here,' he told me. 'I ordered several meals for a party I was having and ended up with a bill for seventy lobsters!' After a pause he added, 'If you fancy one, pop round.'

We ran in to a lot more groupies when we stayed at the Beverly Hills Hotel. The tour personnel would ask me, 'What kind of women do you want? Kinky? What are you into? Anything you want, we can get it for you – just describe what you want and we'll get it.' It was unreal. We were rock stars, and we'd started to behave like rock stars. Sex was available to us day and night and I assume drugs were around, although all I ever did was smoke a bit of weed. Booze was a different story, though.

I drank a lot on this tour, which was a mistake, because I behaved badly when I was drunk. I was quite shy apart from when I was on stage and had a kit in front of me. But then every gig would have a rider, with the best brandy, and the best wine, and if it didn't get drunk it would get thrown out, and it was free – so I just thought, 'Fuck it, I'll have one.' Not that

we drank before gigs, apart from a glass of wine each. Afterwards, though . . . How do you come down after playing for
thousands of people? You're still up there on adrenalin. With
forty people on the crew we often occupied nearly a whole
floor of a hotel; after the show it was one big party involving
many rooms and many guests.

Sometimes we would go out to a club and because the club
owner had been at the concert he would say, 'The drinks are
all free.' At twenty-two years old this seemed like a great perk.
After a few drinks I had no inhibitions. I would go and sit at
tables where I didn't know anybody, and pick up people's
drinks and start talking at them, which isn't great when you're
chatting up someone's wife. I was lucky I never got beaten up.
I always knew I had Stuey, close by, which actually made me
worse as I trusted him to handle any trouble I got into.

I was definitely drinking far too much – even though I
knew I was a pain in the arse when I was drunk. It really made
no sense.

After leaving the 'Pink Palace', as the Beverly Hills was affectionately called, we headed for San Francisco, minus the
flowers in our hair. There we shot the video for 'The Jean
Genie' which Mick Rock filmed and directed. He used live
footage from one of our recent gigs and the rest was shot that
day in a studio he'd hired. It also featured Cyrinda Foxe, a
friend of David's who was now an employee of MainMan and
who had also Monroe character and she fitted the bill. There
was a rumour among the crew that she and Bowie were
having an affair and had spent several nights together earlier

at the Plaza in New York. I knew Bowie was fond of her as he told me she was really good fun to hang out with. When I saw the three of them together Angie didn't seem to have a problem with it. I think she got on with Cyrinda as well.

A week earlier I had bought a book on kabuki theatre and one section had cartoons showing some of the different poses the actors used to portray emotions. One – with the hands making inverted spectacles – looked quite alien to me so I showed David how to do it a couple of days later. He used this in the video and it became a part of the live act, now affectionately known as the 'Ziggy Mask'. *Jean Genie* was one of the first videos made for music TV.

We played the Winterland Auditorium the next night, which was not as well attended as Santa Monica and then from San Francisco we took a train down to Phoenix, Arizona, where we had another couple of days off. The hotel had an outside swimming pool and the desert heat was unbearable so we hung around the pool quenching our thirst on tequila sunrises. It got so bad that Mick and I decided to go for a swim but I guess us northern boys weren't used to the relentless desert sun. By the time we got back to the hotel room Mick looked like a lobster and I wasn't too far behind. The next morning we freaked out: the chlorine in the pool had turned our hair peppermint-green! Wardrobe disaster . . . so Suzi had to come to the rescue. It prompted much piss-taking from the crew, with comments like 'Here come the green genies!'

Some parts of America were dangerous in unexpected ways. For example, back in England I'd always wondered what it would be like to go into one of those classic American diners, where you sit at the bar and drink coffee and order food. In November 1972, we were travelling through Georgia on the bus and we decided to keep an eye open for one of those places. Sure enough, one came along and we pulled over.

We walked in, the Spiders and half the entourage, and the atmosphere immediately became a little tense; we looked outlandish, to put it mildly, with our bleached hair and bright clothes. We all sat at the counter, and the waiter walked over to me, pointed at Stuey and said, 'Whadda ya want? I ain't servin' the nigger.'

I asked, 'What did you just say?'

He repeated, more loudly this time, 'I ain't servin' the nigger.'

Everybody in the diner could hear this, but no one said a word or even looked up.

We all looked at each other in shock for a second. Then we stood up, said, 'Fuck you!' to the waiter, and walked out, giving him the finger. At the time, we thought the civil rights struggle was over; we hadn't encountered any racism of this nature before.

Another time in one of the Southern states Mick, Trev and I were in our hotel suite and there was a knock at the door. I opened it and there were two cops standing there.

'Are you going out on the town tonight, sir?' said one of them.

'Probably,' I said. 'We were thinking about it.'

'We've come to advise you that it's not a good idea. You should stay in the hotel, sir,' he said.

'Why is that?'

'A hippy was shot a few days ago just for having long hair.

We heard you guys were coming to town so we wanted to warn you that if you go out looking like you do, you won't last the night!'

They sounded deadly serious and needless to say we took their advice. It definitely brought us down to earth for a while. I'm pretty sure they visited David's suite too and told him the same.

On a lighter note . . . one day I was sitting in the lobby of one of our hotels with Mick and Trevor. There were many conservative looking business men there, too, with their wives or secretaries. I'd noticed a few giving us condescending glances but we'd got used to that by now. In fact, some of the funniest times were after concerts when we left the stage, jumped in a limo and headed straight back to the hotel. The four of us would get in the lift looking like four versions of technicolour Alice Coopers with sweat and mascara running down our faces. There would often be around ten other hotel guests in the lift already; you could cut the atmosphere with a knife.

Back to the lobby story . . . Leee Black Childers was heading out of the hotel and caught sight of us.

'I'm going shopping, boys, can I get you anything?' he called over in his usual camp voice.

Raising my voice so that it could be heard over all the conversations going on, I asked, quite innocently, 'Can you bring me some fags?'

The whole place went deathly quiet.

'I thought you'd never ask!' he yelled mischievously, clearly relishing the moment.

*

Elsewhere in the world, at the beginning of November *Ziggy Stardust* was released in Japan and towards the end of the month 'The Jean Genie' was released in the UK. It would eventually peak at Number 2 in the charts – our bestselling single to date. By then we'd seen concerts in Dallas and Houston cancelled (Texas wasn't a Ziggy state, it seemed), played places like New Orleans and Florida, and had worked our way across country back to Cleveland, Ohio. Only this time we played at the bigger venue, the Cleveland Public Hall, which had a capacity of 10,000, and due to our growing popularity it sold out for two nights. This was our biggest gig to date. I clearly remember Mick, Trevor and me taking a sneaky look through the curtains at the packed house.

'Fucking hell, that's a lot of people,' Mick said, a note of apprehension in his voice.

'Don't worry,' I told him, 'when the lights go down we can pretend we're at Beverley Regal', a reference to a Yorkshire venue that held a couple of hundred people and where we'd played many times as the Rats!

Cleveland was one of the most exciting and loudest audience responses we'd ever had.

It was around this time, towards the end of the tour, that we found out that Mick and Trevor had been getting the back-up vocals wrong in 'Changes'. We thought Bowie was singing 'Turn and face the strain' during the chorus, until one particular soundcheck when he stopped them halfway through the song.

'What are you guys singing?' he asked. 'It's fucking "strange" not "strain".'

He looked over his shoulder at his own arse, to demonstrate what that meant. We all had a good laugh about this, including Bowie.

The famous Tower Theater in Philadelphia was to be our final venue on this first Bowie and the Spiders US tour. We had sold out the first two dates and a third had to be added, which also sold out. We played three blistering shows in a perfect finale to the most amazing three months of my life so far . . .

But unbeknownst to me there was a cloud on the horizon. Things were about to change.

8

IT AIN'T EASY

On our arrival back in New York at the end of the tour we headed over to RCA Studios where they had arranged a press conference for us. Bowie led us out to a room full of journalists and we took our seats. He introduced us individually and then said, 'These are the Spiders From Mars and I am David Bowie.' I remember it being a bit of a non-event really. It's very obvious how it felt for us if you see the photos taken by Mick Rock. What followed were banal questions like 'What brand of hair colour do you use?' and 'Is it a rinse or a dye?' which I don't remember Bowie even answering. Someone asked Mick, 'Why are you the only one wearing a hat?' to which he answered, 'I didn't have time to wash my hair this morning.'

As no intelligent questions were forthcoming, Bowie announced his second US tour would open at Radio City on Valentine's Day and that he was currently working on a new album that featured songs he'd written while touring America.

As the tour had been extended we were a little behind on recording so Ken Scott flew over to join us in RCA Studios to get some tracks in the can. We recorded 'Drive-In Saturday', which Bowie had written somewhere mid-tour and had already performed acoustically at one of our concerts. It's one of my favourite Bowie songs from this period. It tells of a time in the future where people have lost the art of making love and have to resort to reading books and watching films to remind them. We also recorded 'Prettiest Star' and a version of 'All the Young Dudes'.

With those tracks finished we flew back home on 10 December. Bowie sailed back on the RHMS *Ellinis* with some of the entourage.

I had about ten days off which was fortunate as June was heading down to London and was moving into the flat with me. Ann, Trev's wife, and baby daughter Sarah had already moved into our flat in Beckenham.

June had been working as a window dresser in a big store in Hull and when I met her at King's Cross station she was standing on the platform with a trunk full of her possessions and two three-foot-high cut-out Disney characters made out of some kind of foam. One was Thumper the rabbit and the other was Figaro, a black and white cat, both from a display she'd done. Being made of foam they were very delicate but somehow she'd managed to get them to London without them being damaged! She was going back to clothes designing, which, apart from her brief time as a window dresser, was what she'd done since school. She'd be working with some friends in London and would go on to sell to Harrods' Way In and other boutiques in South Kensington.

I got June, Thumper and Figaro settled in to the flat and then we went Christmas shopping as we knew I'd be busy later in the month, getting ready for two gigs at the Rainbow.

We also planned to spend Christmas in Yorkshire as I hadn't seen my family for a long time.

'Space Oddity' was reissued in mid-December, just in time for our two shows at the Rainbow on 23 and 24 December. Less impressive in production terms than the previous Rainbow shows that summer, the two gigs were still packed with fans who gave a roar of appreciation when we walked on stage.

Bowie asked the crowd to donate money to Barnardo's, the British charity founded to care for vulnerable children and young people. David's dad had worked for the charity until his death in 1969. There was also a piece in *Melody Maker* making the same request. A two-page ad read: 'David Bowie and the Spiders wish everyone a Happy Christmas and request that those attending the Rainbow Concert on 24 December bring a children's toy to be donated to charity.' So truckloads of toys arrived and were duly distributed.

The magazine also cited Bowie as 'THE main man of 1972' and he dominated the issue. Bowie was voted Top Vocalist of the Year (ahead of Rod Stewart and Elton John) while *Ziggy Stardust* was the critics' choice for pop album of 1972.

After the second Rainbow concert June and I jumped in a limousine and headed up to Yorkshire, arriving at my parents' house in Driffield in the early hours of Christmas morning. It was good to see them after so long, and to catch up with my sister. They brought me up to speed on what had been happening with the rest of the family while I told them about the American tour and how great the audiences were.

I also described what it was like staying in places like the

Plaza and the Beverly Hills Hotel, and even how amazing the food was. I should have noticed sooner that I'd gone too far. Mum unfortunately took this personally. While we were talking she'd been busy preparing a meal in the kitchen. Now she walked out with a plate full of food and said, 'You won't be wanting this then.' 'Oh, shit,' I thought. Diplomacy has never been a strong point of mine. It took some clever talking to convince her that no one made a fry-up like she did and that I'd actually missed it.

Even though I'd just toured America and been on TV and in the newspapers the conversations soon got back to: 'How long is it all going to last? When are you going to get a proper job?' There was still nothing I could say that would be satisfactory answers to these questions.

My parents did come to one gig up in Yorkshire, when we played the Bridlington Spa. After the show my dad came up to me and said, 'Bloody hell, lad, you can play them drums', which was a 100 per cent acknowledgement by his standards. That was the one and only time they ever saw me play. Later, my mum told me that my dad had been out with a bunch of his workmates and one of them said to him, 'Your lad's a gay guy in a band, isn't he?' My dad grabbed him and beat the shit out of him. He would rarely compliment me, but he wouldn't let anyone say anything negative about me either, and, back then, being gay was thought of as negative (to put it mildly) in places like Driffield.

We only had three days in Yorkshire before we had to leave and head for Manchester for two gigs at the Hardrock, on 28 and 29 December. Just for a change we opened the show with our version of the Stones' 'Let's Spend the Night

Together'. It was the perfect start and definitely got the message across to a packed audience that it was going to be a great night.

During the American tour we'd got into a routine, for safety and security reasons, of finishing the last song, then running from the stage to a waiting limousine and heading back to our hotel. We'd had several incidents on the tour where we'd been slow leaving the venue and found the limousine surrounded by huge crowds of enthusiastic fans.

One night in particular we'd fought our way into the limousine and were sitting waiting to leave, but the crowd in front refused to move even though there was a cop trying to control the situation. There seemed to be hundreds of hands banging on the windows and we could hear them creaking under the pressure. It was quite scary. Bowie screamed at the driver, 'Just drive, just fuckin' drive.' He did and unfortunately we ran over the cop's foot. We later found out he had fractured a few bones.

The crowd reaction in England was turning out to be just the same as in America: it was pandemonium after the gigs. As we left the stage in Manchester there were two lines of security guards holding back the fans and we had to make our way down the middle of them. Unfortunately the line didn't hold and it felt like we were in a human tumble dryer. Although I understood the fans just wanted to show their love and appreciation, it added up to a very scary scene. I noticed a pair of scissors flashing their way towards Mick's face, until a security guard caught the offending girl's arm inches from Mick's eye. She'd wanted a bit of his hair.

Next was a ride up to Scotland, to the gig in Glasgow.

Greens Playhouse had a reputation: if they liked you, it would be a great night; if they didn't, they would certainly let you know. Although we were riding high and full of confidence, this did give us pause for thought. Thankfully the Glasgow audience absolutely loved it. For some reason we didn't leave immediately that night and I went out the back to have a cigarette and cool down in an area with no public access. Mike Garson was with me and we were deep in conversation about touring in the UK as this was only Mike's fifth gig in UK. Being American, he was still having trouble understanding the British accent. I looked up and was taken aback to see three well-built, tough looking Scottish guys approaching. I took them to be fans, as one was carrying a *Ziggy* album. They spewed forth what seemed like five minutes of anger and antagonism with furious arm and fist motions for emphasis. They spoke with the strongest Scottish accents I'd ever heard. The only word I could understand was 'fuckin', of which there seemed to be quite a lot.

'Did they like us?' Mike asked, under his breath.

I replied in the same manner, 'I've no fuckin' idea.'

We both breathed a sigh of relief when they finally extended their hands for a handshake.

We did three more fantastic shows to end this mini tour by 9 January. The month was shaping up to be a busy one. On 17 January we appeared on *Russell Harty Plus*, a London Weekend TV show, to promote our next single, 'Drive-In Saturday'. We brought along a French make-up artist called Pierre La Roche, who had worked for Elizabeth Arden, and Freddie Burretti to handle clothes. I had a new, more tailored jacket that Freddie had made, a black, white and red striped affair together with red trousers. It looked great but was almost impossible to play in, being too tight around the sleeves. It's a good job we were miming! I also wore a shirt and tie. Mick had a new black satin jacket. Bowie was clad in a multicoloured suit with red velvet lapels, padded shoulders, a green shirt and metallic looking cravat and wore what has been described as a 'chandelier' earring on one ear. He'd also shaved off his eyebrows for this show so he looked even more alien than usual.

We played 'Drive-In Saturday' and Bowie did a live acoustic version of 'My Death'. Between the two numbers he was interviewed by Russell Harty who was – from today's point of view, anyway – completely wrong for an interviewer who was supposed to be in touch with music that teenagers liked. I remember Bowie having to be on his guard during the interview. Harty was obviously trying to trivialize him, asking him pointed questions about the content of fan letters he received, which I thought created a slightly nasty undercurrent given that this was supposed to be an entertainment show.

Bowie didn't bat an eyelid, though, and when questioned about the shoes and tights he was wearing he famously told Harty, 'Don't be silly' . . .

We watched him perform 'My Death' on one of the studio monitors and for me it was probably his best ever version of it. Unfortunately London Weekend managed to lose the recording. That said, our performance on this show was probably responsible for 'Drive-In Saturday' remaining in the charts for ten weeks after its release in April, peaking at Number 3.

That same month we went back to Trident Studios with Ken Scott to complete *Aladdin Sane*. In loose terms it was

Ziggy in America. 'Panic in Detroit' was written in Los Angeles during the period when he was re-mixing *Raw Power* with Iggy Pop. It was the one and only time Bowie had a firm idea of what he wanted from the drums. He'd played the song to us during the tour so I had an idea of the structure and had worked out almost a hard-rock beat for it, very John Bonham-influenced. When we started running through the track in the studio, with me playing the beat I'd worked out, Bowie stopped everything.

'Woody, just play a Bo Diddley beat, on your tom-toms,' he said.

'Anybody can play that, isn't it too simple?' I said.

'I don't want fucking Buddy Rich,' he answered.

This did piss me off as I'd worked out some cool drum fills with my beat that I hadn't played yet. We started playing the song again with me playing the Bo Diddley beat and immediately I knew he was right. It felt great to play and fitted the song perfectly. This was the only time he ever told me what to play.

'Watch That Man' and 'Cracked Actor' both reminded me of Stones songs. Kind of a heavier version of some of the songs on *Exile On Main Street*, just good, straight-ahead rock tunes with a honky-tonk piano and wailing backing vocals supplied by Linda Lewis. The lyrics were very Bowie, though, 'Watch That Man' suggesting to me a decadent, anything-goes-type party, and 'Cracked Actor', about an over-the-hill Hollywood star who had managed to pull some young chick who mistakenly thought he was a drug connection. So I had a no-nonsense approach to both these songs: no frills, just a good rock beat that sounded exciting.

As a genuine nod to the Stones we again did our version of 'Let's Spend the Night Together'. As a result of our time in America the overall sound of the band had got heavier and Mick's guitar sound had naturally got dirtier than it was before. This really helped bring those tracks to life.

The influence of Mike Garson showed up in particular on 'Aladdin Sane', 'Lady Grinning Soul' and 'Time'. On 'Aladdin Sane' Bowie wanted a piano solo in the instrumental section, which consisted of just two chords. We were playing straight-ahead rock 'n' roll through this section. Mike first did a bluesy solo and on hearing it Bowie said, 'No, that's not what I want.' He then tried a Latin approach.

'No, that's not it either,' Bowie said. 'You do this avant-garde jazz, do that.'

'Are you sure?' Mike asked. 'You might never work again.'

So Mike went to town with no holds barred. It was weird and wacky, bordering on 'insane', and at the end of the song we all said, 'Fucking hell, that was amazing.' That first and only take was the one that ended up on the album.

'Time' featured Mike again with kind of avant-garde cabaret piano. When Bowie recorded the vocal on this song he stopped the whole studio with the line 'falls wanking to the floor' . . . We were all busy asking each other, 'Did he just say wanking?' 'It sounded like wanking to me!' At the end, when he'd finished the song, someone asked him if that's what he'd actually said and he just rather coolly replied, 'Yes.' At the time we thought, 'Can you actually sing that in a song?'

'It's definitely not going to get played on the radio, is it!' I said.

'Lady Grinning Soul' was a love song Bowie had written

for someone. I always thought it was for Cyrinda Foxe but I can't confirm that. This track definitely meant a lot to Bowie as it was the only one where he insisted on being in the studio when Ken mixed it, to make sure it sounded the way he wanted it to.

So with the tracks we had already recorded in America during the tour we now had the album. The title *Aladdin Sane* was a take on the phrase 'a lad insane'.

For the album cover RCA employed a company called Duffy Design Concepts, with the legendary photographer Brian Duffy, and Celia Philo, who directed the album cover shoot. Both had worked on Pirelli calendars, and you can see this influence on the inside sleeve. Duffy called in Pierre La Roche for the shoot. I'm pretty sure the inspiration for the 'red flash', which would later become one of Bowie's most iconic images, came from Bowie noticing that the symbol was always present on high-voltage machinery. It was Pierre's idea to put it on Bowie's face, though.

The album had advance orders of 150,000, which made it the biggest advance sale since the Beatles. It would be released on 13 April 1973 and would become our first Number 1 album, staying seventy-two weeks in the UK charts and reaching Number 17 in the US charts.

Recording was followed by rehearsing for the second US leg of the tour. We went back to the Royal Ballroom in Tottenham until 25 January. Bowie was keen to change things up a bit. He wanted someone else to play the acoustic guitar, because that would free him up to do more visual things. He had started to incorporate mime into the act at the end of the UK tour: this was unique to Bowie and had certainly never been seen in a rock 'n' roll band before. Even though I never got to experience this the way the audience did, from my vantage point on the kit I did see their reaction. It caught them by surprise and they loved it. It was another art form he excelled in and it fitted perfectly within chosen sections of the show. He also wanted to add extra dimensions to the sound, and include new songs from *Aladdin Sane*, which meant he needed some more musicians on stage. Because our profile had risen in America, we were playing bigger venues and people expected more from the show and he definitely delivered. However, as soon as the additional musicians were announced, the press got in a froth and said, 'Bowie's adding new Spiders!' He dismissed that in an interview with Charles Shaar Murray in the *NME* on 27 January 1973: 'I'd like to get one thing straight: these aren't additional Spiders. The Spiders are still Trev, Mick and Woody. We've got some back-up men on tenor saxes, piano and voices . . . It's three Spiders, back-up musicians and me.'

So we took on two session musicians, Ken Fordham, a sax player, and Brian Wilshaw, who played sax and flute. We were also joined by Bowie's old school friend Geoff MacCormack on backing vocals and percussion, and John 'Hutch' Hutchinson, who had played with him in the sixties, on rhythm guitar. Rehearsals went well and after a couple of run-throughs of the show it was obvious it wasn't going to take too much work to get it sounding good.

Bowie left for the US on board the *QE2* from Southampton, travelling with Geoff MacCormack, and arriving in New York on 30 January. The rest of us arrived in America in early February with more rehearsals booked at RCA Studios, from

6 until 12 February. Our first gig was to be at Radio City on Valentine's Day. One night after rehearsals Mick, Trev and I decided to go out on the town. We had heard about some of the clubs in Harlem and how they had great music, so we decided that's where we would go. I think Hutch and one of the road crew came with us. We'd flagged down a couple of cabs to take us there and the response had been the same – 'I don't do Harlem.' We thought they were just being awkward New York taxi drivers, but alarm bells should have rung when a third guy said the same thing. However, he agreed to take us to within a few blocks of Harlem and we walked the rest of the way.

Almost immediately we saw a club sign and heard, drifting up from the basement, music that sounded good. We went down the steps, not thinking twice about the fact that we were dressed in pretty far-out clothes and, more importantly, that we were white. As we walked in the entire place went quiet; the band stopped playing and everybody in the room turned to look at us. We were the only white guys in there. We were used to being stared at, of course, but some abusive language was shouted in our direction and the atmosphere was definitely edgy and dangerous. It felt like we might not get out alive.

A guy came up to us and snarled, 'What the fuck are you doing in here?'

'We heard the music and wanted to come in and listen,' I answered.

He obviously noticed the accent and asked, 'What the fuck are you doing in New York?'

I told him we were playing Radio City Music Hall and that we were a band with David Bowie called the Spiders From

Mars. He turned around to everyone else and shouted, 'It's OK, they're in a band', and gave us the thumbs up. Then he told us, 'If you hadn't been in a band, you might have been killed. White guys don't come to this club.' I never knew if he was joking or not . . .

Later I got up and played drums with the house band, just to prove that we weren't lying. It felt like a good move and the audience showed their appreciation. So apart from our initial entrance, we ended up having a great night.

The tour had been streamlined, under RCA's instructions, to only include venues in areas where there had been good record sales, giving us sixteen dates to play. I thought this was a good idea as it guaranteed that we would be playing to sold-out shows everywhere. What obviously influenced this policy was the amount of money that had been spent on the first tour, which RCA had underwritten.

To incorporate the extra musicians into the show visually Freddie Burretti had been busy designing and having outfits made for them. June had made Mike Garson's outfit prior to the tour. It was a light-coloured jacket with tails and trousers and a bright shirt, to complement his flamboyant piano playing. All these additional musicians were mostly out of the spotlight at the back of the stage but they still needed to look good.

David's new costumes had been designed and made by Kansai Yamamoto. Two trunkloads of the new designs were waiting for him when he arrived at his hotel. These were to become an integral part of Bowie's concept for the forthcoming shows. The outfits themselves were sensational without the added bonus of being part of a rock 'n' roll show. One of these outfits was a knitted, multicoloured, one-legged jumpsuit with huge matching bangles for his wrists and ankle. On top of this outfit Bowie would wear a huge, full-length white satin cloak with red and black Japanese characters emblazoned on it. During the show the two wardrobe girls, dressed in black, would come on stage and rip the cloak off to reveal the outfit underneath. There were about four Japanese kimono-style outfits that reached the top of Bowie's thighs, one in white satin with a Japanese design embroidered on it. With this outfit he wore white satin knee-length leggings.

Freddie had also been busy supplying Bowie with various new Ziggy-style outfits, one of which, in red plastic, had huge shoulder 'wings'. Freddie had made new things for the band but I'd had June make me some outfits that would enable me to have freedom of movement when playing drums. One was like a spacey, white Hell's Angels outfit open down the front with chains across the chest. Another was in a green, crocodile-skin-patterned fabric, a two-piece suit with a bomber jacket and skinny trousers. I remember thinking during rehearsals, 'If they don't like the music, they might get off on the fashion show.'

Since working with Pierre La Roche, Bowie's make-up had become more conceptualized to fit in with this bizarre wardrobe. He was quite an expert in applying his cosmetics, which he said was partly due to his time spent with Lindsay Kemp. For this tour he adopted kabuki-style make-up. A friend of his, Calvin Lee, a Chinese American professor who I'd met around the time we recorded *The Man Who Sold the World*, had been involved in inventing a hologram-type of paper with patterns in that was popular in the 1960s. He used to wear a cut-out one-inch circle of it on his forehead which looked like a 'third eye'. Bowie adopted this idea and had a gold circle surrounded by small diamante in the centre of his forehead.

We went over to Radio City for a day of rehearsals before the Valentine's Day gig. Bowie had seen a show there the previous night and during it one of the performers had been slowly lowered from high above the stage in a cage that had lights on it, giving it the appearance of a kaleidoscope. It was part of Radio City's stage equipment, so he decided that was how he wanted to open the show, him being lowered in this cage. During rehearsals I noticed a trapdoor at the front of the stage and asked the house manager if it still worked. He confirmed that it did. I pointed it out to Bowie and said how cool it would look if the four of us ascended to the stage via the trapdoor with the whole venue in darkness, each of us lit by a separate light beaming down from above. He said, 'That's a brilliant idea, let's do it', before realizing we now had two potentially great entrances to the start of the show.

'We have to do both,' he said. 'We'll have an intermission in the show, then we can use both ideas. I'll start the first half descending to the stage and then the four of us will come up through the trapdoor for the second half. They won't be expecting that.

'When our heads arrive at stage level don't smile, just keep as still as you can, looking forward. I'll count to four under my breath and, on four, head for your places on stage.'

We rehearsed both entrances so that everyone knew

exactly what was happening. Needless to say, during the show both entrances received rapturous applause from the audience. What they didn't know, as Ziggy and the Spiders were so dramatically spot-lit, was that Bowie and I were in the middle of a fairly heated argument. It had started during the intermission over a new outfit that Freddie had made me. Bowie was insisting that I wear it that night and I was refusing, having tried the outfit on earlier. It was striped with extremely wide shoulders, and I thought I looked like Lurch from *The Addams Family* crossed with a deckchair.

As we rose up to stage level on the platform various words of abuse were still flying back and forth. Somehow we managed to curse each other without moving our lips, only stopping when Bowie began the count. During the first song after the intermission he made his way to me in front of my drum kit and with a big grin on his face said, 'Fuck you.' We both cracked up.

On the first night we were at the end of the last song, 'Suffragette City', when a fan managed to get up on the stage and grab hold of Bowie who collapsed on the floor and had to be helped from the stage. At the time I wasn't sure if this was a part of his theatrics but I later found out that he had been diagnosed with exhaustion and ordered to rest in bed the next day, which he did. He looked much better when we saw him and was able to pull off the evening show as expertly as he always did.

The two gigs at Radio City had been a resounding success. We even had the artist Salvador Dalí in the audience and I remember wondering if, with all the new stage outfits, especially Bowie's, he was sitting there thinking that one of his paintings had come to life . . .

We moved on to Philadelphia, to the Tower Theater where we'd had such a great time on the first leg of our tour. We were doing seven shows in four days there. We weren't too sure about doing matinees followed by an evening show on three consecutive days, especially not knowing if Bowie was over his exhaustion, but in the end we just said to each other, 'Fuck it, let's just do it and make sure every show is good.' It was incredibly hard physically but really good fun!

Though the shows were amazing and received so well by the crowds, and it felt like rock 'n' roll history was being made, cracks were starting to appear in the established relationship between Bowie and the Spiders. He'd started to go to the venues in a separate limousine whereas previously we'd all travelled together. On several occasions he even stayed in a different hotel from the rest of us.

I remember one time we were all sitting in a dressing room with lots of the crew milling around. Bowie put a cigarette in his mouth and looked directly at the three of us and snapped his fingers, indicating that one of us should jump up and light his cigarette. We'd just been chatting up to this moment and none of us said a word, but gave him a look that said, 'You must be kidding, fuck off.' We carried on talking while two or three of the crew scrambled to put lighters in front of him.

We made many attempts to communicate with him at various times on the tour but he would just look you straight in the eye and completely blank you. I remember once asking him if he'd seen a particular film. He didn't answer and I thought maybe he hadn't heard me, so I repeated the question.

He looked straight at me and blanked me again. His behaviour was definitely changing.

On the earlier tours we'd watched him get into his character of Ziggy Stardust prior to a performance. But the minute the show was over he would drop the character and you could have a laugh and a joke with him. I started to notice that now he seemed to be Ziggy most of the time and I tried to figure out why his attitude and demeanour had changed so drastically. I put it down partly to the fact that as well as all the performances he had to do as Ziggy, he also had to undertake vast numbers of interviews for radio shows and music magazines, national papers, etc., and from my observation the majority of the journalists and DJs didn't seem to want to talk to David Bowie, they wanted an interview with 'Ziggy Stardust'. Bowie seemed to be obliging and I felt that he was like a method actor in a film who couldn't throw off his character.

I guess that along with all this change of behaviour it became clear that Bowie was now separating himself from the band. There were no more meals together prior to the shows. Sometimes we didn't even see him until he arrived for soundcheck. Even the soundchecks weren't fun any more, with hardly any social interaction. We obviously understood that Bowie was the star of the show, but we'd come this far as a 'gang' and now it seemed it was being broken up.

Of course, Bowie's real problem at the time was drugs, as has been widely documented and as he later openly admitted himself.

A new guy had joined the crew at the beginning of the tour. I had never seen him moving equipment or doing anything else, and when I asked what his job was, I was told he was the coke dealer. I was surprised as I'd never seen anybody do coke all the time I was in the band. In fact, the truth is I've never seen anybody do coke at all, apart from in movies! I assumed the coke must be for the crew, who often had to work all night and then travel to the next gig. Mick and Trev certainly never did coke, as far as I knew.

In retrospect, it explains so much but at the time I really didn't have a clue what lay behind Bowie's behaviour. It was much later, after the UK tour, that I found out he was doing coke throughout this period.

And so the touring continued . . . to Nashville, Memphis, on to Detroit.

I met some great people on the road, and attention from female fans and groupies continued to be ever-present. This reached a logical conclusion when a female member of the crew would fill the bus with girls after a gig. It would be driven back to the hotel and we'd meet them in the bar. It was like having our own private harem; we knew if they'd got on the bus they were into sleeping with members of the band. Sometimes I'd single out a pretty one and we'd spend the night together. At first the bus was filled with girls only every now and then, but then it became more regular. Beautiful girls would ask for my room number and I'd happily give it to them. I was selective, though; I didn't sleep with hundreds of girls. I guess we looked at it as one of the perks of being in a famous rock 'n' roll band.

In the morning, we were nearly always woken up by Jamie Andrews who would more often than not have obtained a

master key. He would open the door to our suite and call out
in his camp voice, 'Woody, Trevor, Mick', followed by a string
of obscenities. It was a real circus. He was just so bloody loud
and we never quite got used to it. It was hilarious to see the
confused expressions on the faces of our 'guests'; they weren't
quite sure who they had been sleeping with . . .

Something out of the ordinary seemed to happen every day
when we were touring.

One day Mick, Trev and I were sitting in our suite at a
hotel when all of a sudden the door opened and Tony Frost
entered accompanied by a woman in a green dress. She had
long black hair, black evening gloves and was wearing high
heels. In one hand she had a long cigarette holder; over her
other arm was a black handbag. She was also heavily made
up.

'Have you met Gloria?' Tony asked. 'Can you give her a
light?'

As I looked into her eyes, I noticed the different-sized
pupils and realized that Gloria was in fact Bowie in drag.

'It's nice to meet you, Gloria,' I said politely, as I lit her
cigarette, trying not to smile. This was ridiculous. I didn't
object to Bowie dressing up as a woman, if that's what he
wanted, but I felt it was pretty stupid that I had to pretend not
to know who he was. If anyone else in the band or crew had
done this, it would have been just for a laugh, but Bowie took
this stuff very seriously.

Mick and Trev gave 'Gloria' a polite nod as she turned
round and headed for the door. Before she reached the door I
quickly whispered to both of them, 'It's Bowie.' The look on
their faces was priceless.

Another time, after a gig in San Francisco, the three of us were getting some air outside at the back of the venue. We'd changed into our street clothes and were sitting on a bench just cooling off when three guys stopped in front of us. They were all on roller skates and wearing full-length dresses and with beards that had been sprayed silver. Their faces were fully made up. One of them said in a Southern drawl, 'You guys are so fuckin' weird.'

The band was now so big in America that I could easily have lost my head. I'd walk into a place and there would be literally hundreds of people dressed like us. It was quite unnerving. So much adulation is hard to take; I hadn't banked on that happening. There were mad moments when we thought we were the best thing since sliced bread and that no other band could touch us. The audiences validated those feelings every night, because they went nuts when we played. Even between gigs we had Warhol's lot around us, and everything they said and did was eccentric to say the least. The only people I could communicate with on a real, down-to-earth level were Mick and Trevor and some of the crew. We all managed to stay pretty well grounded, considering. Even though there was now more distance between us and Bowie, I think we still helped anchor him and keep things real. Perhaps it was because he knew we wouldn't accept certain things, so he could only go so far with us. Maybe it was a case of 'I'll try my ideas on these northern lads, and if they can take it, maybe the audiences will too.'

We'd sit down and have a laugh about how far we'd come since the Rats, and that helped us get through it. The northern way of dealing with these things was always to laugh at them and take the piss, so that's what we did. It helped us stay relatively sane.

We were living every young rock musician's dream, but the communication gap between Bowie and the rest of us continued to grow. However, lots of other things were going wrong for him at this point. He was exhausted, and the pressure of coming up with music for a new album must have been considerable. Writing songs while touring, as he'd done for *Aladdin Sane*, is tough, and he also had to do the interviews. Travelling when you can't fly is time-consuming, too. The cracks were getting wider.

A massive, third American tour was now being considered, but it was never booked. Bowie was even talking about taking the Ziggy show to the USSR, Europe and China, but in retrospect I don't think he could have got through it and kept his sanity, with all the drugs as well. I think his way of dealing with the success that he'd been trying for so long to achieve was to do coke, but that just complicated things.

By the spring of 1973, I had started to realize that I didn't enjoy some parts of the rock 'n' roll life that up to then I'd revelled in. I remember looking up at the ceiling, while a groupie was bouncing up and down on me, and thinking, 'I'm the one being used here', which was weird because I always thought that if anyone was being used it was them. It was fun to experience all this, but ultimately I came to understand it was something I didn't want as part of my life. Perhaps I was growing up a bit, and realizing that you need to be a bit responsible in life. At the same time it was hard to keep any kind of mental clarity, because touring was so exhausting.

I'd now been in a bubble for 180-plus gigs, and it was getting both surreal and unreal. A day off doesn't feel like a day off in that situation, because you're in tour mode and you can't snap out of it just like that. It felt like being wired on life, while not being connected with the world because you never get a chance to watch the news on TV or read a newspaper or do anything normal.

I can understand why so many touring musicians resort to drugs to deal with all this, because in such a situation you're either exhausted or too wired to sleep, not helped by all the adrenalin peaks and troughs from the shows, the long journeys and the jet lag. We were either playing a show, sound checking, filming, getting fitted for clothes or travelling somewhere. Drugs just weren't for me, fortunately, but the drinking was becoming a problem. As I mentioned earlier, it had started with all the free booze that was available at the gigs, clubs and parties. For a young bloke like me this was another of the fantastic perks of being on the road. Often the road crew would have six tequila sunrises lined up for me at the bar at a club. That would be just for starters. The next day I'd have no memory of what else I'd drunk. Sometimes one of the crew would say, 'That was a great night last night', and I had to take his word for it. I guess such nights were becoming a bit too frequent and the novelty of all the free booze was beginning to wear off, so I made a decision to curb the drinking, at least to excess. In retrospect, it had partly been an attempt to escape my shyness. I'd just turned twenty-three and I was having to make some big decisions.

I was looking on the whole Ziggy experience as the conclusion of a journey that I'd been on for a few years. As a teenage musician who had been new to the industry, I had concentrated on learning my craft, going to gigs and watching bands. All I really had at that point was a desire to play. Then I'd played in bigger bands, first on the local circuit, then at universities, and I'd honed my skills. All that was sheer pleasure. Then I'd met Bowie, who was always a man on a mission, from the word go. He was willing to do and say anything to get him where he wanted to be. I admired that.

From that point on, I knew that unusual things could and would happen, but I never knew how big it would be, and neither did Bowie, to be honest. Now he was having a hard time with the monster he had created and he was losing control of it, because Ziggy Stardust was more powerful than David Bowie. At least that's how I saw it.

Sadly, relations between the Spiders and Bowie continued to deteriorate during this second American tour. As musicians, it pissed us off that we still weren't allowed to do press, because we wanted to talk about how we created music. The previous year, when we'd first been banned, I understood it and I let it go, but the Spiders were well-known musicians by now, so a lot of journalists wanted to interview us. That never sat well with me, and I could never get a proper explanation of why it wasn't allowed from Angie or Defries.

When I look back, I understand that they probably wanted to keep the mystique alive, and also they didn't want us doing what Mick had done and potentially saying things at odds with whatever Bowie was saying, but it was still incredibly annoying. Plus there was the possibility that our position was going to be reduced as time went on: Bowie told us that he eventually wanted to play funk music and have us dressed in black, so no one would really see us. I wasn't keen on that, obviously, and I thought, 'No way – that's not going to happen.' In retrospect, I don't think Bowie had expected that the Spiders would have a high profile, just as he hadn't expected Ziggy to be such a huge phenomenon.

More seriously, I found out how poorly we were being paid compared to the extra backing musicians. At that point on the second American tour we were still on a pathetically low salary. I was sitting with Mike Garson one day and I saw an article in a magazine about Lamborghinis. I remarked how nice they were, and Mike said to me, 'You can buy one after the tour.'

'Yeah, I wish!' I answered. He seemed surprised.

'You could buy one of those, couldn't you?' he asked.

'Fuck, no!' I replied. 'They cost $20,000.'

'But you've been with Bowie right from the beginning!' he persisted.

I asked him how much he thought I earned.

'Well, I know what I'm on,' he answered. It turned out he was earning ten times as much as me. I then checked with the other backing musicians and found out they were getting almost double what the Spiders were getting.

I couldn't swallow that. I felt I had to do something about it, so Mick, Trevor and I got together and discussed the fact that we were getting screwed. We hadn't expected this to happen: a while back, Bowie had taken us to a club one night and told us, 'I really want to prepare you for what's coming. You're going to be millionaires, and you need to be prepared for that.' He wasn't bullshitting us; I could tell he was absolutely serious.

I know it sounds really naive to say that we hadn't been doing it for the money; the purpose of it all for us was to be out there playing music. We literally never thought about money, because we were working all the time, and anything we needed was paid for. We got the best of everything that existed, plus a bonus cheque after the tour. I wouldn't even pay that cheque into the bank; it would stay in my drawer at home and be joined by another cheque after the next tour. I had enough money to live on, so I never thought about it. It was all done on trust, and we weren't businessmen.

Mick, Trevor and I decided to take care of this. What would happen to us if it all stopped tomorrow? We hadn't done any interviews in the press so although we had a certain profile simply from being Bowie's band members, we didn't feel our futures were secure.

Mick said he knew someone at Lou Reed's management, and had a word with him. The guy came over to our hotel and said to us, 'Look, you're in a brilliant position. You're Bowie's band, the musicians who have put him up there. He wasn't selling any records until you guys came along.' The next day he came back and said he'd been talking to the record label CBS, who had offered us a hundred grand to give them first refusal on a record deal for the three of us as the Spiders From Mars. The money wasn't even for signing the deal – it was just for giving them the first option.

Unfortunately, one of the roadies overheard this discussion and went to Defries and Bowie and told them about it. They called us into Bowie's hotel room for a showdown – and, man, that was a heavy scene. Bowie was sitting there, expression-less. We knew this wouldn't go well.

Usually Mick was the spokesman in these meetings, but that day it was me rather than him, and I couldn't figure out why. So because he wasn't saying anything, and because Trevor was quiet at the best of times, I told Defries, 'This is not right. The new musicians are getting more than us, even though we've been here all the time.'

Defries said, 'I'd rather pay the road crew more than you.' He was serious.

I was really shocked to hear him say this and I was half expecting Bowie to come to our defence. But he just sat there, still expressionless.

'In that case,' I said, 'I'm off the fucking tour. I'm not doing the remaining dates.'

That was it; as far as I was concerned, I was out. I was partly bluffing, in that I was hoping it could be sorted out, obviously, but I felt a drastic statement was needed to match Defries's insult. I looked at Bowie and said, 'What do you think about this?'

Bowie answered, 'You're just a fucking backing band. I could have made it with anybody.'

When someone has just knocked everything you are, you react without thinking. I told him, 'You're a cunt! You didn't make it before we came along and if I wanted to back somebody, I would have picked somebody who can fucking sing, like Elvis Presley.'

He looked shocked. He wasn't used to people talking to him like that. Of course, Elvis was Bowie's idol, although I didn't know that at the time, which obviously made it hit home even harder. When Trev said he felt the same way

Defries said to him, 'You've got a wife and kid, Trev. How are you going to bring up a kid with no money?' which was a shitty thing to do.

Defries then said he'd found out about the CBS offer and had threatened legal action on the parties involved so the deal was no longer there. At this point I said, 'Well, I'm not playing any more dates on this tour or the UK tour if this is how we're going to get treated', and Mick, Trev and I got up and left the room.

I hadn't argued with Bowie before that, apart from that one time over the stage outfits at Radio City. This time, though, I was a threat, because I'd said I wouldn't play the forthcoming dates. That was unacceptable to him. I found out later that he'd said, 'I'm not having them hold me over a barrel.'

Again, in retrospect, we weren't aware of the cocaine problem at this time; I'm sure this situation would have had a different outcome if the conversation had been with David Jones rather than Ziggy Stardust.

I found out years later that RCA had spent so much money on funding Bowie's American tours that they weren't willing to do it again. Because they weren't going to pay for the next tour, there was no money. It put Defries and Bowie in a tough position as everything had been funded by advances – now they had to confront what they had been spending and what they could afford from that point on. Worse for Bowie was that reportedly his deal with Defries was a 50/50 split, but all the touring expenses were coming out of Bowie's percentage.

Defries and Bowie could have told us the money wasn't

there at the time, but they didn't. Instead, we were just insulted and told that Bowie could tour with any old band.

The reason Mick was quiet in that meeting, I later found out, was because, on learning of the CBS deal, Bowie and Defries had taken him aside and told him that they wanted to make him the new Jeff Beck/Elvis, although they weren't quite sure if Trevor and I were going to be included – and he fell for it. That's why he had said nothing and why I had to be the spokesman on his and Trev's behalf.

I thought the only real strength we had at this stage was the fact that the three of us were the Spiders. But Bowie and Defries had managed to split that relationship.

The next day Mick came to me and persuaded me to do the remaining tour dates. He told me that Defries had agreed to give us a good pay rise and a bonus, and that Trevor and he were both happy with that, so I thought 'job done'. I had no idea what was coming. I had no idea what had gone on behind the scenes.

Defries now asked us to sign contracts, which we duly did, in March 1973. These stated that he would be our manager, and that if we got a record deal as the Spiders From Mars, he would be the one who arranged it. We fell for it, like the suckers we were. After all we'd been through, we were still naive boys from Yorkshire who assumed that because you worked with someone you could trust they were going to look after your interests. That's not necessarily true.

Mick, Trevor and I were now put on salaries of £500 a week, plus another £500 as a bonus at the end of each tour, which I was happy with. I would have followed through on my promise not to play the remaining dates but it was the last thing I wanted to do. I still wasn't there for the money, and, yes, I know that still sounds stupid but I was there because I wanted to be out there as part of a band, playing shows.

After that, things with David seemed OK, in as much as we didn't mention it again and he talked to me as much as he had before on that tour. I thought the bad blood was a thing of the past, because we were all talking about touring Europe in the autumn of '73 and recording Bowie's next album, *Pin-Ups*. We started listening to the songs he wanted to include, figuring out what we were going to do with them.

I admit that I didn't like the idea of doing a covers album. I didn't want to cover other people's songs, and nor did the others. Bowie later blamed it on us and said that we'd wanted to do it, but that was untrue; he just hadn't had time to write any new songs and was contractually obliged to do another album!

On the tour, a real turning point came for me when, in the spring of 1973, I came across Scientology. I'm not going to say too much about it because it's a very personal thing, but it has helped me find a life that I'm very happy with, and I'm not bothered what other people think about it.

The way it happened was essentially as the end point of a journey, which I'd been on since I was a kid. As I mentioned earlier, I was raised as a Methodist but grew out of that pretty quickly. Soon after that I became interested in Buddhism, the writings of Khalil Gibran and anything along those lines that might offer some answers. Some of it was interesting and offered new viewpoints, but nothing really grabbed me.

I was still searching for something spiritual, though. I looked for things that were true for me – things that meshed with my experience, or enabled me to see things from another angle and help me understand life better.

When Mike Garson joined us we knew he was part of some religion, although we didn't know what it was. All we knew was that he didn't drink and was anti-drugs, and once we got to know him he seemed relatively sane. For fun we nicknamed him 'Garson the Parson' which Mike took in the spirit in which it was intended. Many mornings at breakfast on the tour the whole crew would wait for Mike to come down and we would ask him to say grace before we ate.

'For what you miserable drug-taking scumbags with no morals are about to receive, may you all go to hell. Amen!' he would say.

We never got tired of this joke and neither did Mike.

During a conversation with Mike in Los Angeles, he told me he was a Scientologist. Putting it very simply, he said that Scientology was a religion developed by its founder, the humanitarian L. Ron Hubbard. He said it takes any area of life that you're having problems with, and it uses exact principles and exact technologies to address self-confidence, intelligence and ability. I thought that sounded interesting, because, as I mentioned before, I'd always been really shy. It hadn't gone away, even after all our success; in social situations it was always painful meeting new people. I covered it up well but it was becoming a major problem for me. The bigger the band got, the more of those situations I had to deal with and the shyness had become even more of an Achilles heel.

Mike told me that there was a Scientology course in LA that was designed to help exactly the kind of problem that I had. He said, 'I'm not promising anything, but it might be worth checking out.'

After the tour finished with dates in Long Beach and the Hollywood Palladium I stayed in LA and did the course Mike had mentioned. At the beginning of the course I'd read, 'If what I say works for you, great; if not, throw this book in the waste bin', or words to that effect. I thought to myself, 'That's a very Yorkshire way of putting it.' I liked that.

After a week, it began to make sense to me, and I went from always thinking that life had dealt me a lousy hand, and that I would carry it with me as long as I lived, to the reverse. It was incredible. That one week of study really paid off. It didn't take much effort on my part; it was simply data that I'd never received before from anywhere, and it completely changed the way I dealt with people.

This evolution was as important to me as being in a band, because it was about me as an individual. All parts of my life would be better if I mastered this problem – and that is exactly what happened. I couldn't quite believe it; I'd almost given up hope of finding a solution. It genuinely changed my life and continues to do so to this day. I'm definitely not shy any more!

Since then I'm continually being asked 'what's Scientology all about?' I tell people to read one of the books. The one I usually recommend is L. Ron Hubbard's *A New Slant On Life*.

So this tour had brought many changes to my life. Little did I know but even more changes were just around the corner.

9

WATCH THAT MAN

I flew home in mid-March, arriving at Heathrow where June was waiting for me with a taxi. We'd barely seen each other over the last twelve months thanks to the crazy touring schedule, so it was nice to be back on British soil with the prospect of spending the next ten days with her before I had to leave for Japan.

I filled her in with stories from the US tour and brought her up to speed on all the changes that had taken place, with more detail than I had been able to do on the long-distance phone calls I'd made during the tours. She was shocked to hear what had happened at the band's meeting with Defries and Bowie.

I told her that the relationship between Bowie and the band had definitely changed and our 'gang' no longer existed, apart from during the performances, but I reassured her that even though some of his behaviour was hard to deal with at times, we had quickly developed a mutually friendly and professional approach that seemed like it was going to be workable.

She was happy to hear I'd curbed the drinking and stopped the weed and said she thought I looked healthier for it. That's before I mentioned my epiphany on the groupies . . . I coughed up everything, and needless to say I didn't look so healthy any more at this point. That was a hard thing for me to say and for June to hear, but we both survived the revelations and the hurt healed. It felt right and a relief not to have those kind of secrets any more in our relationship.

The ten days passed in a blur and before I knew it the Spiders, the auxiliary musicians and entourage had all convened at Heathrow airport once more. We were heading for Japan, the Far East, land of the rising sun. We were all in high spirits, eagerly discussing the exotic journey ahead of us. What would it be like? Did anyone speak English? What would the food be like . . . did they even have vanilla ice cream? It made my childhood holidays in Filey seem like another lifetime.

We took a flight to Paris and then Air France would carry us to Japan via Moscow, where we would stop for refuelling. Bowie had left America at the end of the US tour with his travelling companion Geoff MacCormack and sailed from LA on the SS *Oronsay*, arriving in Tokyo on 5 April.

As we were preparing to land for refuelling at Moscow airport one of the air hostesses told all the Spiders and a couple of the crew that upon landing all the passengers would be vacating the aeroplane, but they would like us to remain seated until everyone had left. I asked why and she said someone would be attending to us. We landed and stayed put as instructed. I thought they must know who we were and this must be some kind of VIP treatment, so I wasn't worried until two soldiers in uniform armed with rifles appeared at the front of the plane. They made their way towards us and, signalling with their weapons, insisted we follow them. They took us through passageways under the airport to a room where an unsmiling, uniformed guy who could speak English awaited us.

'We were informed you were on the plane and we also know that you have caused riots in other countries. We cannot allow the people of Russia to see how you look,' he said. So we were detained in what I presumed was an international lounge for the duration of the refuelling of the aircraft. They then escorted us back to the aeroplane to continue our journey. It had been quite scary; those guns were real after all. We'd had police escorts during the US tour and at one place we'd persuaded a couple of the officers to let us handle their guns (they were surprisingly weighty), but the atmosphere during this incident was so far from friendly that we knew better than to try that again.

We were met at Tokyo airport by representatives of the Japanese promoters, who greeted us with lots of bowing. We'd been told beforehand that it was customary for the Japanese hosts to make the last bow as a sign of respect; we weren't sure if this was true so we tested it out . . . It *was* true and quite funny. We were staying at the famous Imperial Hotel in the centre of Tokyo, overlooking Hibiya Park and the Imperial Palace. It was quite luxurious and the rooms themselves were decorated in a westernized Japanese style.

My first impression of Tokyo was that it was just like a US city, the only difference being that all the signs and billboards were in Japanese, which was a little disorienting. I noticed extremely wide zebra crossings at road junctions where literally hundreds of people would cross when the lights changed.

There didn't seem to be anyone jay-walking. It seemed very orderly. Then I realized that everyone had black hair; there didn't appear to be anyone of a different race, which was strange as most cities are quite cosmopolitan, at least the ones I'd visited.

Interest in the band had been growing in Japan before our arrival. 'Starman' was a huge hit there and *Aladdin Sane* would go on to have a two-year run in the Japanese charts. I was told that before Bowie's arrival a 60- by 90-foot poster was hung from a building in Tokyo, making it the biggest poster in the world.

Our reputation for being a debauched rock 'n' roll band had preceded us and security staff were stationed around the hotel to prevent any misbehaviour. All 'guests' would have to pass through a stiff security check before being allowed into the lifts. It was clear that the promoters and the hotel staff were going to make sure that it was a well-behaved tour, though I did see one Japanese 'lady' in full kimono who appeared just to be hanging around the lobby day and night. When I asked who she was I was told she was the hotel prostitute . . . so I guess to some degree they were still being 'service-oriented'.

We had a day off on the 7th and as we weren't going to be in Japan for that long – for just nine concerts in fact – Mick, Trev and I and a couple of the crew had decided to get up early as we wanted to cram in as much as we could during our stay. We had breakfast at the hotel, which luckily served western cuisine as I was pretty sure I wasn't going to be able to eat raw fish, and still can't to this day. This could be due to the fact that one of my hobbies is carp fishing!

Then we hit the streets of Tokyo and got used to being stared at continually as we walked around. Mick and I stood out in particular, having blond hair. In among the skyscrapers and bustling streets we found a Japanese Buddhist temple with a courtyard where people could light candles and tie ribbons onto the branches of a couple of trees. It seemed out of place in this modern metropolis but had a real air of tranquillity about it.

I needed a new hairbrush so I checked out one of the huge department stores to see what I could find. I handed my brush to the sales girl who bowed politely and disappeared with it through one of the doors. She returned after what seemed like ten minutes with an intricately wrapped present with a huge bow on it, presented on a silver platter. I thought at first that she'd made a mistake as the packaging seemed to be more expensive than my hairbrush. It turned out this was normal service which impressed me no end and definitely made me want to do some more shopping. The Japanese had turned buying a simple item into an aesthetic experience. I bought a couple of kimonos for June, some Japanese fabric I knew she would like and some porcelain buttons that had Japanese faces hand-painted on them.

Bowie, meanwhile, was spending some family time with Angie and Zowie, who had flown in from London. They also hung out with Kansai Yamamoto's family. We met up with them later in the afternoon and went to see a performance of kabuki theatre. After the show some of the cast came out into the foyer and we were introduced by an RCA rep. David got some make-up advice from one of the actors, who, it turned out, was famous. One of the hairdressers from the show was fascinated by Trevor's long black hair and offered to come and style it like a traditional Samurai warrior for the gig. Trev thought it was a great idea and that it would work perfectly with the stage outfit that June had made him for the tour. It was a kimono-style jacket with huge 'wings' on the shoulders. When he walked out in front of the Japanese audiences later they were absolutely blown away.

That evening we had a short rehearsal, including 'Starman', which Bowie wanted to include in the set. We also went over various songs that others wanted to brush up on. Then, on 8 April, we did our first gig of the tour at the Shinjuku Koseinenkin Hall. The response was wild. Unlike our other shows, the audience was predominantly young girls and their screams were so high-pitched my ears were ringing by the end.

As the show had progressed, Bowie had gone through his various Japanese costume changes. Some of the outfits had been presented to him when he got to Japan and at one point he was wearing only a diamond-studded jock strap (an homage to sumo wrestlers) by which time the audience was almost at fever pitch. The next two nights at the Shinjuku Koseinenkin were equally successful and we were told there'd been a rave review in the *Japanese Times* which said, 'Musically he is the most exciting thing to have happened since the fragmentation of the Beatles, and theatrically he is perhaps the most interesting performer ever in the pop music genre.'

We did two more equally successful shows at the same venue on the next two nights.

I was thinking very much of June at this time, knowing how much she would have loved Japan and its culture. It was time for another life-changing decision, I decided. I called her

Bowie photographed at RCA Studios in New York, 1973
at the start of our second US tour.

Iggy Pop and Angie. Iggy was around quite a bit.

On stage in Los Angeles, March 1973.

Clockwise, from top left:

Mick in America.

Back in London,
on my way home from LA.

With June, who had moved into
the Beckenham Road flat.

Trying out the Ziggy mask.

At home with Trevor, his wife Ann
and daughter Sarah.

Waiting for the bullet train in Japan. Stuey George is on the far left.

With Trevor at the Dorchester.

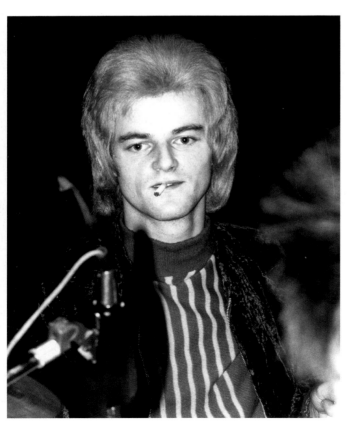

Feeling like a rock star, 1973.

Photo © Mick Rock 1973, 2016

Stopping off at Stonehenge on our 1973 British tour.

With June – now my fiancée – at Stonehenge.

The last time I played with Bowie and the night he killed off Ziggy – Hammersmith, 3 July, 1973.

The U-Boat album cover.

Newly-weds. With June
at Bridlington Register Office.

With Nicky Hopkins in 1986. He was a great friend.

June with our sons Nicky, Joe and Danny in 1990.

The last time I saw Trevor, 2013.

Holy Holy at Shepherd's Bush, 2015. Left to right: Berenice Scott, James Stevenson, Tony Visconti, me, Glenn Gregory, Steve Norman, Hannah Berridge, Terry Edwards and Lisa Ronson. Front right, Paul Cuddeford, Jessica Lee Morgan, Morgan Visconti.

On stage with Holy Holy. All I ever wanted was to be a drummer.

from my hotel room and asked her if she would marry me. It was a romantic gesture for me – I'm not the demonstrative type – but Tokyo with the cherry trees in blossom was inspiring me. Of course, the romance of the city was lost on June but I did try to include her by describing the scene. She said yes and we agreed to do it after the UK tour finished. Later when I got back and gave her the presents I'd bought in Japan, she said jokingly, 'Most girls get engagement rings. I get buttons!'

The next gig was Nagoya followed by Hiroshima. All of us, Bowie, Angie, Zowie, the Spiders et al., travelled on the famous bullet train. It was an eye-opener: they give you a ticket with the platform and seat number on it, and you walk along the platform to your designated number. The train pulls in, the door opens in front of you and your seat is right there! And it leaves bang on time. As the second hand on the station clock hits the twelve, the train starts to move – they don't do late trains. It's a completely different culture there.

It was particularly emotional arriving in Hiroshima, where the Americans had dropped the first atomic bomb in 1945, obliterating the city and its people and ultimately bringing about the end of the war against Japan. The city had obviously been rebuilt and across from the hotel was a park around the area where the bomb had hit the earth. It's called the Peace Park. I visited the museum at the park's centre and saw some of the horrific photos taken of that event, images that have stayed with me.

Next was Kobe and then Osaka before returning to Tokyo. The concerts continued to be wild. When Bowie sang 'Like some cat from Japan . . .' in 'Ziggy Stardust', the audiences went completely insane.

Our final concert in Japan was at Shibuya Kokaido, a different venue in Tokyo. As had started to happen in America, Bowie kept himself separate from us a lot of the time. Often he would arrive at a soundcheck, wave or give us a quick nod, sing half a song and disappear. Only occasionally would he stay and have a conversation with us. But he would socialize at the after-show get-togethers, especially if there were pretty girls around . . . at least until he'd pulled one of them.

This night was particularly memorable: the crowd seemed wilder than ever and when we left the stage we received a standing ovation that just didn't seem like it was ever going to stop. It lasted for fifteen minutes. We went back on and did two encores, then we came off again but the stomping continued, getting louder and louder.

We went back on to do a third encore of Chuck Berry's 'Round and Round' and almost immediately a dozen fans managed to climb up on the stage, grabbing Bowie and Mick – in fact, anyone they could get to. The bodyguards, Stuey and Tony, had their hands full trying to control the situation by either hauling the fans off to the side of the stage or by throwing them back into the audience.

The stomping had continued throughout this invasion of the stage and suddenly the first ten rows of the audience, which had been visible up to this point, disappeared from view . . . There were more fans than ever on the stage, some even getting as far as my kit.

I think Mick was the one who shouted, 'Let's get the fuck out of here!' and we all dropped everything and ran from the stage. It transpired that all the stomping had caused the floor at the front of the stage to give way, seats and all.

By this stage the theatre was in a state of pandemonium with police, road crew and Angie helping the kids, some of whom were trapped by their seats. Fortunately no one was seriously hurt. We, meanwhile, were back in our dressing rooms in relative safety.

The police, who were now calling this a riot, wanted to investigate whether anyone in our entourage had incited the audience, as it was thought that some of our crew had encouraged the fans to rush the stage for a better finale. The next day the Tokyo police called RCA to question them about who could be responsible for this. At this point it was thought that warrants for the arrest of Angie and Tony Zanetta had been issued so Leee bundled Tony, Angie and Zowie off to the airport so as to avoid any potential trouble. On returning he told us that the police were watching all the flights to London and the US and in fact warrants had been issued, but he had managed to get them all on a flight to Honolulu.

So Japan had been really wild and the Tokyo concert was not the finale to the tour we were expecting but it was exciting nonetheless. I really loved Japan and I've been back several times since then. I'm still enamoured of both the people and the country.

Trev, Mick, myself and the rest of the entourage flew back to London while, on the 21st, Bowie took a ferry from Yokohama to Nahodka, then caught a train to Vladivostok to join the Trans-Siberian Express to Moscow, a 6,000-mile journey. Again he was travelling with Geoff and also Leee Black Childers who would make a photographic record of the trip. They took the Orient Express to Paris and then home to London. He later told us that it was a mixed experience for him: he saw a lot of poverty-stricken people and towns on that journey, and couldn't wait to arrive at the other end of the line in Berlin. On the other hand, it gave him a new appreciation for his position as a VIP, sleeping in 'soft class' cabins (sonamed because they had beds) as opposed to 'hard class' where Russian peasants sat for days on end on wooden benches.

We now had about three weeks before we started our biggest tour ever, sixty shows in the UK between 12 May and 3 July. Many were matinee shows, meaning we had to perform twice a day.

In May we regrouped in London for rehearsals for the run of English dates, which was scheduled to kick off with a sold-out show at London's Earl's Court Exhibition Centre. It was the first time this venue had been used for a rock concert. It was an 18,000-seater, at the time the biggest indoor venue in the UK. The prospect of playing to that many people on our home turf was exciting for all of us and was an indication of how popular we'd become since being out of the country.

Earl's Court was like a vast cathedral inside, and its ceiling was so high that they had suspended huge parachutes spread out to try to reduce the amount of space and hopefully make it more controllable soundwise. Unfortunately no one had done their homework on what it would actually take to provide a good sound in a venue of this nature. Our sound man, Robin Mayhew, had been with us since the very beginning and had always managed to get us an amazing sound everywhere we'd played. He did his best, using the in-house PA system and adding all our regular touring equipment, including PA, to it, hoping this would be adequate. It wasn't and the gig turned out to be a complete disaster.

As soon as we started to play the first song I knew we were in trouble: all the guts and definition of the instruments was missing and it was just a wishy-washy, thin sound that sounded as if there were three or four bands all playing at the same time. Also there were no big screens around the hall like you get today at concerts and festivals, so seeing us was a problem, too.

Fighting broke out towards the back of the hall where fans were growing frustrated at not being able to see or hear us properly and had started to surge forward. Bowie did try a couple of times to calm everything down but to no avail.

Needless to say reviews the next day were not that favourable! We were scheduled to return to do another gig at Earl's Court later on the tour which had already sold out, but this was immediately cancelled. We were all pissed off, including Bowie, that what should have been an amazing first gig back in the UK, to our largest audience at that point, had gone so badly. But we had a monster tour in front of us to get on with, so we quickly got down to business as usual. We were like a well-oiled machine where everyone involved knew their parts and were able to deliver at the drop of a hat a show that they knew would work, and create the intended effects. The routine soon became established: we'd travel to the next gig, sound-check at 5 p.m., for a performance at 9 p.m. unless we had a matinee, in which case we'd still sound-check at 5 p.m., play at 7 p.m. and then again at 9 p.m., leave and get back to the hotel.

For any long journeys between cities we'd take the train, with even Bowie joining us in a reserved first-class compartment. We had our own bus for the tour but this was before the days of the custom, luxury band buses which are available nowadays. It had half a dozen tables each with its own table lamp, an area to make coffee at the back as well as a toilet. Each window had curtains you could draw for a bit of privacy. Unless it was a long journey involving a train, however, Bowie was still travelling from city to city, and from hotel to gig, exclusively by limousine. The Spiders would still leave the gig after the show with him in the limo, back to the hotel.

Obviously because of the overspending on the US tour we were no longer staying in the 'best' hotels in a city but they were still nice. There were many times when the hotels were on the outskirts of the city but the tradition continued of filling the bus with girls after the show, so it meant that there would be a party of sorts before retiring to your room.

And so we rocked our way through the tour, many times playing two gigs a day as more matinees had been added to keep up with the demand for tickets. The audiences were loving it and for me that time on stage was what being in a rock 'n' roll band was all about. Seeing so many people every night getting off on the show was amazing.

Remember, this was the early seventies. It was a gloomy period politically and economically and the future wasn't looking too bright. All it took was for someone with ideas, like Bowie, who wanted to brighten things up and create some excitement, to say, 'This is the future, we'll take it somewhere.'

We had all received thousands of letters from fans who wanted to tell us how much the music and shows meant to them. In many cases they described how it had changed their lives for the better, how it helped them to decide who they really wanted to be and that it had inspired them to pursue their ambitions. One in particular read, 'I was in Vietnam and I only had the *Ziggy* album. Listening to it was what got me through it.' There were many stories like this. I guess at the time the letters were a confirmation that what we were doing was having a positive effect on so many people. Over the last four decades, with the advent of the internet, I have seen countless emails, tweets and Facebook messages reiterating the sentiments of the Vietnam vet which continue to this day. I still find this humbling.

On 23 May we played a matinee concert at the Brighton Dome. The venue had a huge mirror ball suspended high up above the middle of the hall. As we started 'Space Oddity' a light hit the ball and the effect was magnificent, giving the appearance of thousands of stars circling the whole place, totally integrating with the song. The crowd went crazy. After an evening show that was just as brilliant, however, we were informed that David Bowie had been banned from ever appearing at the Dome again. Apparently overenthusiastic fans had done considerable damage to a section of the seating and this was too much for the Dome's proprietors.

On 6 June we checked in to the Hallam Hotel in Sheffield, as we were playing the City Hall later that day. We found out that Lulu and Labi Siffre were also staying at the same hotel as they were both playing gigs in the area. After our gig we all convened in the bar for an after-show party, and Lulu and Labi joined us. The bar happened to have a baby grand piano which Labi began playing – he was soon joined by Lulu and Bowie singing 'My Funny Valentine'. They followed this up with some blues standards which allowed Lulu to demonstrate her vocal abilities. It was nice to hear her singing in a non-pop voice, being as ballsy as on her 1965 single 'Shout'. Later on, I heard Angie asking where Bowie was: had anyone seen him? I didn't say that I had seen him get into the hotel lift with Lulu half an hour earlier. Apparently she later found out they'd disappeared up to his room.

June had arrived earlier that day to spend the rest of the tour with me. I remember the next morning we went down to the lobby and saw three young fans waiting there. We went to talk to them and found out they had been following us from gig to gig and had now run out of money to get home – they couldn't even ring their parents. June got the number of one of their parents and called them up, letting them know the kids were all OK and making arrangements to get them home. She then packed them off to the station in a cab. This kind of thing happened a few times on this tour.

On our way to Salisbury in Wiltshire, where we had a gig at the City Hall on 14 June, the driver happened to mention that we were passing close to Stonehenge. Seeing Stonehenge struck us as a brilliant idea so we asked him to take a detour and arrived at the site like a typical busload of tourists. Back then the stones themselves hadn't been cordoned off from the public. We all bought ice creams and had various silly photos taken lying on the stones. For an hour and a half it actually felt like we were on holiday. We even had a group photo taken outside, alongside the bus.

So after two more weeks of concerts during which we played twenty-two performances, obviously with quite a few matinees to fit that many in, we headed back to London. As we were nearing the end of this British tour there were rumours circulating among the band and crew, supposedly originating with Defries, that other tours were already being looked at. Forty dates in the US was being mentioned, as was a tour of Europe, and Bowie had actually told me that he wanted to take Ziggy to Russia and China.

'Life on Mars?' had been released as a single on 22 June. It went straight in at Number 21 and had jumped to Number 4 by the beginning of July. (It climbed to Number 3 in the UK charts and stayed in the charts for thirteen weeks.) It felt as if we could do no wrong.

Our third UK tour had been all we hoped it would be and more. The finale was two nights at Hammersmith Odeon on 2 and 3 July.

The first show was brilliant, probably spurred on by it being a London gig and that extra adrenalin you seem to find when the finishing line is in sight. These two gigs had been added to replace the cancelled Earl's Court gig – the disaster a distant memory by now.

There's a great story about that first night at Hammersmith, which has been around the music scene for all these years but I was not aware of it until April 2016, when Tony Visconti and I appeared on *Jonesy's Jukebox*, an LA radio show presented by DJ and former Sex Pistols guitarist Steve Jones.

After Tony and I had answered many questions regarding our time working with Bowie, Steve looked at me and asked, 'Woody, what about Hammersmith?'

At first I thought maybe he'd been at the concert, so I said, 'Yeah, a great night.'

'You don't know what I'm talking about, do you?' he said.

'Not really,' I replied.

He then proceeded to tell me that he lived in Hammer-smith at the time and he knew the Odeon like the back of his hand. He and a friend had got into the theatre after the show on the first night and pinched Bowie's vocal mic, Trevor's spare bass amp and two of my cymbals. He said it was just a thing he did, but they only stole things from bands they liked . . .

'This is a British thing, right?' Tony said, laughing. 'You like someone so you steal from them.'

'I want to make amends for that, on air,' Steve said. 'How much do I owe you for the cymbals?'

I still thought he was joking at this point, so with a straight face I replied, 'A hundred and twenty thousand pounds.'

'No, I'm serious,' he said, taking a sheaf of dollars out of his pocket,

'Two hundred dollars,' I said, which he promptly handed me.

'Good, I feel better about that,' he said. 'It's been on my conscience since then.'

I thanked him and we carried on with the interview.

For the final concert at Hammersmith Defries had arranged for director D. A. Pennebaker to film the show and an RCA mobile unit was there to record it. Ken Scott was in charge of the recording that night and had brought in another Trident engineer, Roy Baker, to assist him. This would eventually become *Ziggy Stardust and the Spiders From Mars: The Motion Picture*, which was released in 1983.

That last night was probably one of the best shows we'd ever done. We tore through the set and everything just seemed to fall into place. Bowie was particularly on form. Every move he made was delivered with an extra something that made the whole show electrifying. After a blistering version of 'White Light/White Heat' the Hammersmith audience were going berserk.

It got even wilder when Bowie stepped up to the microphone and announced, 'As this is our last concert of the tour we thought we'd do something special for you, so we invited one of our friends and I know you'll give a big, warm welcome to Jeff Beck.'

Jeff walked on to thunderous applause and Mick started the riff to 'The Jean Genie'. It was a particularly special moment as Jeff Beck was one of Mick's guitar heroes. We did an extended version of the song where they each took it in turn to solo back and forth. It was 'The Jean Genie' like we'd never played it before. Jeff stayed on for 'Round and Round' and then left the stage to great applause.

Then there was a longer than usual gap but luckily the audience were still making one hell of a noise. Bowie then stepped up to his microphone and signalled with his hands that he wanted the audience to be quiet. They immediately calmed down.

'Everybody . . . this has been one of the greatest tours of our lives,' he said. 'I would like to thank the band. I would like to thank our road crew. I would like to thank our lighting people. Of all the shows on this tour, this particular show will remain with us the longest because not only is it the last show of the tour, it's the last show we'll ever do. Thank you.'

My first thought was, 'What did he just say? Did he just say it's the last show we'll ever do?' My eyes went to Trevor who, judging by the look of confusion on his face, was thinking exactly the same. I looked around at the other guys on the stage and most of them wore the same bemused expression. Some of the audience began shouting out, 'No, no, no' and I could see many of the fans close to the stage in tears.

Then Hutch, the auxiliary rhythm guitarist, started playing the intro chords to 'Rock 'n' Roll Suicide' and we were into the final song of the show.

Throughout the song I was wondering if it was just another of Bowie's publicity stunts. Had he planned this or was it just spur of the moment? He'd done many things like this before without informing us. By the end of the number I was actually quite annoyed so I threw one of my drumsticks in his direction, obviously with no malice intended as it missed his head by about six feet . . .

Then Bowie said to the audience, 'Bye bye, we love you', and we left the stage.

As Trevor and I walked back to the dressing room we quizzed each other about what he'd said and what it was all about. I guess there was still not enough information at that point for us to reach a conclusion. When we questioned Mick in the dressing room he said, 'As far as I know he's quit but I'm not sure what it all means. You need to ask him.'

We then went around asking various crew members if they had any more concrete information. Some said they'd been told that was it, he'd finished with Ziggy, others said they thought it was just a big stunt and many were just as confused as we were. Bowie had already left the venue by this time.

So I decided that, as there was an after-show party, I would catch up with him there and hopefully get an answer.

The party was held at the Café Royal on Regent Street and I'd already seen the guest list which included Ringo, Lulu, Jagger, Lou Reed, Jeff Beck, Cat Stevens, Peter Cook, Britt Ekland, Elliott Gould and Keith Moon, one of my heroes.

Mick had already left for the party so Trevor and I went together in a cab. As well as getting the truth about that statement I had another important mission in mind. I was leaving the following morning to go home to Yorkshire to get married . . . June and I had planned to get married at the end of the tour and had finally settled on a date. We would have a register office wedding on 5 July with close family and friends from Yorkshire. We had also planned a short service down in Sussex for our friends on 7 July, at a Scientology church. I had asked Mick to be my best man for that and had also invited David, who'd said he'd be there. As we'd done all this at real short notice, due to not knowing when the tour would actually finish, we hadn't got together any official invitations, it was all verbal. So I wanted to remind David and Mick about the wedding that night.

Arriving at the Café Royal, we were confronted by a red carpet and a bunch of photographers madly flashing away as we exited the cab. The place was jam-packed with guests. I'd hoped to see Keith Moon but there were so many people I never did, and we tried to get to Bowie but he was surrounded by the likes of Jagger, Lou Reed, Jeff Beck and Ringo. It soon became clear to us that this wasn't the time or place for any serious band discussions, or wedding reminders for that matter.

June and I were married as planned in Bridlington Register Office with both sets of our parents and our families and a few old friends present. June had made me a suit as well as her wedding dress over the previous two days. She added the porcelain buttons to her dress that I'd brought from Japan.

Then we came back down to Sussex for the second ceremony. However, Mick and David didn't show up. We didn't know what had happened to them, but we couldn't wait any longer so Trevor stepped in as best man and Geoff MacCormack gave June away. Some of the road crew and entourage were guests, too. Trevor's daughter, Sarah, was a flower girl, along with Mike Garson's daughter, Jenny.

I got a call about an hour and a half after the wedding ceremony, while I was getting changed at the house of a friend of myself and Mick. I assumed it was someone phoning to say congratulations. But, no, it was Tony Defries, who said, 'I'm calling to tell you that you won't be going to France to record the *Pin Ups* album.'

'Why not?' I said. I was a little shocked. It was not a statement I was expecting to hear, especially on my wedding day.

'Well, you said you didn't want to be in the band any more.'

He was referring to the moment six months earlier when I'd refused to do the remaining dates during the second US tour unless we got a pay rise.

'Yes, but we got through all that, and sorted out the money, didn't we?' I said. 'And we've done two tours since then.'

'But you said you didn't want to do it,' he repeated.

I could tell by his tone that this wasn't something I could argue my way out of. Standing there, it struck me suddenly that I'd had enough of this insanity. Not as a musician or a rock star, just as a person. I'd had enough. I really didn't feel like fighting it. I asked if David and Mick were there with him as I honestly just wanted to say something like, 'No hard feelings, all the best.' After all, we had been close friends for some time.

'Yes, they are both here,' he said.

'OK, can I speak to David?' I asked.

After a few seconds of silence he answered, 'He doesn't want to speak to you.'

'All right,' I said, 'put Mick on.'

'He doesn't want to speak to you either,' he said.

I just said, 'OK', and put the phone down. I was speechless.

Trevor came in and I said to him, 'Do you know who's just called me?'

He could see by my face that something terrible had happened. 'Defries? I knew you were going to get that call, but I didn't want to spoil your wedding, so I didn't tell you about it.'

'Why the fuck would they call me right now?'

He just looked at me unhappily. My mind was reeling. It was hard to believe they would sack me on what should be such a happy day.

10

SO WHERE WERE THE SPIDERS?

I spent the rest of our wedding day trying to keep it together, mostly for June's sake but also for the rest of our friends and guests who were not aware of the latest news. The last three and a half years had taken me on an extraordinary adventure, reaching beyond my wildest dreams. Our wedding was meant to be the cherry on the cake. I needed time for my severe reality adjustment to sink in.

I'd worked hard with a group of close friends who had more or less become my only family due to the nature of our schedule. Together we'd produced four studio albums that were all now successful. In fact, towards the end of July all those albums plus the first *David Bowie* one were in the top forty, three of them were in the top fifteen and *Aladdin Sane* was at Number 1, an unheard-of achievement by an individual British recording artist. We'd played somewhere in the region of two hundred concerts, we'd appeared on prestigious radio and TV shows, including *Top of the Pops*. The ride to the top had taken years; the trip down took a few minutes. It knocked the shit out of me. I was lower than I'd ever felt in my life.

A honeymoon, which should obviously have been on the agenda, didn't even once cross my mind. June and I were back at the flat in Beckenham and it was just the two of us. I'd spoken to Trev at the wedding and he'd said he found out from the crew that the 'mysterious' coke dealer on the tours had in fact been Bowie's supplier, which had added more shock to an already confusing scene.

Trevor was staying with Mick at his friend's flat in London prior to leaving to go to France, to a studio at Château d'Hérouville, to start recording *Pin Ups*. He phoned me at the flat and told me he hadn't really thought the 'wedding phone call' scenario through properly, and now, on seeing the effect it had had on me, it really made him angry. He had stormed into MainMan's office where Mick, Bowie and several others were having a meeting.

'That was fucking disgusting what you did to Woody at his wedding. How could you do that?' he said to Bowie.

'If you don't like it,' Bowie replied, 'you can fuck off as well. I'll easily get another bass player.'

At that point Mick dragged Trev into one of the other rooms and told him not to say anything more or he would be out of a job too.

Over the next couple of weeks, and with June's help, I was able to start picking myself up from the floor. I decided to do my own post-mortem on the situation; even though I might still be missing vital pieces of the jigsaw, getting it straight in my own mind had to be better than feeling mystified by my sacking. After all, the only explanation I'd been given for my dismissal was Defries' statement, quoting me six months earlier: 'You said you didn't want to be in the band.'

The shock news that Bowie had been on cocaine through-out the last US tour did explain his strange and often antisocial mood and behavioural changes, his distancing himself from the band. And it helped me to begin to understand his refusal to defend the Spiders when Defries had been so dismissive in the meeting over financial matters.

I had also noticed his inability to be in control of 'Ziggy' and that he appeared more and more in character 24/7. I had thought at the time that 'Ziggy in America', as he described the *Aladdin Sane* album, was a bit of a compromise for him and he'd wanted to move on. I looked back now and realized even at that point that he was looking for a way out of Ziggy Star-dust and back to David Bowie, but 'Ziggy' was so huge I don't think he could see how to do it without potentially disastrous consequences for his career.

When he learned of RCA's refusal to continue funding the tours, I think that pushed him into making the decision to end 'Ziggy' as neither he nor Defries liked being dictated to by the record company. So if Ziggy's death was on the cards, he would have to make a clean break, which meant he wouldn't really be able to continue with a band that had, by this time, created its own profile as 'the Spiders From Mars'. Therefore we had to go, along with Ziggy.

I also thought that my reactive outbursts during the wages discussions had not done me any favours. I was probably seen as an unpredictable element, something I'm sure led to the secrecy about that last Hammersmith gig and put me first in line for the firing squad. Yet, in retrospect, it's now obvious that events had been set in motion even before that. But I had been unaware of a lot of things at that time.

The other thing I looked at was the fact that Defries had wanted to fire the band after *The Man Who Sold the World*, and I don't think he put any value whatsoever on the Spiders and what we actually contributed, which I would put down to lack of awareness, plain and simple. I was never convinced he had always acted in Bowie's interests.

It was a shame that it was considered necessary to bring about my exit from the band in such a hurtful way. But in the end my personal take on all this was that I was extremely proud of what Mick, Trev and I had contributed to Bowie's music and in helping him realize his vision. Mick, with his incredible guitar playing, string arrangements and his talents as a performer, along with Trevor and myself as the rhythm section and backbone on all those amazing songs and shows. I never dreamed back then that, four decades later, the songs from this period would still be a part of weekly radio play.

June and I moved out of the flat we'd shared with Trevor and Mick in Beckenham and got our own place in Sussex, while I tried to decide what I was going to do next musically. I got to know a few local musicians around the area and started playing gigs in pubs and sports clubs, performing a mix of original material and covers. It felt good to play purely for pleasure, with no extra pressures. I'd been learning to play the acoustic guitar on my last few tours with Bowie, sitting in my hotel room while Mick shouted at me to shut the fuck up. He eventually stopped shouting at me so I figured I'd got to a good point . . . I could do it reasonably well and started writing some songs. After a few months I decided to try the songs in front of an audience and put a little four-piece together, taking on the job of lead vocals. Often the people who came to see us would shout, 'Get on the drums, Woody!' which I tried not to take as a reflection on my singing. All this, I think, was a sign that I still wasn't ready to get too serious about my career.

Meanwhile, Trev and Mick had come back from recording *Pin Ups* in France, which proved to be the last Bowie album the two of them would play on. In October 1973 they joined Bowie in a new production he was doing for NBC TV, a *Midnight Special* called 'The 1980 Floor Show', which was filmed at the Marquee on Wardour Street, London. RCA wanted it to promote *Pin Ups* as there was no upcoming tour. I'd stayed in touch with Trev quite regularly since the last Hammersmith gig; he was keeping me updated on what they were doing and I knew he was working with Mick on Mick's solo material.

The next time I saw Mick was when he invited June and me to his new flat In Hyde Park. He'd got together with Suzi Fussey by now, although she wasn't there that evening. He'd also left Bowie and was into his solo career. His first solo album, *Slaughter On 10th Avenue*, had come out in March 1974 and had sold reasonably well, but the critics didn't like his vocals much. I think Mick was reeling a bit from the fact that his solo career wasn't going quite as well as he'd planned. When I raised the issue of his involvement in me being sacked he shrugged and said, 'Well, it couldn't have lasted forever', which was very Yorkshire of him. I dropped the subject because he had enough problems of his own. We were still close friends, after all, and the past was the past.

I'd gone to see one of his gigs earlier at the Rainbow in London with June, who had made all the costumes for everyone in the show, including Mick. I found it uncomfortable watching him in the role of lead vocalist/frontman because, having known him for so many years, I could see he was incredibly nervous. It was good to see him attacking the guitar solos with his usual flair, though. I've often wished that he'd been advised to follow a more Jeff Beck approach to his solo career and concentrated on guitar instrumentals.

Not long after this Trevor phoned me and said he'd just spent a few minutes with Mick in the MainMan office in Fulham where he'd told him he wasn't continuing with his solo career and had joined Mott the Hoople, leaving Trev out of work. Trev said he now knew what I'd felt like on my wedding day. It was so abrupt.

Trevor came down with his family that autumn to live near June and me, because he and I were discussing putting a band together, although we didn't yet have a name for it. We needed a singer and a guitarist and asked Mick to join. He wasn't interested in that, but offered to come down and play a bit of guitar on the album and help to produce it. Instead, Trevor and I found two musicians on Cube Records. Dave Black was the guitarist – he was a bit like Mick, but jazzier. Pete MacDonald was the singer, and Mike Garson came in on keyboards. So Trevor and Pete started writing songs, and I wrote a couple, too. We went up to Hull and demoed the tracks in a few days at Keith Herd's studio.

We also took on a manager who'd been recommended to us. After a while I realized he was answering 'It's all going nicely' to whatever question I asked him, so I knew something a bit weird was going on, although he had a London office and could talk the talk. After a while I said, 'What do you mean, it's going nicely? I'm skint!' Believe it or not, he told me that he had a meeting with an Indian aristocrat who he was going to ask to invest in the band.

'Do you know this guy?' I demanded.

'No, I'm just going to go up to his hotel and get into his room somehow and ask him.'

'Fucking hell. That's your plan?'

The wealthy Indian declined to fund us but the demos were good, so our manager booked time at Trident Studios for us, even though we didn't have a record deal. We started to record the album and quickly racked up about £10,000 of costs, including hotel bills. At that point Trident wanted to know when our manager was going to start paying them, but when I asked him I didn't get a meaningful answer. I'd had enough – the situation needed handling by someone. I went to the hotel manager and explained that neither we, the band, nor our manager had any money. The hotel manager was really nice. She was a friend, or perhaps a mistress, of Spike Milligan – we had dinner with him one evening and he was hilarious. She liked me, so she arranged a deal whereby we all shared a single room, and as long as we didn't order the most expensive things on the menu we could eat in the hotel restaurant and pay the bill when we got our record deal. It was very generous of her.

That sorted, I took on the role of band manager and started booking appointments at record companies. I had a few finished songs, and the backing tracks had been completed. I didn't have a clue what I was doing, but I was good at bluffing. Some of the people I met were really annoying: they'd listen to the first eight seconds of a song and then skip to the next one. Typically the meeting would then go like this:

'Didn't you want to hear the full song?' I'd ask.

'That song isn't a single,' they'd reply.

'You can tell if a song is a single from the first eight seconds?' I'd say incredulously.

'Yes, we can.'

I'd take the tape back off them. 'You're a wanker', I'd say and walk out.

There was a lot of that. I was slogging around record companies and getting zero results. Then one day a friend from the Bowie days phoned out of the blue to say hello. She told me she was working at Pye Records for the head of A&R and happened to mention in conversation that they were looking for a rock band. I immediately said, 'Book me an appointment for tomorrow!' and she did.

I took the songs over, walked into the Pye executive's office and said, 'You need a rock band.'

'We do,' he said. 'Talk to me!'

And I was in. Just in time, too. Norman Sheffield, one of the owners of Trident, was a tough man with a reputation for ruthlessness. He called me in about this huge debt we'd incurred and said, 'It's very hard to play the drums without feet, isn't it?'

Dennis McKay, our tape operator from the Bowie days, was producing the album and he went as white as a sheet when he heard this.

'Woody, we're both going to end up wearing concrete boots!' he said.

Fortunately, Pye gave us £80,000 for the album. I had no idea about royalty points and so on, and just pretended that I knew what they were talking about. I'd told them how much I needed for the studio, the hotel, the gear and living expenses and Pye agreed to it. I calmly said, 'That's great, thanks', but inside I was going mad, thinking, 'Thank fuck – I can keep my feet and I can still play the drums!'

I did the same thing with the publishing companies: eventually I got us a 75/25 deal, which is unheard-of. I had managers phoning me up saying, 'How the fucking hell did you get a 75/25 deal?' I had no idea.

We decided to call the new band the Spiders From Mars; Trevor registered the name. Our self-titled album was recorded in 1975. Mick did come in and play some guitar and helped with some production ideas but unfortunately those tracks never made it to the finished album. We did a short tour of the UK and the album was released in 1976. 'White Man, Black Man' was the single, but it didn't get much airplay. It soon became clear that the record company didn't really have a clue how to market a rock band. The album didn't do well outside Japan and stayed underground.

I argued with Trevor a little about the situation, the first and only time he and I fell out. He wanted to stick with the band after the album came out, but I didn't think it was going anywhere, and I was also doing all the work – drumming, writing and managing – while the rest of them sat around playing cards. I said that if I was going to manage the band I wanted an extra 5 per cent; they hit the roof and that was that. I left the band and they continued gigging with a drummer they knew from Newcastle.

Around this time I received a phone call from one of Paul McCartney's secretaries. She said Paul was auditioning drummers for his band Wings and wanted to know if I was interested. I told her I was and she said I had to be at the studio at eleven o'clock on the Monday morning. To this day I don't know what I was thinking, but I didn't go. On the Monday afternoon the girl phoned me up and said, 'Where were you? Paul was expecting you.' I apologized and said that I thought the Wings gig wasn't for me. I asked her what deal the new drummer was getting; when she told me I realized I had made a mistake!

Then in 1976 I met a guy called Brian Leahy, who had been an agent in Australia and suggested that I put my own band together. As I had now written quite a few songs, it seemed like a good idea. I started looking for musicians for my new band, which I called U-Boat, and began demoing songs. Leahy took them into Bronze Records, who announced that the first song I'd written was a hit and signed us up.

The owner of Bronze Records was Gerry Bron; he was also the manager of Uriah Heep and Manfred Mann. He produced the U-Boat album, called *U1*, and unfortunately made the mix really compressed, whereas I'd wanted a raw sound with no frills, almost like punk rock, which was then all over the charts. We ended up falling out over it. The album came out and we did quite a few sold-out gigs in this country, although most of the people at the shows were obviously there because of the Bowie connection.

While we were making the album Gerry told me he was having trouble finding a suitable bass player for Uriah Heep. I'd recently spoken to Trevor, who had moved back to Hull after the Spiders had finished. He told me he was on the dole, and that every time he went into the dole office to pick up his cheque the whole place would break out into 'Starman', which really upset him. This pissed me off, too, so on my mental list of things to do I'd added: find a gig for Trev . . . He didn't deserve that shit.

I immediately recommended Trevor for Uriah Heep. I knew he'd fit, and he got the gig, staying with the band for the rest of his life apart from a brief stint with Wishbone Ash. He was grateful and after that, for a good few years, he and I would chat regularly on the phone, no matter where we both were. We'd talk about everything: family, band members, music, whatever else was happening in our lives, generally putting the world to rights.

I didn't actually see or hear from Bowie until autumn 1976. I was in France doing some session work when one of the studio engineers mentioned that Bowie was at Château d'Hérouville again, recording his next album with Tony Visconti. This would be *Low*, which came out in January 1977.

I decided to give Tony a ring as I hadn't seen him since 1971, when I'd visited him at his flat in Penge a couple of times, and the château wasn't too far away from where I was working. He was excited to hear from me but said, 'Give me your number and I'll call you back as we're under pressure to get the album completed.'

He rang just ten minutes later.

'David says why don't you come down to the studio, it'll be nice to see you.'

I booked a cab and headed for the château, an eighteenth-century mansion that was quite imposing from the outside but had a more relaxed and bohemian feel inside. They called through from reception and Tony came out to meet me. He looked the same as ever. We hugged and then he took me through to a kind of banqueting area with a lounge section alongside it. There were about eight other people sitting on the sofa and chairs, chatting.

A voice said, 'Hello', and I recognized it as Bowie's, so quickly checked all the faces in the room to find him. He saw my confusion and cracked up. He was sitting in an armchair next to the wall.

'Fucking hell, I didn't recognize you,' I said.

He had very short brown hair, quite a scruffy-looking beard and he was wearing a checked shirt, baggy denim jeans and what looked like hiking boots. Definitely not what I was expecting. He stood up and we gave each other a friendly hug. He seemed very pleased to see me, too.

'Have you eaten?' he asked.

'No,' I said.

'We've just stopped for our evening meal so you can eat with us.'

After dinner he said, 'Woody, let's go and talk.'

I followed him through a door into one of the editing suites. We just chatted generally, about who he had been working with, how it was good to be working with Tony again. He said he'd been in a 'bit of a state' with the drugs, obviously assuming I knew all about it, and he was doing everything he could to get clean.

'I had no idea you were doing coke on the Ziggy tours,' I said.

'No, I was very discreet,' he replied.

He said he'd realized recently that those were the best times. There was something special about the first time you go for success and you make it, and he didn't think he could ever capture that feeling again.

He asked what Trev and Mick were doing. When I told him Trev was with Uriah Heep, he said, 'I can see him doing that.' I told him I didn't know what Mick was up to at that moment. Mott the Hoople had broken up shortly after he'd joined, but he did collaborate with Ian Hunter on his first solo album which came out in 1975, the same year they formed the Hunter Ronson Band. He'd recently released his own second album, *Play Don't Worry*, which hadn't really worked; by now I'd not heard from him for months.

Bowie asked how my band was doing, how was June?

Tony popped his head around the door after about half an hour and said, 'We need to get back to work, David, otherwise we're not going to get these tracks finished.'

'It's been really good to see you,' Bowie said. 'I'm glad you're all right, and if you ever need to get hold of me for anything, whatever, ring the office. Depending on what I'm doing it might take a couple of weeks, but I will get back to you.'

I hadn't felt there was any need to bring up what had happened three years earlier. He had acknowledged it in his own way. I said goodbye to Tony and him, and called a cab. As I headed back to my studio, I felt that the old wounds had been healed.

*

U-Boat were the first band to get a residency at the Marquee; we sold it out every night for two weeks, which was gratifying. I was told Gary Numan had come to see us and was a fan, and also the Sex Pistols had sent us a telegram saying they'd like to support us.

We toured Europe supporting Uriah Heep, and did pretty well; we were selling more albums in Europe than they were at one point. I also got to see a lot of Trevor on that tour, but it was pretty weird, us both being in different bands. We used to play tricks on each other during each other's set. One night, during one of our serious ballads, a near-naked woman came onto the stage. She then proceeded to walk around to each band member caressing them while they tried to concentrate and not fuck up the song. It turned out the Heep guys had hired her. They also filled my snare drum with marbles one night, so when I hit it there was a horrendous noise. I quickly had to switch to my spare snare drum while they all stood in the wings killing themselves.

In retaliation we grabbed two fire extinguishers and set them both off under the drummer's stool; he disappeared from view for quite some time. We also grabbed Trevor one night while he was doing a bass solo. He was standing near the back-drop, so we pulled his leg through, wrapped gaffer tape around it and attached him to a scaffolding pole. He had to get one of his roadies to come and cut him loose.

One of U-Boat's last appearances was at the Reading Festival in 1977. We were planning a second album when everything went belly up. There were serious musical differences between us – I wanted to go in more of a rock direction, others wanted to be more pop – which ended up causing a rift with the management and U-Boat sank without a trace.

It had been good fun, though. Would I change anything about it, looking back? No, I have no regrets. I did turn down a gig with Meat Loaf around this time, which was probably another mistake, but you accept your mistakes and move on.

The rest of the seventies went by in a bit of a blur. I did sessions here and there, and June set up an interior design business. I'd made money from U-Boat, so we were doing OK. My first son, Nick, was born in 1975, and his brother Joe arrived two years later, and my youngest, Dan, came along in 1985. I loved being a father, and tried to spend as much time with them as I could.

I didn't know this until after the fact, but Bowie apparently wanted to put the Spiders From Mars back together around 1978. Mick told Trevor that Bowie had phoned him up and asked him. But Mick had said he didn't want to do it. He was still collaborating with Ian Hunter, and was in demand as a guitarist and a producer, working with artists like Sparks, Roger Daltrey, John Cougar Mellencamp and the Rich Kids. He told Trevor he'd said to Bowie that he didn't want to go backwards and he was too busy anyway and happy with what he was doing. A reformed Spiders would have been an interesting scenario! At least it proved that there were no bad feelings between Bowie and us.

The ad said 'Twelve-piece professional band seeks drummer with feel and good attitude'. It was 1984 and I was now an established freelance drummer for hire who was in-between jobs, so I gave them a call out of professional curiosity. The band turned out to be Dexy's Midnight Runners, who'd had a couple of big hits. The manager recognized my name and told me that they'd auditioned 250 drummers, but had just found one the day before that the singer, Kevin Rowland, was happy with. He passed my number on to Kevin anyway, and the next day the manager phoned again, asking me if I would come up to Birmingham and audition if they paid my expenses.

I hadn't played the drums for three months, so I was a bit rusty, but I went up there and met Kevin Rowland, who seemed a bit eccentric. He took me into a room where his entire band was waiting, and showed me their drum kit. It was the worst I'd ever seen.

'I can't play that,' I told him.

'Well, two hundred and fifty other drummers have had no problem with it,' he replied.

I told him I'd need fifteen minutes to set it up, tune it and make it playable. He reluctantly said yes and I fixed the kit.

The atmosphere in the audition room was as you'd expect after eleven people have just spent two weeks playing with 250 drummers – good ones, bad ones and indifferent ones. They were fed up with drummers, and now some other fucker had come in to audition, just when they thought they'd found the right guy. That was the vibe: it was really uncomfortable. Then I noticed a tray with eleven cups on it and a big teapot and I was parched, so I poured myself a cup. A roadie came in, did a double take and said, 'Who's poured a fucking cup of tea?'

'I did.'

'You've fucked it,' he said. 'Kevin pours the tea, and it hasn't brewed properly yet!'

Then we started playing a song, but it had so many changes that I stopped the band.

'Look, I will get this song right,' I said, 'but I need a few minutes to go through it with someone who knows it.'

The guitarist showed me the song, and we went through it again. I got it all right, and Kevin seemed moderately impressed, enough at least to ask me to try another one. We did that correctly, too, but the organist, who was pretty cocky, said, 'You're speeding up!', which I wasn't.

'I may be playing it wrong,' I said to him, 'but I don't fucking speed up.' Probably not the best thing to say at an audition! By this time I assumed I'd failed but we carried on and did a few more songs. At the end Kevin said, 'Thanks for coming, I'll give you a ring tomorrow.'

All the way home I thought I'd wasted my time, so when he called me the next day I said, 'You're calling to tell me I didn't get the gig, right?'

He went silent then asked, 'Why do you say that?'

'I could tell I'd fucked it up.'

'Well, I just wanted to let you know that I've gone with another drummer,' he said.

'Thanks for telling me. It was nice to meet you,' I said, and thought no more of it until he called again three weeks later, out of the blue.

'I'm just calling to apologize to you.'

'Why?'

'I picked the wrong drummer: it should have been you. Will you come up and do the album?'

'I will but since I screwed up the audition, why have you changed your mind?'

'Out of those two hundred and fifty drummers that we auditioned, you were the only one who was prepared to put up with shit and get it right.'

So I worked on the album, which was called *Don't Stand Me Down,* for a few months. We demoed some fucking great songs, which never got released. The album took two years to complete and in the end I think I was only on one song, 'The Waltz', which got some radio play. I rocked the song up to the level I thought it should be, and I thought it was brilliant. It was interesting to play with a brass section, which I hadn't done before. There was no drum booth so they built me one, made of sheet plastic, in the middle of the studio floor. It had a door and a large plastic window so I could see the rest of the band and it was like my own little house. I found a couple of milk bottles and wrote '2 pints please' on a piece of paper, stuck it in one of the bottles and put them outside my door. This didn't go down well at all.

It was a bit odd at times in the studio. It soon became clear that when a song was recorded, no one was supposed to tap a foot, or even move a muscle, until Kevin said it was a good take. I didn't know this, and was enthusiastically moving around, and saying 'Yes!' because it was good shit. Initially Kevin looked at me suspiciously but then he gave me a big smile. I got on fine with him.

The number of tempo changes during a song was equally strange. During rehearsals I would be given a chart showing all the arrangements to the songs we were going to be recording. Alongside each section of the song was written the bpm (beats per minute), in other words the tempo, that it had to be played in. Each of the sections, like verse, chorus and bridge, had different tempos. A song would start in 120bpm for so many bars, then go to 122bpm for the verse, 118bpm for the bridge and 124bpm for the chorus . . . playing to a click track hadn't yet become a part of the recording process at this stage. Now it is a standard way of recording bass and drums, as many programmed keyboard parts are used and they have to be set to a specific bpm.

The first time this happened it really threw me. I'm a good timekeeper but changing the tempo four or five times during a song seemed like an impossibility. I actually went home that night and played countless records, from Phil Collins to Billy Cobham, to see if anyone had actually done this. After three hours I hadn't found a song that had.

The next day I told Kevin what I'd done but he insisted that he wanted the tempo changes so I told him I'd have to rehearse for a few days with a metronome on my own. When we rehearsed the songs he recorded them on a little portable recorder and after each song he would play it back and check the tempo changes with a metronome. I found it pretty stressful having my playing scrutinized to this degree, but by the end of the week I had actually got there. But I have to say, from my point of view it did knock out a lot of the potential feel that would have been achieved by not using this method.

Kevin had a unique voice but even more importantly he had an amazing ability to communicate with it. I thought the Dexys sound was unlike any other, and if he'd continued in the same direction, they would still be successful today. I also hit it off with Helen O'Hara, who was the violinist in the band. I thought she was very sweet and an amazing player. I later programmed all the drums for her solo album.

Then, in 1984, I got a call from a friend in LA who told me that Nicky Hopkins, who had played piano with just about everybody including the Beatles, the Stones, the Kinks, the Who and the Jeff Beck Group, had asked about me. The Who and the Jeff Beck Group are two of my favourite groups ever so I was impressed. It turned out that the songwriter and multi-instrumentalist Edgar Winter needed a drummer for some open-air events and Nicky wanted to know if I'd be up for doing it. I thought, 'Cool', and said, 'Yes, I'll be there.'

However, after flying to LA and arriving at the studio, I found twenty-five drummers in a corridor practising on their drum pads. I was annoyed; I hadn't known I was coming to an audition. I thought I had the gig. Nicky told me apologetically that Edgar's management had just continued contacting as many drummers as they could. They were panicking because Edgar was going to pull out of the shows unless he found the right drummer.

All these drummers were American, and the name of the game seemed to be who could shout the loudest to the guy who was in charge of scheduling about the famous people they'd played with. I thought, 'This isn't me. I'm British and we don't do that. If that's what they want, I've wasted my time.' As I sat waiting my turn I was listening to a cassette on the studio tape player of two songs I was to play on. Just as I'd got to a complex part at the end of one of the songs, there was a power cut in the studio and the tape stopped rolling. I started panicking as I knew it was almost my turn to audition.

At that moment, a guy called me into the audition room and he told me which song I was to play, which was neither of the ones I'd been learning. 'I've never heard this song!' I protested.

He just shrugged so I walked into the studio where Edgar and the band were waiting. The drummer who was in there put some headphones on me and I heard about eight seconds of the song before they said, 'You're on!'

Edgar turned to me and said, 'You start this song.'

I hadn't noticed that the whole intro was just drums. I hadn't even grabbed hold of the actual beat. In order not to look like an idiot, I said, 'Yeah, I know.' The other musicians were all staring at me in anticipation.

I started the song and the whole band played a few bars of it until Edgar put his hand up and signalled for everyone to stop. I assumed I'd fucked up and wasted my time and everyone else's. Then Edgar came over to me and said, 'You played that beat, man! No one plays that beat unless they're from Memphis. Where you from?'

'England!' I said. And that was it. I had no idea what I'd done that was so great, but I got the gig.

The next major gig that came along was thanks to Nicky, too. We'd become great friends by this time. Nicky was Art Garfunkel's pianist and MD and when he was asked to put a band together for a tour of Europe he suggested me. I hadn't been a folk fan, as I've said previously, but I had fond memories of listening to Simon and Garfunkel on the jukebox back in the infamous coffee bar in Driffield.

Nicky gave me a tape of the set list for the show and at first listen they didn't seem too complex. But once I got into them I realized that, although some of the parts sounded simple, they required quite a bit of technique to get right. A particularly well-known session drummer called Steve Gadd was the drummer on the majority of Art's songs. Steve's one of the most incredibly skilled players around, and he plays with a very laid-back and behind-the-beat feel that I initially had real problems duplicating. It was only after lots of practice that I was able finally to master it.

When we practised for a couple of days before Art's arrival, Nicky kept telling me to play more quietly or I wouldn't get the gig. That was tough: I was already playing as quietly as I could. When he got to the studio Art walked right up to the kit and said, 'Playing drums for me is like walking on eggshells. If you understand that, we're going to get on.'

'No problem,' I said. I didn't know what he meant, but it didn't sound good. It did focus my mind on not playing too loudly, as Nicky had advised. Most other musicians that I've played with would probably say, 'Woody doesn't have a volume control, he's stuck at eleven' . . .

Art was not unlike Bowie in that he didn't seem to have the musical vocabulary to explain what he wanted, so he'd say to me something like, 'In the chorus, I want you to think of the words "blue" and "icebergs" . . .' Or he'd say, 'Think "butterflies" on the bridge.' You can't say to Art Garfunkel, 'What the fuck?' so I'd just nod thoughtfully and carry on. It was hard not to crack a smile sometimes, though.

All the band, including myself, passed the audition with flying colours. When we were in Spain we had a *Midnight*

Special show to do on 16 October. I honestly can't remember if this was for TV or radio. We recorded the songs in a really nice studio and we got an incredible sound. Art was very pleased with it.

Back in my hotel room I was watching the BBC news when I saw there had been a major hurricane across Britain which had hit the South of England especially badly. I called home to see if everyone was all right and June told me that the big beech tree that used to stand in the garden was now parked on the roof! They were all OK but a little shaken up; two of the boys had joined her in the middle of the night because they were scared, but Nick, our eldest, had slept through it all.

The power was out and lots of other trees in the vicinity were down, too, so you couldn't drive down the street. I travelled home the next day, a beautiful sunny one, but the landscape had changed. The local authorities had obviously been out in the morning and cleared a lot of the roads of fallen trees, so it was no problem getting home – except that I couldn't get in through the front door because it was blocked by a massive tree.

Our next performance with Art was a Royal Command Performance for the Prince's Trust at the London Palladium. This was on 4 December 1987. We played 'Bridge Over Troubled Water' with Prince Charles and Lady Diana in the royal box. Elton John was appearing that night, as was Ray Cooper, Robin Williams, Chris De Burgh, Sarah Brightman, Rowan Atkinson, James Taylor, Belinda Carlisle, Amy Grant, Mel Smith and Griff Rhys: the host was David Frost.

I lent Elton John's drummer my kit because his drums had got held up somewhere. Elton came over and said,

'Woody Woodmansey! The last time I saw you was outside the Beverly Hills Hotel in 1972.'

'Yeah, that's right – too many lobsters!' I said and he laughed.

During the performance I looked up towards the royal box and noticed Princess Diana was smiling. I thought to myself, 'I'm probably never going to play in front of her again' so I gave her a wink and a nod of the head. I'm fairly sure her smile got bigger.

We followed this up with a tour of the UK and then Japan where we appeared at the Tokyo Dome with Billy Joel, Boz Scaggs, the Hooters and Impellitteri for the twentieth anniversary of CBS/Sony Records. It was in front of an audience of 42,000 which was my biggest yet . . . so I was really excited. We were doing an hour-long set, opening with 'The Sound of Silence' by Simon and Garfunkel.

While we were sound-checking I was taking in the enormity of the venue when I suddenly had an idea for the opening song. Normally we just went on as a band and started playing, then Art would walk in with a spotlight on him, so I wasn't really sure if he would be receptive, but I said to him, 'What if we turn all the lights off in the Dome with no lights on stage and then you just start singing "Hello darkness, my old friend", and then the following line which is "I've come to talk to you again". Then a spotlight hits you, then the band comes in.'

He said, 'I love it, let's do it!' So we opened up the show in that way, by the third and fourth line in the song at least 20,000 lighters had appeared, and Art turned round and gave me a nice smile of approval. It was an emotional sight I'll never forget.

In September that year Nicky, June and I were invited to Art's wedding to Kim Cermak, an actress and singer, held at the Brooklyn Botanical Gardens in New York. It was all a mad rush as our scheduled flight was cancelled, so we raced around to get another flight, which we did, but that meant we arrived late in New York and therefore had to get changed into our wedding outfits at JFK as we had no time to go to the hotel first. Luckily we arrived just as the service started. Art was really happy that we'd made it. It was beautiful and in a fabulous venue.

Just over a year later, in October 1989, we headed over to Antwerp where we were doing a 'Night of the Proms' at the Sports Palace, an enormous stadium that held 23,000 people. The one-hundred-piece Royal Philharmonic Orchestra of Flanders were accompanying us.

To polish up the music on our side we had rehearsed for five days in London and were sounding pretty damn good. When we got to the soundcheck at the stadium the orchestra was already in place behind us. All our equipment, including my drums, was in place ready and the famous Dutch conductor Roland Kieft was on his podium. It was the first time I had ever played with a full orchestra. I'd done sessions with string quartets before but nothing like this. It was a little daunting.

As I fiddled about with my drums and did a bit of tuning, I noticed the conductor handing out piles of sheet music to the orchestra and some of our band. He then proceeded to walk in my direction and I thought, 'Shit, I hope they're not for me.'

He stopped in front of the drums and said, 'Your music', hand-ing me the pages.

I started to panic a bit as I didn't read music, although I could tell from looking at some of the songs that the drums had been written to come in at different places from what we had rehearsed. I could also tell that some of the beats had been simplified. I thought, 'Hell, I'm really in the shit if these arrangements are how it has to be played', so I went to Art and said, 'I've just got the drum parts for tonight.'

'Are they any good?' he asked.

'They're quite a bit different from what we rehearsed,' I said.

'Just play whichever you think is the best', he told me. I walked back to my drums thinking, 'Thank fuck for that', wiping my brow.

When we started the show I noticed the conductor cueing the orchestra and members of our band to bring them in. He then turned to me and did the same, but according to our rehearsals I wasn't due to start playing till several bars later so I just stared at him and kept my arms folded. I'm not sure what he was thinking – he was pretty poker-faced – but after a couple of songs he didn't bother to cue me in any more.

Luckily the original drum parts all fitted perfectly with the arrangements, although I did fuck up during 'Bridge Over Troubled Water'. Sitting in the middle of a one-hundred-piece orchestra, with Nicky Hopkins' incredible piano playing and Art's amazing voice, I got completely lost in the moment and didn't realize I'd become a spectator. When it came to my turn to bring my drums in I completely missed my cue. If I hadn't noticed Nicky glaring at me from behind his piano, I would probably not have played at all. I would have stood up at the end and applauded along with the audience. I was able to ride over the cock-up and I don't think many people noticed.

I was with Art for a few years. I got on with him really well and found him to be a real gentleman and quite an intellectual, yet also eccentric. It was a real pleasure, musically: and every night I would be blown away by the absolute quality of his voice. No other singer has that same purity. June came to many of the shows and was a big fan of Art's voice, especially when he came to dinner one night and started singing 'Mrs Robinson' to her in the kitchen while helping with the food.

Nicky Hopkins was a real character and I loved him. He moved to England and lived with us for about a year. We soon found we had the same sense of humour, which was due to the fact we'd both grown up enjoying the Goons, Monty Python, Tony Hancock, Peter Cook and Dudley Moore, to name a few. He was a very modest guy even though he was one of the world's best piano players. I think he played on more than five hundred albums in his career. We were walking around Tunbridge Wells one day when a guy came up to him and said, 'Excuse me, I hope you don't mind me saying this but you really do look like Nicky Hopkins.'

Nicky didn't even crack a smile, and just said earnestly, 'You know, sometimes I *feel* like Nicky Hopkins.'

The guy looked confused and sloped off.

I worked on some of Nicky's solo stuff and several gigs, mainly in LA. In 1988 Nicky had written a song with a friend of his for Children in Need. He was doing some work with Paul McCartney at the time and mentioned the song to him.

Paul suggested Nicky recorded it in his studio and offered to play bass on it.

'Who have you got to play drums on it?' he asked.

'Woody,' Nicky said.

'Woody? Why don't you get a real drummer?' Paul said.

Taken aback, Nicky replied, 'He is a drummer, a great drummer! You know Woody Woodmansey, don't you?'

'Course I do, I thought you were talking about Ronnie Wood. We call him Woody, too.'

When I got to his studio, McCartney said, 'The last time I saw you was when you were rehearsing for the Ziggy Stardust tour. Have you still got the same kit?'

'No, that one got lost somewhere in the ether. I'm playing Premier now.'

'Well, hurry up and set up and we can do some jamming.'

I did this as quickly as I could and we jammed for about half an hour, everything from reggae to old-school rock 'n' roll with Nicky accompanying on piano. Paul really loved Nicky's piano playing. I kept feeling the urge to play drum fills like Ringo would have done.

A local girls' choir came along to record vocals for the session, and Paul and Linda had laid on a load of crisps and buns and sausage rolls and whatever for them. It turned out there were twenty-five kids but only twenty-four bags of crisps, and we were a long way from any shops. They both panicked because some child was going to have to go without crisps. That was touching: it showed me what they were really like. I said, 'Paul – look how many cakes and things are on the table. I'm sure one of them will manage without crisps!'

*

Mick Ronson and I hadn't been in touch for probably ten years, partly because he had moved to America, where he was living with his wife Suzi and daughter Lisa. Then I heard on the grapevine that he had moved to Sweden with his new girl-friend.

I think it was sometime in February 1993 when I got a call from Suzi Ronson. She told me that Mick had been diagnosed with liver cancer a couple of years earlier and the two of them had got back together and they were living in London. He had been trying alternative remedies and was now under-going chemotherapy.

This was a big shock. Although she hadn't given me many details, her tone had seemed more desperate than optimistic. She said he wanted to speak to me when he felt a bit better.

He phoned me a couple of days later and told me about it. He said he'd been having back pains a couple of years before and there were times when he was so exhausted that his sister Maggi arranged for him to see a doctor. That's when he'd found out it was cancer and since then he'd been trying every-thing to beat it. He sounded really confident that he was going to win the battle and I backed up his confidence by saying that was the right attitude to have and not to give in.

He did say one thing that made me think he hadn't actu-ally faced up to the situation. He told me he'd been down Portobello market and bought a healing crystal that he was wearing around his neck. I didn't have any experience or knowledge of this kind of treatment, so all I could do was say, 'Try everything.' I could tell he didn't really want to talk any more about his situation so we started reminiscing happily about the old days, from the Rats to the Spiders. He also said he'd had a great time in the Hunter Ronson band, and Ian Hunter had become a really good mate. He told me he was working on another solo album and mentioned the musicians he'd been working with although he hadn't got all the tracks done yet.

'I'd like it if you and Trev would do something on the album, Woods,' he said. 'I'd really like that.'

'That would be brilliant and I'm sure Trev would be up for it as well.'

'I'll get back to you with some dates.'

'It would be good to see you anyway. When can we meet up?' I said.

'I'll get Suzi to let you know because sometimes I'm too knackered to do anything.'

Later I had a chat with Trev and we were both waiting for a call to tell us the studio dates. Unfortunately the next time I heard from Suzi it was to tell me that it didn't look like it was going to happen. They didn't honestly know how long Mick had to live.

Suzi called me shortly afterwards to say Mick had passed away in his sleep. He died on 29 April 1993. He was only forty-seven. Even though I was half prepared for it by Suzi's earlier phone call it was still devastating news. I tried to look at it positively, in that he'd passed away in his sleep surrounded by people who loved him and we'd had a chance to talk and remember the good times. Still, it hit me pretty hard.

On 6 May Trevor, June and I attended Mick's memorial service at the Church of Jesus Christ of the Latter-Day Saints in London. He was buried in Hull the following day. Bowie was in America doing promotion for his new album, *Black Tie*

White Noise, but he did give Mick a tribute on Arsenio Hall's TV chat show in America, praising him as the early 1970s most influential guitar hero, which was pretty accurate.

There was a memorial concert for Mick at the Hammersmith Apollo exactly a year after he died, organized by his sister Maggi and writer Kevin Cann, who had initially suggested the idea to her. Trev and I became Spiders again for the night and were joined by Joe Elliott and Phil Collen from Def Leppard, and Phil Lanzon, the keyboard player with Uriah Heep. We played seven tracks, four Bowie numbers from our Spider days, one by Lou Reed and two of Mick's songs, 'Angel No. 9' and 'Don't Look Down'. We were also joined, for two songs, by Bill Nelson from Be Bop Deluxe and Billy Rankin from Nazareth.

Among those appearing that night were Tony Visconti, who played with the remaining members of the Rats, Dana Gillespie, Glen Matlock, Steve Harley, Roger Taylor from Queen, Roger Daltrey, Bill Wyman, Ian Hunter, Bob Harris, Johnnie Walker, Mick Jones and Big Audio Dynamite. Bowie didn't appear, and rumour has it that he thought his presence would have turned the event into a circus. If that's true, then I think he was right, and it would have been disrespectful to Mick. As it was, the whole evening had a great vibe to it, and it was obvious all the musicians were there because they wanted to celebrate Mick as an artist and an individual in the best way they could.

It was very surreal for me to be playing songs which Mick had been such an integral part of. To be on stage at the Apollo, which used to be called Hammersmith Odeon and was the scene of Bowie and the Spiders' last gig, made it even more poignant. Several times during the set I looked up expecting to see Mick standing there with his Les Paul, pulling one of his faces. Afterwards Trevor said he'd felt the same thing.

We all went over to Bill Wyman's restaurant, Sticky Fingers, in High Street Kensington afterwards and shared our memories of Mick.

Nicky Hopkins also died prematurely, in September 1994. He was only fifty and died needlessly of complications from surgery for Crohn's disease, from which he'd suffered for most of his life. I was incredibly sad to see him go. The range of work that Nicky did during his career was remarkable. He was a true legend. I'm privileged to have known him and to have had him as a friend.

11

HOLY DAYS

Playing at Mick's memorial concert at Hammersmith, and getting to know Joe Elliott and Phil Collen during rehearsals, was a bittersweet experience for Trev and me. We'd lost an old friend with whom we'd shared some of the most exciting times of our lives and we were focused on making sure that we did justice to Mick on the big night. Any worries we'd had were immediately dispelled as we started running through the songs with Joe and Phil. It was obvious they were big fans of both Mick and Bowie. In fact, they knew the songs as well as Trevor and me, so it all came together quickly and without any hassles and they sounded shit hot. On top of that we all hit it off as individuals and the banter was as if we'd been together for years.

After the Hammersmith gig we all agreed it had felt really special and that if the opportunity came up it would be fun to do more concerts.

That opportunity did come up in 1997 when an agent I knew in Birmingham was able to arrange a small series of UK dates for us, playing as the Spiders, plus an evening at the

Olympia in Dublin on 7 August. By a strange coincidence, Bowie was due to play there on 8 and 9 August on his *Earthling* tour.

On the flight over to Ireland Joe mentioned that as he lived close to Dublin it might be a nice idea if we all stayed at his place. It would be more relaxing and we'd save on hotel rooms, so Trev and I agreed.

As I was about to start unpacking my bags, Joe came into the room and said, 'Are you wearing a baseball cap tomorrow night for the gig?'

'Yeah, probably, haven't made up my mind yet.'

'Check out the cabinet,' he said. 'Just grab one if you want.'

I opened the doors to the large cabinet in my bedroom and blinked at the sight of about fifty baseball caps in every colour and design imaginable. I spent about fifteen minutes trying on different ones. Then Joe came back into the room with a leather cowboy hat in his hand.

'What do you think to this?' he asked. It wasn't something I saw myself wearing for a show . . . but I didn't want to offend him so I said, 'Actually Joe, I always preferred playing the Indian when I was a kid.'

'No, you prat,' he said, 'read it.' He handed me the hat and I saw that on its rim was written 'Just go for it, kid. Cheers, Woody Woodmansey.'

'Where did you get this?' I asked.

'I queued up with two of my mates after watching you in concert with U-Boat at the Top Rank in Sheffield, in 1976. We had a chat and you were really encouraging and you signed my hat for me and I've kept it ever since.'

This really touched me, especially the fact that he still had it all these years later.

The gigs had been going so well that Joe had the idea of recording the show at the Olympia. He had the gear at his place and arranged for it to be brought to the venue. We were so happy with the result we decided to go in to Bow Lane Studios while we were in Dublin and record four more songs, including 'All the Young Dudes', which Joe said was his favourite song in the whole world.

The evening after our show Joe, Phil, Trev and I went back to the Olympia to watch Bowie. His people got us the royal box and as Bowie walked on Joe and I were leaning on the rail, looking at him. He glanced in our direction and gave us a friendly nod.

I'd never sat in the audience watching a Bowie concert; my only previous experience of him performing live was when I was actually on stage with him. It was electrifying. He didn't have a rock band with him, as such, and the musicians didn't create the same effect that we'd created as the Spiders, but it was just as powerful. He was a charismatic frontman with complete control over his audience. He could create any effect he wanted, and it made me realize yet again what a true artist he was. He was unique.

We flew back to England the next morning, and travelled up to Hull, where Maggi Ronson had organized another concert to raise money for the Mick Ronson Memorial Stage in Queens Gardens. Dick Decent joined us on keyboards. Many of the artists were the same as at the first memorial but there was the addition of a Japanese rock band called Yellow Monkey, who had even brought 600 of their Japanese fans with them. The Saturday night concert was at the Hull Arena, and all the bands seemed to be on form that night, no doubt encouraged by being in Mick's home town. The audience response was fantastic.

The recording we'd made in Dublin was released in June 2001 as *Cybernauts Live,* a limited edition album available in Japan only, on Universal Music. Earlier we'd talked about the fact that we needed a name for the band and the album. We were driving to one of the gigs one day and talking about *Dr Who* and the Cybermen when a truck overtook us. Emblazoned on the back was the word Cybernaut . . . and we all laughed and said, 'That's really spooky . . . That's got to be the name for the band.' It was a sign.

Sales in Japan were healthy enough for us to be offered a few dates over a two-week period and so in 2001 we left for Tokyo. The audiences were a mix of Leppard, Bowie and Spiders fans and the show went down brilliantly every night. While we were there we had the opportunity to record 'Panic in Detroit', 'Lady Grinning Soul' and 'Time', which were finished off in California and Dublin for an internet-only release called *The Further Adventures of the Cybernauts.*

On one of our nights off in Tokyo we decided that, as we were in the home of karaoke, we had to try it out. Our two Japanese translators booked us into one of the best karaoke clubs, which was only about eighty yards from the hotel. It was a great night and a brilliant way to relax, singing songs we knew and many we just about knew. We'd agreed that everyone in our party should have a turn, whether or not they could sing. Our two translators tried to wriggle out of it but we told them it was a matter of honour, that it would be considered disrespectful if they didn't join in. They reluctantly agreed to sing together.

They chose that old karaoke favourite 'The Final Countdown' and were doing quite well until Joe nudged me. 'Watch this,' he said. There was a key change control under the desk which Joe proceeded to turn up. This meant our two Japanese friends now had to sing the next verse in a higher register, which they almost managed. But Joe didn't stop there, turning the knob further and further, the key getting higher and higher. By about the third chorus their faces were bright red and you could see the veins standing out on their foreheads as they strained to reach the notes. It had become increasingly funny as the song went on and by the end the entire band was rolling around on the floor holding our sides from laughing so much.

'For fuck's sake, don't do it any more, we can't take it,' I said to Joe.

We stood up and gave the Japanese guys a round of applause and admitted what Joe had done, which they took in good spirits.

Most of us had been drinking sake at the club, but no one seemed drunk until we left and stepped out into the warm evening air. Trevor asked if anyone wanted to join him in a taxi back to the hotel as he didn't think he could walk very far.

'Trev, that's the hotel,' I said, pointing to it across the roundabout directly in front of us.

'No,' he said, 'that's not it, it's miles from here.'

We all tried to convince him but he was determined to hail a cab. The rest of us strolled across the road and arrived at the hotel minutes later, just as Trev's cab pulled up next to us.

'I thought you weren't getting a taxi,' he said as he got out.

'We didn't, we walked,' we told him. It then dawned on him what had happened . . .

'Fucking hell,' he groaned, 'it's just cost me $15.'

The perfect way to round off a great night.

My youngest son Dan and my oldest son Nick both play drums – although I'd made a point of never encouraging them to become drummers, after hearing a cautionary tale from a friend. Geoff Appleby, the bass player in the Hunter Ronson band and one of the original bass players in the Rats, had two kids and lived in Hull. Geoff was a frustrated lead guitarist, and wanted his son to play lead guitar. His son was quite keen so Geoff bought him a guitar for his eleventh birthday. Geoff would hear his son practising in his bedroom and if the guitar was out of tune or he was playing the wrong chords, he couldn't help taking the instrument off the boy and showing him what to do.

'One day,' he told me, 'I went into his room to correct something and Shane threw the guitar against the wall and smashed it to bits. I was totally shocked but when I thought about it I realized I'd been the interfering dad.'

A short while later Geoff's wife, Moira, had asked him if he was coming to his daughter's piano recital at the school. 'I didn't even know she played piano; she was really good and had just passed a high grade!'

The moral to this story for me was 'don't interfere'. I'd be really pleased if any of my sons wanted to be a drummer but it should be their choice, and I'd answer any questions they had about drums or drumming but leave it at that. When Nicky was small he would watch me practising at home for a few minutes and ask questions like, 'What is that thing called that you play with your left foot?' I'd say, 'It's a hi-hat' and give him a quick demo, after which he'd walk away quite happy and continue playing with his toys. Much as I wanted to show him how to hold the sticks and play, if one of my older relations had tried to do that to me when I was a kid I would have thrown the sticks away.

Then June came in one day and told me that Nick had asked if she knew anyone who could give him drum lessons. Somehow he hadn't made the connection that Dad could teach him. To be honest, all I did was show him a couple of simple beats and he took to it like a duck to water. He now has his own jazz fusion band called Emanative and he's a great drummer.

As for Dan, when he was eleven he watched me do a solo at a festival in front of a couple of hundred people, which went down really well. He came up to me and said that he wanted to go up on the stage and play a drum solo. I stared at him blankly, because as far as I knew he'd never even sat at a drum kit before or expressed any interest in the drums. I didn't want to knock his confidence, though, so I said, 'It's not up to me, Danny; we'll need to ask the promoter, because he decides who plays.'

He ran off, found the promoter and came back saying, 'I'm on after this band!'

Now June and I were panicking. Did he think that you just sat at a drum kit and a solo magically happened? We couldn't face being in the hall so we found a side door where we could watch the stage from outside. Dan walked on, cool as you like, and played a 4/4 beat. The audience started singing 'We Will Rock You' and he added drum fills. June and I couldn't believe our eyes and went back in, clapping along with everybody else, the very proud parents.

Afterwards I asked him how he did it, and he said, 'I've been playing in my bedroom, hitting my legs with sticks. I just figured I could do it.'

I thought it was incredible – six months later, I'd ask him how to play a part by Nine Inch Nails or someone, and he'd teach it to me. He can listen to a beat and get it instantly.

By 2006 I was mainly concentrating on session work. Martin Smith, who had been the lead guitarist with U-Boat, had a recording studio called the Garage close to where we lived and he would often call me to do stuff. A lot of it was music for commercials and soundtracks for film and TV, with sessions for the occasional band or solo artist.

I had kept up the 'solo' drum performances at small local festivals like 'Battle of the Bands' and 'Say No to Drugs'. All three of my boys were into cutting-edge artists like DJ Krush, DJ Shadow as well as hip hop and electronic music. My middle son, Joe, was DJing in London clubs. They were continually playing new music to me which definitely influenced me and broadened my tastes.

I suggested to Dan and Nick that we get together and create some instrumental tracks based solely on drums and percussion and it was a real joy to be playing drums with two of my sons. We've played together live in the UK and USA – including an appearance at the Womad Festival where we had great fun trying to get three drum kits across a very muddy site and onto the stage – and even recorded an album called *Future Primitive* under the name 3-D. The album fused traditional drum rhythms with electronic samples and live instruments, drawing on influences as diverse as tribal, Latin, jazz and funk.

I'd stayed in touch with Ken Scott ever since we recorded the Bowie albums and in 2007 he asked if I'd take part in his new project. Sonic Reality, a sounds sampling company in the US, wanted him to create a package of drum samples called 'The Ken Scott Collection, EpiK DrumS', featuring the drummers he had worked with during his career as a producer. I told him I'd love to do it.

It was typical of Ken that he wanted to meticulously recreate the exact conditions and equipment originally used by the drummers involved. My silver-sparkle Ludwig kit from the Bowie era had mysteriously disappeared after that last Hammersmith concert. I did occur to me while writing this chapter that maybe Steve Jones had made a second visit to the Odeon after that farewell gig, and maybe he has another confession to make to clear his conscience completely – but I'm sure he would have mentioned it during that LA radio interview.

Ross Garfield, who has a company in LA that supplies kits to drummers, managed to find a vintage kit that was a duplicate of my old one and even got hold of all the same skins I had used in those Bowie recordings. Meanwhile, Ken managed to locate a studio called Emblem, in Calabasas, LA, that had the same Trident A Range desk (only thirteen were ever made) that he'd had in the studio originally, so we were all set.

As we worked we couldn't help recalling the original

recording sessions and how we had tuned the drums and used whatever was available at the time to eliminate any unwanted tones or odd ringing sounds, using masking tape to stick cigarette packets or pieces of tissue paper to various skins. This time around, though, we were both more experienced and I was able to eliminate unwanted tones through better tuning and only the odd piece of masking tape. The drums really did sound exactly the same as they had all those years ago. As my style had obviously developed since that time, Ken had me play along with the tracks from the Bowie albums so that I could reproduce what I'd done, and this was recorded for the samples. So now any artist or producer wanting that sound and style as part of their own music could use Ken's program to achieve it, without all the blood, sweat and tears we had gone through creating it. And it preserved it as part of rock 'n' roll history.

I also did a project with Ken in LA for movie director Steven Soderbergh, a soundtrack for a film that has not materialized . . . so far. Steven had specifically asked for the drum sound and style that was on *Ziggy* so Ken had said to him, 'Well, as a matter of fact . . .'

My parents finally reconciled themselves to the fact that I was a drummer and eventually stopped asking me if I was going to get a proper job. Throughout the late eighties we kept in touch regularly by phone and I would pop back to Driffield now and then. I even went on a few fishing trips with my dad who had definitely mellowed. During one of these he said if he had to raise a family again he would probably do it a lot differently, and thought he'd been too tough as a father. Knowing him, this was his way of trying to make up, which we did. My parents had both passed away by the early 2000s which meant that they didn't have to suffer the death in 2010 of my sister Pamela. That was a really dark time for me. There had been a period of some years when she and I weren't in touch, because she stayed up north and I was always down in Sussex or touring abroad. Four years before she died, we became close again and I spent some time in Yorkshire with her and my youngest son, who she loved, just catching up. I realized that there had been a big hole in both our lives as a result of this distance and getting to know her husband and her kids better was really nice.

She told me that she clearly remembered the day I left Driffield to go and live with Bowie in London. She was fourteen at the time, and was watching out of the window as I walked off down the road. We'd been close when we were kids and now she didn't know when she'd see me again. She didn't want me to leave – but she didn't communicate that at the time, and I guess I was so wrapped up in myself and my plans to become a rock star that I didn't notice how she felt.

Pamela died when she and her husband were visiting Madeira on a walking holiday. It was the first time she'd left England. A month's worth of rain fell in a matter of hours, and their taxi was swept away in a torrent. Pamela's husband managed to get her out of the taxi and onto safe ground, but then he was pulled away by the water. He was dragged out of the floodwater about a mile away and taken to hospital by his rescuers. Pamela's body was found later; the whole area where she had been standing had been swept away as well. It was a terrible thing to happen.

I worked with Trevor again early in 2013, getting him in to play bass on a week's worth of sessions that I was doing. We'd always had a natural affinity, getting an amazing sound without even thinking about it, but we didn't know if that feeling would still be there. It was, immediately. And, as ever, when we worked together we had to make an effort not to sit up all night just chatting. We still called each other nearly every week to catch up, something I think we both looked forward to.

During these sessions he told me that he had to go for a medical checkup when he got back to Hull, because he thought he might be anaemic. He called me up a couple of days later and told me the awful news that he had pancreatic cancer. He had surgery to remove some of it, and then he had chemotherapy, but it made him feel worse. The next thing I heard was that he was taking some tablets in place of the chemo, but they were making him feel terrible.

'Maybe you should be on a lower dose?' I said.

He went to see the doctors and they told him that he was indeed on too high a dosage, and reduced it. I wondered what the hell they were playing at.

He and I talked a lot through that period, but in May he went downhill really fast. After a few days of being seriously ill, he was gone. He was only sixty-two. It hit me hard. His wife, Shelly, told me that Bowie had rung him a couple of days before he died and said some really nice things to him and I was glad about that. I was also glad I was able to say a few words at his funeral up in Yorkshire, even if I only just got through it and ended up breaking down at one point.

I thought of Mick and Trevor when I found myself on stage the next year, at the Latitude festival, playing 'Five Years' and 'Ziggy Stardust'. I was there thanks to Tom Wilcox, the financial director of the ICA. As part of their 2012 Bowiefest he'd asked me to do a two-hour interview in front of a live audience, which would cover the 'cultural impact of the Ziggy Stardust period and my contribution to it'. I jokingly said to him, 'After that, what are we going to talk about for the next hour and fifty-five minutes!' As it turned out, I really enjoyed the event and agreed to be interviewed for another ICA outing at Latitude, this time by Miranda Sawyer. Tom had also put a band of musicians together to cover songs from those four albums, including Steve Norman of Spandau Ballet and Clem Burke, the drummer from Blondie, both of whom were fans of Bowie's early albums. They asked me to join them as a special guest for a couple of songs, and I really enjoyed myself. In fact, it was incredibly difficult standing at the side of the stage watching Clem playing all my drum parts to a dozen other Bowie songs during the set.

After the festival they got quite a few offers to do more gigs. Clem wasn't available as he was committed to a tour with Blondie so they asked me if I would take over the drum stool. It was an exciting prospect and interesting to me that the work I'd done with Bowie all those years ago kept finding its way back into my life.

The shows had all sold out and I was blown away by the fact that the audiences knew every single word of the songs and sang along with us. That hadn't happened on the Ziggy tours; at least I hadn't noticed it. Maybe they hadn't had a chance to learn them that early on . . . The other thing that surprised me was that the audience ranged from sixteen to sixty-five; in fact, quite a lot of the younger ones had brought albums to sign. I remember thinking not only were they not born when we were on the road as Ziggy and the Spiders, but their parents may have still been in nursery.

As much as I enjoyed playing the shows I didn't want to continue with what was almost a tribute band. However, Tom had reminded me that we'd never performed *The Man Who Sold the World* live with Bowie, although we had done a couple of songs from it during the Ziggy tours. I thought this was the perfect way to do some more touring but realized it would only work with the original bass player and producer on that album, the one and only Tony Visconti. I emailed Tony putting forward my idea, expecting to have to do a lot of persuading to get him on board. Instead, he replied saying, 'Whatever you want to do with it, I'll be there . . . It was one of the biggest regrets of my career that we never went on tour with that album. Bowie and I have spoken about it many times over the years.'

When he then told Bowie about it, Bowie asked him, 'Why are you doing it?'

'Because we never did,' Tony answered.

'Sounds like a good enough reason to me,' Bowie said.

Tony immediately suggested we bring onboard Glenn Gregory from Heaven 17.

'He's got one of the best voices I've ever worked with and I know he'll do a fantastic job,' said Tony.

We kicked off in September 2014 with another talk

arranged at the ICA by Tom, this time Tony and me talking
about the making of *The Man Who Sold the World* followed
by four gigs in London, Sheffield, Glasgow and culminating at
the Shepherd's Bush Empire, London. Tom suggested we call
the band 'Holy Holy' after the Bowie song. It then became
'Woody Woodmansey's Holy Holy' simply because not everyone knew this early song and therefore wouldn't know who
we were. The band, which had evolved during its short time
because of difficulties in scheduling, now also consisted of
Steve Norman, Erdal Kizilcay (who had done extensive work
with Bowie, including two world tours and three albums),
James Stevenson (the Cult, the Alarm and Gene Loves Jez-
ebel), Paul Cuddeford (Bob Geldof, Ian Hunter) Rod Melvin
(Kilburn and the Highroads), Malcolm Doherty, and the
Ronson girls, Mick's sister Maggi, his niece Hannah and
daughter Lisa.

At the first rehearsal – with Tony just in from New York,
having stopped only to drop his bags off at the hotel – we
started with 'Width of a Circle'. Seven minutes later, as we hit
the last chords, everyone in the room had a grin on their face.
It sounded so fucking powerful – everyone had obviously
done their homework. Tony and I sounded like we'd been
playing together for years and we'd managed to put a contemporary edge on it, probably because we'd improved as players
over the years. By the time we'd finished rehearsing we were
sounding shit hot.

So we did the first three gigs which were a phenomenal
success. At the Garage, the first one in London, we had
Marc Almond, Billy Duffy (the Cult) and Glen Matlock (the
Sex Pistols) join us as special guests. And on backing vocals

Daphne Guinness (model, fashion muse, singer), which definitely added some glamour to the show. The fourth and final gig at the Shepherd's Bush Empire was recorded. Our special guests again included Marc Almond, plus Gary Kemp and Benny Marshall (the Rats). Tony's son Morgan and daughter Jessica Lee Morgan sang backing vocals as well as being the support act. Tony mixed the album, *The Man Who Sold the World, Live in London*, back in New York and he played it for Bowie, who wanted to hear it. Tony told me Bowie was smiling all the way through it.

'I really like this. It's how we would have sounded if we'd gone out and played the songs after the album,' Bowie said, adding, 'I think my career might have taken a different turn if we'd done that.'

It meant a lot to get such a positive response from him.

The next tour Tom planned was fourteen dates, starting on 12 June at the Isle of Wight Festival and finishing again at the Shepherd's Bush Empire on 30 June. Joining us for this tour was Berenice Scott (Heaven 17) on piano and synthesizer and Terry Edwards (too many to mention!) on twelve-string guitar and saxophone.

Once again the audience response was amazing. Again I was surprised at how many young fans there were and how they even knew some of the darker, more dystopian lyrics from *The Man Who Sold the World* and sang along as though they were all commercial hits. During the show we made a special point of acknowledging Mick and Trev for their contribution to the music and Bowie as the creator of all those fantastic songs. At the meet and greet afterwards, which often lasted a couple of hours, we'd sign albums and various items fans had brought along. I met some genuinely lovely people who often just wanted to say thank you for all the music which had meant so much to them while they were growing up.

Before the end of the tour, Tom Wilcox had already arranged four dates in Tokyo at the Billboard Live, the venue being many floors up in a skyscraper, offering a fantastic view from behind my drum stool. After the success of Japan the whole band was eager to get another tour going. We had talked several times about the possibility of playing in the US, having received so many requests via Facebook and other sites from American fans who wanted to see us. After talking it through with Tom, we realized it was unfeasible for him to organize this, given that he already had three day jobs: senior partner at a financial consultancy called Counterculture, his record label Maniac Squat and the ICA role. He had done an amazing job for us, and had had a great knack of bringing people together, but it was time for us to move on.

James Stevenson, our lead guitarist, had played with the Cult and knew their manager, Tom Vitorino. I asked James to check out if Tom would be interested in helping us set up a tour in the US. James played him the live album from Shepherd's Bush and a video of us doing 'Width of a Circle' at the same gig and he was on board. He suggested we start with a smallish East Coast tour, and if we got good reviews he could use them to get other promoters interested. That seemed like a fair and decent plan . . .

While Tom went about the business of putting the tour in place, it was my job to get back to confirming who would be available in the band to actually do the tour, given that everyone had other projects and gigs they were often committed to.

In the end we had the band down to an eight-piece – Tony, Glenn, James, Paul, Berenice, Jessica and Terry and myself.

We left for New York on 4 January 2016, for an eleven-date tour. The tour bus was definitely of a different class from the ones we'd had back in the seventies on those Ziggy tours. For starters it had twelve bunk beds, fully equipped. It had a lounge at the back and a kitchen with big American fridges, a sink and food storage areas and a bathroom towards the front, where there was yet another lounge. This could be expanded when the coach parked up; it slid out and almost doubled the width of the bus. It had huge TV screens, wi-fi, a music system and a selection of mood lighting, some of which was a bit too disco and psychedelic for my taste. It made me feel like I should be dancing all the way to the next city . . . All our stage equipment was in a separate trailer on the back of the bus. Our personal luggage was stored in two or three bays underneath the bus. We had our own driver, a seasoned band tour bus driver called John Glas who we would all grow fond of.

The tour started on 7 January at the Asylum in Portland, Maine, a fitting place to play 'All the Madmen', I thought. The audience were really up for it, and their determination to have a good night and our intention to make our first US date special was a perfect combination.

Our second gig was back in New York at the Highline Ballroom on 8 January, which was, coincidentally, Bowie's birthday. There were rumours among some of the staff there that Bowie would be making an appearance but that it was unlikely he would be performing. We figured these had probably started on Facebook, as we had seen a few optimistic posts.

The Highline was sold out and again the New York audience was definitely in high spirits – and many of them had the Ziggy flash on their faces. After we played the whole of *The Man Who Sold the World*, Tony did his usual mid-set speech about the recording sessions all those years ago, with a few anecdotes about working with Mick, Bowie and myself, which the audience always enjoyed.

He then surprised us (and Bowie) when he said, 'Let's give Bowie a call', to which the audience gave an enormous cheer. Bowie answered and Tony said, 'We're on stage at the Highline right now.' He then asked the audience to sing 'Happy Birthday' which they did enthusiastically as he held up his phone for Bowie to hear.

'Thank you,' Bowie said, then added, 'Ask them what they think of *Blackstar*.' Tony relayed this and another enormous cheer went up from the crowd.

'Good luck with the tour,' Bowie said, and he was gone. It was a really nice moment and I thought it was very cool of him to do it.

Next was a concert in Ridgefield, Connecticut, followed by a ten-hour journey to Toronto, crossing the border in the wee small hours. We were woken by our tour manager and had to get off the bus into the heavy snow. We were made to sit in a waiting room until the border service officials called us up one by one to check our passports and ask us questions like 'Where did you play last night?' which I only just managed to answer, being half asleep and not quite sure where I was.

We arrived in Toronto late morning and, because the next day was free, we checked into a hotel. It's hard to describe the sense of relief I felt at being in a space that didn't have another eleven people in it, with a bed that was wider than a yard and a room that wasn't moving! Heaven for a few hours at least. Outside it was so cold that even this northern boy couldn't take it for more than a couple of minutes. I only managed a few puffs on a cigarette before I had to give up and head back indoors. June and I went to bed early, looking forward to our day off.

The first clue that something had happened was the constant beeping of our mobile phones disturbing our sleep. At about five in the morning we finally put the light on and took a look at the screen, seeing parts of messages that read 'sorry for your loss', 'our condolences', 'our thoughts are with you'. We instantly thought it was something family-related and tried to open the phone. Then the phone rang and it was our son Danny.

'I've been trying to get hold of you,' he said. 'Did you know that Bowie just died?'

He filled us in on what he'd heard on the BBC news earlier that night back home in the UK, that Bowie had died from cancer. After we ended the call, we sat there stunned. It took quite a few minutes to actually grasp the reality of the situation. It was surreal, made worse by the fact that we were still half asleep. I decided I should go and wake Tony and see if he knew and check that he was OK. Terry was outside Tony's room and said, 'Yeah, Tony found out a little while ago. He's upset but I think he's gone back to bed.' Terry had a key so he let me into Tony's room, where I found him in bed with his eyes closed. I gave him a gentle nudge and he opened his eyes and I asked him if he was OK. By now the news was starting to sink in and both of us were devastated. We talked for a while and then parted with a big hug.

It turned out that Tony had known Bowie was ill and had been having treatment for cancer, but he was under the impression that he was beating it. So the news had really come out of left field.

We then rounded up the rest of the band, who by this time had all heard the news, and sat in the hotel restaurant trying to figure out what to do. Should we cancel the tour out of respect for Bowie or should we do the gigs in his memory? Tony pointed out that Bowie had worked right up to the end of his life on the new album and the video for the 'Lazarus' single, even though he was very ill. He would work until he couldn't work any more, take some time out to regain some energy, and then work even harder. I remembered that he always had the attitude that the show must go on. In the end we decided it felt right to continue – the more so when we checked our social media and saw thousands of messages telling us that his fans needed us to play the music more than ever now. We were dreading the show, though, as we knew it would be hard to get through.

Tony and I spoke beforehand and decided to go on stage and talk to the audience before we started.

'Thank you for coming out in the cold,' Tony said. 'Listen, yesterday was the worst, well, almost the worst, day in my life and I think it was for most of you here, too. We actually had to talk about whether we were going to perform more on this tour, but there's no better way to work through grief than through music.

'Music is magic. It's better than any pill you can take. It's better than any drug and this music is some of the best music that's ever been written. I'm so glad to see you are so upbeat. I didn't want to see a sea of sad faces. So we're going to celebrate the life of David Bowie.'

I then stepped up and added, 'We really appreciate it. It's good for us, as well as you. I know we all feel the same in this room, so as Tony just said it's a celebration of David and his music. You're supposed to have a good time tonight. So that's a fucking order, all right?'

This was met by a huge cheer, and it felt so good to have connected with the audience that we repeated that introduction on the rest of the tour dates.

At some stages the show was so emotional it was tough to carry on – when we began playing 'Five Years', for example. All the songs now took on a different meaning for us. But we hoped that the music was helping people, making Bowie's loss easier to face. Thankfully, at the end of the show, when we did our meet and greets, this was confirmed by the hundreds of fans we talked to. We finished the remaining eight dates, ending in Boston on 21 January, and returned home to England.

Before Bowie's passing Tony had agreed to be the musical director for an annual charity event that was to celebrate Bowie's music and would take place at the Carnegie Hall in New York on 31 March. He had asked us, the band, if we would join him as the house band, to which we had all agreed. The planned promo for this event was due to go public on 10 January. That same day it was also announced that David had died and suddenly this event became something else altogether. Tickets were sold out almost immediately. In fact, the demand was so great that the organizers added another date, at Radio City Music Hall on 1 April. When this too sold out almost instantly they added the Winery, New York, on 30 March where the public could come and watch us rehearse for these two gigs.

Holy Holy would open the show playing 'Width of a Circle' and then would back most of the other artists. Apart from three songs, 'Space Oddity' sung by Ann Wilson of Heart, 'Suffragette City' sung by Cyndi Lauper and 'Starman' featuring Debbie Harry, the rest of the set were songs from later periods in Bowie's musical career. Esmeralda Spalding's choice of 'If You Can See Me' was a real challenge for me, being an incredibly fast drum and bass track. She is an amazing bass player and has a fabulous voice. I honestly didn't feel I played it well until the actual performance itself at Radio City, which was just as well as there was an audience of 6,000. That night was filled with memories of the first time I'd played there in 1973. I found myself smiling when I remembered my row with Bowie over Freddie Burretti's spectacularly striped outfit.

Ann Wilson was also doing 'Let's Dance', another of those songs where the drums sound easy until you have to play it and suddenly realize it's not what you thought on first listen. That one took some time to get right.

But Perry Farrell's 'Rebel Rebel' was a real joy to play. I always thought the single sounded like it was the Spiders playing, even though it was done after we had all left Bowie.

Both nights went down a storm with very few mishaps considering how many changeovers occurred. What was obvious was the eclectic mix of songs and artists which exemplified both Bowie's songwriting diversity and how far-reaching his influence was. All the artists seemed genuinely thrilled to be able to contribute to this celebration of Bowie's music. Though some of it was a little crazy, in a bizarre way it all worked and afterwards it was apparent everyone had risen to the occasion.

After the shows, it was time to 'get the fuck out of Dodge', board our luxury hotel on wheels and hit the road on a twenty-five-date tour across the USA from east to west, and back through Canada. Our first show was the Tower Theater in Philadelphia, scene of some of our best gigs on the Ziggy tour. The crowd at the Tower left us in no doubt that Philly was a Bowie city!

As we made our way through Boston, Baltimore and Richmond, Virginia, the band got better and better. We were definitely being energized by the audience reactions; it was becoming an organic and almost spiritual interchange. The heartfelt appreciation each night was almost overwhelming. Many, it seemed, had waited over forty years to say 'thank you for the music' and to express how much hearing the songs that night had meant to them. Many nights it was like being a rock star drummer and a counsellor when needed. It really did feel like we were helping people through the loss of a family member. That was how much Bowie had meant to them.

Chicago, House of Blues concert was a wild one, the venue itself looking like the devil's own apartment, decorated with statues and gargoyles, and every wall – including those of our dressing room – covered by paintings or murals of naked bodies and demons cavorting, signs of the zodiac everywhere. The crowd were fantastic.

We made our way through Milwaukee, Minneapolis, Kansas City, all of which were amazing nights. Then on to Texas, where our shows on the Ziggy tour had been cancelled all those years ago. Texas is huge. I would look out of the bus window and wonder at the flatness of the landscape, stretching forever in all directions, with nothing to engage the eye except the occasional lone tree and a couple of cows. I lay down on my bunk for a few hours, then came back and the scenery was exactly the same. Twenty minutes later, whoa . . . another tree, another cow.

We had a great night at Dallas, too, then headed for Arizona. In no time at all we were in cowboys and Indians country, beautiful red and ochre sandstone cliffs carved over the centuries into fantastic shapes. Our gig was at Scottsdale, just outside Phoenix. It turned out to be in a high-class casino owned by Native Americans. We had rooms in the hotel adjoining the casino itself and they were the ultimate in luxury. Every appliance, from lights to the coffee machine, was sensor-operated. Obviously they had been designed to encourage the longest possible stay for the gamblers occupying them. I didn't want to leave; the place was bordering on perfection.

Next it was San Diego, then we set off for Los Angeles where we were playing the Wiltern, a fabulous art deco building. It was in LA that Tony and I did the radio interview with Steve Jones on *Jonesy's Jukebox* which may have helped sell out the gig, although Rodney Bingenheimer had been promoting us on his KROQ show for weeks so that was probably the real reason.

Rodney had asked if he could be MC at the gig as he really wanted to introduce us. After all his help in the early days with Bowie and the Spiders, and all he did in later years, we felt this would be perfect. He did a fabulous job.

Steve Jones actually came to the gig that night and brought friends Billy Duffy and John Tempesta from the Cult with him. Steve, in his usual cool manner, said, 'I don't ever come to gigs of people I've interviewed but I made an exception.'

'That's great, Steve,' I said. 'I'm glad you did, but just stay away from our equipment, all right?' He thought that was funny.

On 29 April we hit the Fillmore in San Francisco. This is an iconic venue and the huge old walls are covered with posters of all the bands that have graced its stage since the sixties. It was a bit of a moment for all the band when it dawned on us we were playing there. The place was jam-packed and I could see the silhouettes of people squashed against the back wall. The crowd went ballistic many times during the show. I could see that not a single person was standing still; the whole place was rocking throughout the entire set even though there wasn't much extra space. The atmosphere was magic.

We finished up the American part of the tour in the friendly city of Portland, Oregon, where I'd appeared some years earlier with Edgar Winter. After a fantastic show, we drove for over nine hours, crossing the border into Canada for our next two dates in Calgary and then on to Edmonton. We passed through some of the most amazing scenery any of us had ever seen, with peaks that have been cut by massive glaciers and rapids racing alongside the road.

The last leg of the journey to Toronto was a solid two full

days' drive and so the band and crew flew, leaving our intrepid driver, John, plus an additional driver, to make that journey alone. We completed our final gig at the Phoenix Theater, Toronto, and as I flew back to England scenes from the tour kept replaying themselves in my mind. I thought about meeting the many fans who told me how Bowie's songs, and his unique creations in many media, had been inspirational and had, they felt, changed their lives for the better. Hearing their heartfelt accounts was quite humbling and made me wish that Mick and Trev had been present to receive that kind of acknowledgement for their own contributions. I was happy the tour had gone so well and that I'd been in the right place at the right time to be able to play Bowie's songs to thousands of people who needed a hand through this traumatic loss, who felt that hearing his music live was the best possible solution.

I also felt very proud of the band, Holy Holy, who had been magnificent, true pros every one of them. Tony's daughter Jessica could possibly do anything you asked of her musically and pull it off. I was blown away by her voice and natural talent as an artist. She not only supported us on the gigs with her partner Chris Thomas – joined sometimes by her brother Morgan – but as well as backing vocals she had taken on the job of playing twelve-string acoustic guitar and sax when Terry left us in Boston to join PJ Harvey on her tour, something he had committed to before our plans were in place. Terry did a brilliant job while he was with us, and his musicality, especially on the sax, was a real pleasure to play along with.

Glenn had taken on the daunting task of singing Bowie's

songs to a Bowie audience night after night and pulled it off with incredible style and elegance. I personally don't know of another vocalist who could have done it better, and he's a fellow Yorkshireman as well.

Tony played bass from the heart for over two hours every night and never strayed from the groove; he played every note as if his life depended on it and everyone got it and loved it. His passion for great music was obvious to anyone watching him play. It was great to work with him as a rhythm section again after all this time.

James and Paul had both stepped into the spotlight knowing they were being asked to fill Mick Ronson's shoes. It must have been intimidating to play the solos he had created on those Bowie albums but they did them justice. They were the ultimate professionals and entertaining to boot. Mick would have been proud.

Berenice played parts that were created by virtuoso pianists, one being Rick Wakeman, the other Mike Garson, plus synth lead solos that no one has ever played live, and seemed to take it all in her stride with an air of 'That's what I do, what's next?'

I was honoured every night to be sharing the stage with such an outstanding band of musicians and singers. I can honestly say it was one of the most enjoyable tours I've ever done.

We returned to England in mid-May with many requests for us to do more back home. Obviously the whole band had individual commitments and tours take time to plan, but one particular proposal came along that was a no-brainer.

In 2017 the city of Hull becomes Britain's City of Culture for a year. Of course the Spiders From Mars were Hull's most famous export and there was only one answer I could give when I was asked if Holy Holy would play a big concert in City Hall on 25 March 2017. We will be playing *The Rise and Fall of Ziggy Stardust and the Spiders From Mars* in its entirety. It will be a first for us as a group. I can't wait.

Over the past four decades I'd watched Bowie stay on the cutting edge of music, often creating a completely new character to go with his new musical direction, but always managing to retain that unique quality that was David Bowie.

I always admired his refusal to rest on his laurels as an artist. There were many times in his career where he could have said, 'Eureka, that's it, I'll stick with this form.' But change had always been a part of his psyche and always would be.

I remember during the sixties when everyone was waiting for the next Beatles release, the excitement, the anticipation: what will it sound like, will I like it? I thought Bowie as a solo artist had managed to create that same buzz and kept it going right up to *Blackstar*. Always surprising and, true to character, always unpredictable.

I am extremely proud to have been part of what has become regarded by many as an iconic and seminal period of Bowie's career. From being a gang of friends trying to make ends meet on a meagre seven pounds a week, the Spiders set off on what would become the adventure of a lifetime. I was twenty years old, the others not much older. We used our individual skills to help create music that we loved – for me drumming was and always has been my passion and to create along with Mick's incredible artistry on guitar and arranging skills as well as forming rhythm sections with first Tony and then Trevor was an absolute joy. We experienced a lifetime in a few short years.

We shared that first taste of success, the incredible feeling when a song you helped create is a hit. We were there for the TV and radio shows, the sell-out tours. We worked hard and partied hard. As many wise men have said, 'Trying to achieve something, trying to be somebody, that's the real adventure', and it certainly was.

Afterword
by Joe Elliott

The first time I saw Woody Woodmansey's ugly mug, it was in the four-square pictures of him, David Bowie, Mick Ronson and Trevor Bolder on the inside sleeve of *Ziggy Stardust*. I was lying on my bed, aged twelve, listening to him play.

I met him for the first time three years later. As you've just read in Woody's book, I have a leather cowboy hat that I used to wear to all the gigs when I was a kid. Whenever I saw a rock star coming out of the back door, I used to say, 'Sign my hat!' When Woody's band U-Boat were playing the Top Rank in Sheffield in 1976, me and my buddies all went down there because we were into anything connected with Bowie.

There was a crowd of about twenty Bowie freaks, all dressed like Ziggy Stardust, bopping up and down like nutters when they played 'Suffragette City' – but I wanted to hear the original U-Boat songs: I think *U1* is a great album.

I joined the music industry eight years after *Ziggy Stardust* came out. When Def Leppard became successful, I became known as a big Bowie fan because I was always going on about him and Mott the Hoople and Mick Ronson. I was an enormous fan of Mick's, and I worked on his *Heaven and Hull* album with him before he died.

A year later Mick's sister Maggi organized a memorial gig for him at Hammersmith. She said, 'Do you think you and Phil Collen would stand in for Ronno and Bowie, and play with Woody and Trevor?' That was the first time Woody and I got together and played. Even though we'd never met, there was a kind of instant mutual understanding, we looked at each other and the bond was there straight away. We had exactly the same sense of humour and we had a great laugh together. He's my kind of musician: he doesn't talk shop all the time.

Woody is a phenomenal drummer. Bowie only did three takes in the studio, so Woody had to pull his best performance out in that time – there was no room for error. He's like Ringo Starr: one of those drummers who isn't all flash like, say, John Bonham. That said, when I watched him playing drum solos when Cybernaut played Japan in 2001, it was incredible – and, trust me, I fucking hate drum solos! Woody's is one of the very few that I can watch.

Once our paths had crossed, we were destined to become friends. We're as thick as thieves. Woody is a good man.

Joe Elliott, 2016

Select Discography

DAVID BOWIE

The Man Who Sold the World, 1971
The Width of a Circle / All the Madmen / Black Country Rock / After All / Running Gun Blues / Saviour Machine / She Shook Me Cold / The Man Who Sold the World / The Supermen

Hunky Dory, 1971
Changes / Oh! You Pretty Things / Eight Line Poem / Life on Mars? / Kooks / Quicksand / Fill Your Heart / Andy Warhol / Song For Bob Dylan / Queen Bitch / The Bewlay Brothers

The Rise and Fall of Ziggy Stardust and the Spiders From Mars, 1972
Five Years / Soul Love / Moonage Daydream / Starman / It Ain't Easy / Lady Stardust / Star / Hang On To Yourself / Ziggy Stardust / Suffragette City / Rock 'n' Roll Suicide

Aladdin Sane, 1973
Watch That Man / Aladdin Sane (1913–1938–197?) / Drive-In Saturday / Panic in Detroit / Cracked Actor / Time / The Prettiest Star / Let's Spend the Night Together / The Jean Genie / Lady Grinning Soul

Ziggy Stardust: The Motion Picture, 1983
Hang On To Yourself / Ziggy Stardust / Watch That Man /
Wild Eyed Boy From Freecloud / All the Young Dudes / Oh! You
Pretty Things / Moonage Daydream / Space Oddity / My Death /
Cracked Actor / Time / Width of a Circle / Changes / Let's Spend
the Night Together / Suffragette City / White Light/White Heat /
Rock 'n' Roll Suicide

Santa Monica '72, 1994
Intro / Hang On To Yourself / Ziggy Stardust / Changes / The
Supermen / Life on Mars? / Five Years / Space Oddity / Andy
Warhol / My Death / The Width of a Circle / Queen Bitch /
Moonage Daydream / John, I'm Only Dancing / I'm Waiting
For the Man / The Jean Genie / Suffragette City / Rock 'n' Roll
Suicide

Sweet Head / Velvet Goldmine / Black Hole Kids / Bombers /
Shadow Man / Looking for a Friend

SPIDERS FROM MARS

Spiders From Mars, 1976
Red Eyes / Shine a Light / White Man, Black Man / Fallen Star /
Summers of Gold (US LP only) / Prisoner / (I Don't Wanna
Do No) Limbo / Stranger To My Door / Good Day America /
Rainbow / Can It Be Far / Running Round in Circles (US LP only)

WOODY WOODMANSEY'S U-BOAT

U1, 1976
U-Boat / Movie Star / Slow Down / Star Machine / I'm in Love /
Rock Show / Let You Be / Hope They Come Back / Oo La La /
From the Top

Acknowledgements

These are individuals, friends and artists who I consider have had a positive effect on my life, in no particular order:

Graham Cardwell, John Butler, Uncle Harold,
Uncle Ernie, Tony Visconti, Ken Scott, Nick Hopkins,
Tom Wilcox, Joe Elliott, Phil Collen, Tom Vitorino,
Rick Wakeman, Art Garfunkel, Chris Cavanagh,
Paul Nash, Jenny Scarfe Becket, L. Ron Hubbard,
my co-writer Joel McIver, my agent Matthew Hamilton,
Ingrid Connell and the team at Pan Macmillan

THE MUTATIONS
John Flintoff, Frank Theakston, Paul Richardson,
Michael Grice

THE ROADRUNNERS
John Hall, Dave Lawson, Dave Westaway, Brian Weeldon
Road crew: Chris Cooper, Dave Simpson, Phil Dukes,
Dave Owen

THE RATS
Benny Marshall, Keith Cheeseman, Geoff Appleby,
John Cambridge (without whose courage to venture south,

Ziggy and the Spiders might never have existed)
Road crew: Dave Walkley, Pete Hunsley, Stuey George

HOLY HOLY 2016
Tony Visconti, Glenn Gregory, Paul Cuddeford, James
Stevenson, Berenice Scott, Jessica Lee Morgan, Terry Edwards

HOLY HOLY 2013–2015
Paul Fryer, Malcolm Doherty, Rod Melvin, Maggi Ronson,
Lisa Ronson, Hannah Berridge Ronson, David Donley,
Erdal Kizilcay, Steve Norman, Gary Stonadge, Liz Westward,
Tracie Hunter, Clem Burke

TOUR SUPPORT
Steve McGuire (Sound USA), Hutch Hutchinson (Sound UK)
Clark Becker (drum tech USA), David Donley (drum tech UK)
Wendy Woo (merchandise UK)

DRUMMERS
Charlie Watts, Bobby Elliott, Keith Moon, Ginger Baker,
Mitch Mitchell, John Bonham, Mike Giles, Simon Kirke,
Carter Beaufort, Dave Grohl, Steve Smith, Sandy Nelson

My sons Danny, Nick and Joe

My wife June for being the perfect partner for me in life
(I love ya, hun)

David Bowie, Mick Ronson and Trevor Bolder for their
friendship and the incredible journey . . .

Index

USA:
  Bowie visits (1971) 82–3
  Ziggy Stardust tour of (1972–3)
    61, 149, 151–70, 171–2, 175,
    180–202, 203, 204

Vanilla, Cherry 154–5
Velvet Underground 82, 83, 103, 144
Vertigo Records 58, 75
Visconti, Morgan 272, 283
Visconti, Tony xi–xiii, 45, 46, 52,
  55–6, 57, 58, 59, 60, 63, 65–8,
  70, 71, 72, 73, 77–8, 81, 82,
  89, 152, 217–18, 235–6, 237,
  255, 270, 272, 274–5, 276,
  277–8, 281, 283, 285

Wakeman, Rick 99, 156, 284
Warhol, Andy 103, 105, 146, 156,
  158, 165, 191
'Watch That Man' (David Bowie)
  178
Westaway, Dave 'Les' 30
Wheeldon, Brian 30
'White Light/White Heat' (Lou Reed)
  143, 219
'Width of a Circle' (David Bowie) 71,
  137, 271, 273, 279
Wilcox, Tom 269, 271, 273
'Wild Eyed Boy From Freecloud'
  (David Bowie) 53
Williams, Paul 103
Wilshaw, Brian 181
Wilson, Ann 279
Wings 234
Winter, Edgar 244–5, 282
Wood, Ronnie 84, 252
Woodmansey (née Bradley), Annie
  (mother) 4–5, 6–7, 8, 11–12,
  19–20, 23, 25, 28, 34, 35, 43,
  49, 77, 173–4, 266, 267
Woodmansey, Dan (son) 239, 262,
  263–5, 276
Woodmansey, Douglas (father) 4, 5,
  6–9, 11–12, 19–20, 23, 25, 26,
  27, 33–5, 43, 49, 77, 173–4,
  266–7
Woodmansey, Joe (son) 239, 264

Woodmansey, June (wife) 21–2, 26,
  28, 31, 35, 47–8, 50, 76–7, 87,
  88, 130, 140, 151, 172, 183,
  184, 203–4, 207, 208–9, 215,
  216, 221–2, 225, 226, 228,
  229, 230, 237, 239, 247, 249,
  251, 254, 263, 264, 276
Woodmansey, Nick (son) 239, 247,
  262, 263, 264–5
Woodmansey, Pamela (sister) 7, 11,
  267
Woodmansey, Woody:
  albums, bands and songs involved
    with see under individual
    album, band and song name
  ambition to become a rock
    musician, birth of 1–3
  apprenticeship 26, 27–8
  birth 5
  Bowie and see Bowie, David
  childhood 5–22, 200
  drinking/drugs and 40–1, 61–2,
    69, 164–5, 204
  drum kits, first 15, 30–1
  drum theory, first encounters 80
  fame 142–3, 150, 175–6, 189–90,
    191–2
  family see under individual family
    member name
  fired from Spiders From Mars
    (1973) 222–3, 225–6
  first band 14–15
  first gigs 21, 26–7
  first plays drums 6
  hair, grows 17–19
  last concert with Bowie (1973)
    217–21
  leaves home for London 50–1
  Haddon Hall, life at see Haddon
    Hall
  love/sex life 21–2, 26, 28, 35,
    47–8, 50, 60–1, 140, 164, 172,
    189, 192, 204
  marriage 208–9, 221–3, 224, 226
  musical taste 1, 16–17, 29, 46, 244
  name xi, 6
  pay dispute with Bowie 195–200,
    203, 222–3, 227

PICTURE CREDITS